STEROIDS

STEROIDS

A New Look at Performance-Enhancing Drugs

Rob Beamish

PRAEGER

AN IMPRINT OF ABC-CLIO, LLC
Santa Barbara, California • Denver, Colorado • Oxford, England

Library of Congress Cataloging-in-Publication Data

Beamish, Rob.
   Steroids : a new look at performance-enhancing drugs / Rob Beamish.
      p. cm.
   Includes bibliographical references and index.
   ISBN 978–0–313–38024–2 (hard copy : alk. paper) — ISBN 978-0-313-38025-9 (ebook)
1. Anabolic steroids. 2. Doping in sports. 3. Olympics—Political aspects. 4. Olympics—Social aspects. I. Title.
RC1230.B454   2011
362.29′9—dc22   2011010791

ISBN: 978–0–313–38024–2
EISBN: 978–0–313–38025–9

15 14 13 12   2 3 4 5

This book is also available on the World Wide Web as an eBook.
Visit www.abc-clio.com for details.

Praeger
An Imprint of ABC-CLIO, LLC

ABC-CLIO, LLC
130 Cremona Drive, P.O. Box 1911
Santa Barbara, California 93116-1911

This book is printed on acid-free paper ∞

Manufactured in the United States of America

Contents

Preface

C. Wright Mills urged students and scholars to aspire to be craftsworkers. In his essay "On Intellectual Craftsmanship," Mills (1959) encouraged sociologists to keep files because the very act of writing is inescapably creative. By simply jotting something down to put into a file, one pauses and reflects, considers the idea, sees links to other ideas and experiences, and develops new associations.

Mills emphasized an active engagement with one's files: going through them from time to time, physically spreading a file out on a desk, reassessing and rearranging it. In the physical manipulation of the file, one sparks associations and connections never seen before. All of Mills' (1959) projects began and ended with his files; his books, Mills noted, were "simply organized releases from the continuous work that goes into those files" (pp. 200–1). This book is no different.

As Ian Ritchie and I finished *Fastest, Highest, Strongest*, I was already adding new material to my files on performance-enhancing substances. Various requests for essays, chapters, and editorials encouraged me to add more and to consider steroids and other substances from different perspectives. The ongoing world of high-performance sports also generated new examples, problems, regulations, interpretations, and concerns over the social construction of steroid use in sports. As a result, this is another periodic, organized release from my own files; it is one that I hope will stimulate other researchers, athletes, and policymakers struggling with the dilemmas and contradictions that exist in high-performance sports to open files of their own from which they may contribute to the debates over high-performance sports and performance-enhancing practices.

As this organized release comes to completion, I am indebted to several individuals. I have learned a great deal from the lively, spirited discussions in my graduate seminar: KHS 869: The Body and Social Theory. As an interdisciplinary group, the students in that seminar have continually inspired me with their enthusiasm for comprehensively studying the body and embodiment. While we were supportive of each other, no idea went unchallenged or underexplored. While I am indebted to all the students in KHS 869, I have benefited in particular from lengthy discussions, at a variety of locations across the campus, with Stephanie Cork, Paloma Holmes, Melanie Kurrein, Jackie Orsetto, and Carolyn Prouse—a fine group of young craftswomen who embody the rich future for critical scholarship directed at the social construction of the human body.

Bill Munn has carefully read the entire manuscript, asked the right questions when others would have shied away, and provided the intellectual support that is so vital to the solitary task of writing. My debts to Bill extend well beyond this book, and words could never adequately express my thanks.

I also want to thank Michael Atkinson for suggesting to Dan Harmon that I might be a person who could undertake this project and Dan for following through on that suggestion—even though it took longer to complete the manuscript than I had anticipated.

Most of this book was written within a compressed period of time, involving long hours, seven days a week, over several months. I am truly fortunate that my lifelong partner, Nada, fully understands the demands of writing and gives me the intellectual and emotional support needed to work through every obstacle that I encountered along the way. While Nada may justifiably think "I've heard that before," I am looking forward to enjoying her love freed from all the external pressures and deadlines we have had to negotiate over the past few years.

Finally, it is safe to say that Travis, Stephanie, and Ryan Beamish have each become fully involved in their lives as young adults, charting futures that will follow dreams that they will realize over the next few years. In the past, they have been close by, and I've drawn support from their proximity; this time, it has been a different form of support that I have felt—the sense of satisfaction and well-being that arise while watching them on a phase of the life course that Nada and I can recall like it was yesterday. Knowing they are so well on their way is deeply satisfying and rewarding.

Before taking full responsibility for all the arguments presented in this book, there is one particular issue that I should address: On the basis of the material that follows, am I advocating the use of steroids? The short answer is no—but there is also a longer answer.

The decision to use steroids is complex. It is currently clouded in a good deal of misinformation as well as the absence of reliable scientific knowledge. Nevertheless, no matter what the state of the available information and despite the powerful social forces that impinge on athletes' and others' decisions, before any individual ever chooses to introduce powerful hormones, such as anabolic-androgenic steroids into his or her body, he or she should have absolute certainty on three points.

First, the individual must be absolutely positive that he or she has gone as far as possible toward meeting his or her particular goals without using such powerful synthetic hormones. In addition, the individual must have compelling arguments that will persuade his or her close family and friends that there is a genuine need to use steroids to further the individual's goals and objectives.

Second, if it still seems appropriate to use steroids to enhance one's performance or appearance, then the individual should thoroughly study the most authoritative scientific information possible; seek the wisdom, experience, and guidance of the appropriate medical and health professionals; and ensure that his or her physiological responses to the substances used are closely and regularly monitored. Steroids are powerful hormones, and they should not be used lightly.

Finally, no individual below the age of majority should take steroids. To begin with, a teenager has not matured enough physiologically to know whether steroids are necessary to reach his or her particular performance or appearance goals. Second, no matter how socially sophisticated and informed a teenager may be, he or she still lacks enough life experience to make a fully informed decision about substances that will have such a significant long-term impact. Steroids affect more than one's physiology, and it is their influence on one's social psychology and perception of self that are really the most significant and far-reaching outcomes. Lastly, at the present time, without a medical prescription, possession of steroids is illegal, and within the current social climate, steroid users are marginalized individuals. Dealing with the guilt, uncertainty, and social stigma currently associated with steroids become additional (and unnecessary) problems for teenagers already struggling to navigate those difficult years of emotional, personal, and social development.

With my views on steroid use clear, despite all the support and advice I have received in writing this book, I remain solely responsible for each of the arguments presented. Now back to my files. . . .

Introduction

Testifying before the Committee on Government Reform (CoGR) on March 17, 2005, Denise and Raymond Garibaldi were unequivocal: "There is no doubt in our minds that steroids killed our son" (CoGR, 2005, p. 115). That sound bite defined the committee's investigation into steroid use in baseball: Steroids are lethal substances that must be eradicated from sports.

How did it ever come to this? That simple question is deceptively complex. It is one that this book addresses within the context of several more questions.

First, how did sports ever become so focused on performance and victory at any cost? That critical question leads into several more. What were the reasons for banning performance-enhancing substances in the first place? Do those reasons still apply? Through what processes did steroids—more than any other substance—become so demonized? Finally, what are the real implications of the existing ban on steroids in sports?

This book focuses on five major themes: the nature of sports within the modern world; the manner in which the Olympic Games have shaped the performance imperative in modern sports; the role the Olympic Games have played in establishing the predominant attitudes toward performance-enhancing substances; the processes that have defined the current understanding of steroid use in sports; and the unintended consequences resulting from the current ban on steroids.

Although steroids affect athletes' physiology, their use is really a socially based phenomenon. Surprisingly, however, sociologists have not played a predominant role in the formation of policies proscribing steroids in sports and other areas of social life. Their absence is unfortunate because sociology provides a unique and important perspective on sports, human performance, and the social construction of attitudes and beliefs. This book seeks to redress that absence and demonstrate what sociology can contribute to contemporary discussions of steroids and sports.

Although numerous sociologists' ideas inform this study, the works of Raymond Williams, Michel Foucault, Anthony Giddens, Peter Berger, and Thomas Luckmann are of particular significance. All five are decidedly historical in their approaches to understanding social processes; each has made issues of social power (what it is, where it "resides," and how it is exercised) central to their work; and each is highly sensitive to the interpretive dimensions of social life and the significance of socially constructed meaning in the contouring of social action. In addition, the positions of all five are antireductionist (no explanation can be reduced to a single cause), materialist (the understanding of social processes only arises from an examination of real social practices that men and women enact within a particular sociohistorical context), and nonessentialist (there are no inner, essential, transhistorical, pure elements that, through their expression or "coming into being," direct and/or guide social processes to a particular, ultimate *telos*, or final, "true" outcome). Finally, all five have continually emphasized the interpenetration of social processes with the specific social actions they have been examining—whether that involves the nature of culture, specific genres of literature, prisons, asylums, war, the formation of self, or the nature of high modernity. All these features also inform this study.

However, of the five, it is the perspectives of Williams, Berger, and Luckmann that are most predominant. Williams' (1977, 1980) conceptualization of the dominant, residual, and emergent nature of sociocultural practices provides the underlying framework within which Berger and Luckmann's social constructionist position is employed.

Many sociological analyses tend to separate past, present, and potential future practices from one another, but Williams continually emphasized the complexity of social life in which elements of the past remain within the present and, despite their declining influence, still shape emerging forms of social action. According to Williams, social processes and social action are complex, messy, and interconnected. Thus, while every analysis focuses on certain aspects of that complex reality, it should not draw attention completely away from the intricate interpenetration of dominant, residual, and emergent that actually exists in real social processes.

The notion of "the social construction" of what people consider their "reality" has a long history in sociology, but Berger and Luckmann's (1966) *The Social Construction of Reality* gave the perspective genuine, contemporary prominence. Berger and Luckmann argued that all forms of knowledge—from the most scientific to the everyday, taken-for-granted common sense understandings that people routinely employ in their daily activities—arise from and are maintained by social interaction. It is only on the basis of shared perceptions of the world within which people live that they can meaningfully engage with one another. Knowledge is socially created and negotiated; it is through "knowledge frameworks" that the objective, material world is "known."

Building on Berger and Luckmann's analysis of the social construction of everyday life, such sociologists as Karin Knorr-Cetina (1981, 1999) and Bruno Latour (1987, 1991) have detailed how science and scientific knowledge about objective "entities" are also socially constructed. Their work has produced a thoroughly argued, carefully considered body of scholarship that demonstrates that people do not "know" the world within which they live directly; their knowledge is mediated by social conventions and social constructions. This applies to all the unwritten, informal rules that are used when holding a simple conversation to scientists' conceptions of the atom, DNA, or way testosterone influences muscle development.

While social constructionism has been used to demonstrate how profoundly people's knowledge of the natural world is shaped by socially constructed understandings of each and every entity under scientific scrutiny and while it has focused on the social construction of everyday life, social constructionism has also been used to focus on the nature of social problems. And it is within this work that the use of steroids in sports may be profitably explored.

Social Constructionism and Social Problems

In people's daily lives, through the constitution and reconstitution of social action, they encounter, create, and recreate social relationships that have consequences for their lives and further action. Some of those consequences are positive, some neutral, and some quite problematic. These consequences are "real"; they matter, and they cannot simply be wished away. Those who argue about the social construction of social problems do not deny this dimension of the "reality" of the problems that people encounter in the world. There are people who commit robbery, assault, live in material poverty, experience discrimination based on sex, racialization, or ethnicity—to name a few examples. Thus, there is an "objective" dimension to social problems. But social constructionists argue that there is more to know about social problems. By focusing on only the objective nature of social problems, one has not really analyzed them.

For social constructionists, how people *think* about a problem—how they perceive it—is at least as important—if not more—than the "objective" characteristics of the problem itself. In fact, social constructionists maintain that it is through the creation of particular perceptions that many of the "objective" characteristics of a problem are created; the relevant "objective" characteristics of a situation are part of its social construction/definition.

Focusing on the socially constructed dimensions of problems leads to such critical questions as: What have people done or said that has defined a particular action as problematic, and why are these particular aspects of those actions the ones receiving attention? Why those aspects and not others? Why do people worry far more about one issue (the use of steroids, for example) and invoke rules and legislation to curb or prevent it rather than another (the continual risk that lugers face every time they hurtle down a track at maximum velocity)? Social constructionists believe that the way an issue becomes a problem is through a process called *claims-making*.

As incredible as it may seem, in many respects, no actions or individuals are in and of themselves problematic or deviant. What people "recognize" as problematic behaviors or as deviant actions are socially constructed. Consider an extreme example: killing another person. Depending on how it is socially constructed, killing another human may be horrifically abhorrent, courageously heroic, or impossible to evaluate.

A soldier in combat is expected to kill the enemy. Failing to do so may result in severe punishment. And under some circumstances, taking people's lives is deemed heroic. The social construction of the situation and thus the act determines how that action is understood (or judged).

When a person engages in an apparent rampage shooting in a school—the label "rampage shooting" is a social construction of the event—the act is most often constructed as horrific. But that assessment may change as more is learned about the mental state of the perpetrator and his or her relationship with the victims. If the shooter belonged to a particular political movement that felt it was compelled to take dramatic action in aid of its cause, then those within the movement would construct and judge the event differently than those outside the movement. The public at large receiving news of the event may make one judgment but then change that initial assessment as the event is more fully "explained" (that is, more elaborately constructed) by the media.

Finally, if another person in the school overcame the shooter and killed him or her in the ensuing scuffle, that act would be viewed through another constructive lens. Assessing it as just or unjust, immoral or heroic, could be very complex and perplexing because it brings together a variety of social definitions and social constructions of taking a life. As a result, in all these instances, the apparently "objective" act of taking a life is never assessed in isolation from the social definition or social construction of the situation, the circumstances, and the nature of the act. The pure, unmediated act and result of taking a life does not actually exist. Every single instance is encountered and then framed and perceived through a particular social construction.

Few acts are as dramatic as taking a life, and while there is, in most cultures, a deeply imbedded prohibition of taking another's life, that is not the case for most actions that may or may not be constructed as problematic or deviant. Alcohol consumption, smoking, premarital sex, marijuana use, and downloading music or movies have all been socially constructed at different times as forms of legitimate behavior, then as deviant, even illegal behavior, and then redefined yet again. The same is true of steroid use in sports, blood boosting (now constructed as blood doping), and the use of caffeine—all were fully acceptable practices in high-performance sports, all three were later banned, and caffeine was then socially reconstructed and removed from the list of prohibited substances in 2009 (World Anti-Doping Association, 2009, p. 8).

In order for members of the temperance league, smokers anonymous, the sexual freedom club, marijuana advocates, or the pirate entertainment lobby to change the existing regulations and practices affecting alcohol consumption, smoking, sexual freedom, marijuana use, or the legality of downloads, they would have to successfully engage in a process of claims-making. Each group would have to succeed in making specific claims that would change the existing socially constructed knowledge or understanding of alcohol, tobacco, premarital sex, marijuana use, or free entertainment that has led to their restriction.

In the claims-making process, claims-makers must successfully achieve three objectives if their social construction of the phenomenon or action is to prevail. First, the claims-makers must successfully publicize the behavior they see as problematic if they want it banned or as unproblematic and perhaps even beneficial if they want to free it from prohibition and sanction. Those seeking to prohibit substances or acts must convince others that certain substances, people, or behaviors are dangerous, irresponsible, contagious, and/or undermine the welfare of the community in some other way. There does not have to be a genuinely factual basis for the claim, but the claims-makers must convince others that the behavior certainly appears to be deviant and undesired. Indeed, one of the key methods in critically assessing a particular claim is to look at the evidence on which the claim is based. How credible is the case being made? How reliable are the data supporting the claim? Are there flaws in the arguments presented or are there alternative interpretations of the data that make more sense? Are there data missing?

Claims-makers must also successfully shape a specific conception of the problem that they have identified. Generally, claims-makers want to convince people that there is not only a general problem but that there is a *specific* one that is of *particular* concern. Thus, for example, it is not just smoking that is harmful to people's health but the specific dangers of secondhand smoke to which smokers subject nonsmokers without their consent. Antismoking advocates have successfully claimed that it is due to the hazards of secondhand smoke that smoking in the workplace, for example, must be either banned or restricted to specific locations outside and away from nonsmokers.

Finally, claims-makers have to build a consensus around a new moral category. As a well-established, trusted authority, the American Medical Association (AMA), in the early descriptions of synthetic testosterone and its effects, built a very effective consensus around the potential sexually based dangers testosterone posed to some of the United States' most firmly held bedrock values and moral imperatives. The current status of marijuana appears to be in flux because growing claims about the medical benefit of cannabis have begun to erode what was once a widely held, unquestioned position. However, at the same time, the ominous scenario that marijuana use is simply the first step toward more harmful, addictive drugs still stands as a powerful claim that resists the reconstruction of cannabis as no more dangerous than alcohol (even though marijuana has the added benefit of its use in medical treatments).

The current, predominant perception of steroids is the result of a number of highly influential and well-resourced claims-makers, who portray steroids negatively by focusing on steroids from a variety of different perspectives and using all the media outlets possible to establish their specific claims and build support for their position. Chapters 4, 5, and 6 examine different aspects of the social construction of steroids as demonized substances in detail.

The Early "Truth" about Steroids: The Social Construction of Perception

From the time that testosterone was first synthesized in 1935, anabolic-androgenic steroids have provoked "fantasies of hormonal rejuvenation, sexual excitement, and supernormal human performance" (Hoberman, 2005, p. 2). Although the reaction to its potential was mixed, testosterone certainly had its early supporters and influential advocates. The highly successful, popular science author Paul de Kruif (1945a) wrote in *The Male Hormone* that steroids could "extend the prime life of men"; the phrase was even emblazoned on the book's dust jacket (p. 208). Among testosterone's many virtues, Kruif emphasized its performance-enhancing capacity. Commenting on how the St. Louis Cardinals and St. Louis Browns had won championships "super-charged by vitamins," Kruif (1945) postulated that it would be interesting to see "the productive power of an industry or a professional group" that "would try a systematic supercharge with testosterone" (p. 223).

Kruif's enthusiasm received considerable positive press. *Newsweek* published a full page review that emphasized the benefits of testosterone and its future potential (Hormones for he-men, 1945). His position gained further support and wider coverage when an excerpt appeared in one of the most highly successful, widely read, mass market magazines in the United States: *Reader's Digest* (see Kruif, 1945b).

Kruif's optimism was not restricted to journalists and the masses in the United States. Members of the medical community emphasized the positive benefits of the sense of well-being that testosterone produced. By the early 1940s, John Hoberman (2005) has substantiated that "testosterone was hailed as a mood-altering drug whose primary purpose was the sexual restoration and reenergizing of aging males" (p. 3). Even a decade after Kruif's book appeared, a gerontologist wrote that the results of steroid therapy were "astonishing." "Their future possibilities," he continued, "stagger the imagination" (Hormones in geriatrics, 1954, p. 1336). When one began to consider the potential market, it quickly became clear that there were lots of reasons to promote synthesized testosterone.

Nevertheless, what many saw as the beauty and benefits of synthetic testosterone, its detractors viewed as testosterone's and steroids' most sinister qualities. In a period of social conservatism and sexual repression, testosterone and steroids posed a serious threat to several bedrock values in the United States. By the mid-1940s, sensationalist commentary on testosterone's impact on sex drive and performance had resulted in "a quasi-pornographic image" for testosterone therapy (Hoberman, 2005, p. 8).

In response to its growing "unsavoury reputation," Dr. Albert Hemming (1946), writing in *Science Digest*, felt compelled to emphasize that even though "the uninformed continue to believe that the sole use of this

innocent chemical is to turn sexual weaklings into wolves, and octogenarians into sexual athletes," testosterone had a legitimate and positive place
in hormone therapy (p. 75). But the image of hypersexed octogenarians
and hormone-driven sexual predators did not reside solely among the
"uninformed." The ultraconservative U.S. medical establishment was reluc-
tant to support a drug that might extend the sexual activity of aging males
when it could also jeopardize the predominant sexual mores of Americans
in the 1940s.

Although the pharmaceutical companies tried to counter the negative
publicity and fear within the medical profession, they were limited in what
they could do. It was illegal for the companies to advertise directly to the
public and create a demand for synthetic testosterone. Moreover, as
Hoberman (2005) has documented, even when aging men in the 1940s
requested prescriptions for steroids, the preponderantly male medical profession had little interest in "salvaging the sex lives of middle-aged or older
people" (p. 9).

From the outset then, steroids have been recognized for their therapeutic benefits as well as their potential to enhance physical performance.
They have had their ardent supporters and advocates. At the same time,
the properties that appeal to their supporters are the same ones that their
detractors fear and stigmatize. From the time of their first synthesis and
use to right up to the present, steroids have been involved in a struggle
over vastly differing perceptions of what they are, what they represent,
and their legitimate practical use. The current concern over steroid use
in sports exists because some individuals and groups have successfully
defined their use as problematic, unethical, and even dangerous. In other
words, people's perceptions of steroids have been "socially constructed"
in a very particular manner. Where the process of social construction
began is the focus of the next chapter.

Chapter 1

Coubertin's Olympic Project

Olympism: Born on the Banks of the Alphaeus

The concern over steroids in sports has its roots in the modern Olympic Games. That much is well known. However, what needs to be emphasized is that it is impossible to fully understand the profound opposition to steroid use in sports without putting the modern Olympic Games within their full social context. Baron Pierre de Coubertin's goal in launching the modern Olympics extended well beyond the desire to create an international sporting spectacle. Coubertin wanted to resurrect the ancient Olympic Games to oppose and overturn the modernist forces that had fundamentally shaped Europe by the end of the nineteenth century. It is this opposition to modernity—the direct opposition between Coubertin's goals and the prevailing reality of European modernity—that one must keep in focus to fully understand the origins of contemporary opposition to steroids and significant elements of their social construction as detrimental to the true spirit of sports. As a result, this chapter examines the nature of Coubertin's Olympic project while also exploring what is meant by modernity and how the forces of modernity created important tensions—indeed oppositions—to Coubertin's desired goals. Once this background is in place, one can then begin to appreciate the opposition to steroids once they are first introduced into Olympic competition in the post–World War II period.

Coubertin's aspirations for the modern Olympic Games and the reason he felt they could serve as a major factor in the transformation of Europe rested fundamentally on one simple yet inspired and inspiring image: "The athlete enjoys his effort," Coubertin (2000) noted with great flourish. "He likes the constraint that he imposes on his muscles and nerves, through which he comes close to victory even if he does not manage to achieve it" (p. 552). The feeling, he continued, remains internal—almost "egotistical." But imagine, Coubertin enthused, if that experience were to be expanded outward, "becoming intertwined with the joy of nature and the flights of art. Picture it radiant with sunlight, exalted by music, framed in the architecture of porticoes." "It was thus,"

Coubertin assured his audience, "that the glittering dream of ancient Olympism was born on the banks of the Alphaeus, the vision of which dominated ancient society for so many centuries" (p. 552).

With just about 100 words, Coubertin drew together a number of compelling images, emotions, and possibilities. Anyone who has ever engaged in an athletic contest can instantly identify with the physical and emotional collage that Coubertin sketched: Coubertin vividly reawakens the feelings one has as he or she fully embraces the demands of physical exertion, fights back a growing fatigue, and disciplines mind, muscle, and will in the quest for victory. The athletic experience is internal, deeply personal, and becomes even more indelible as the level of competitive intensity increases along with the commitment to perform at the outer edge of one's physical and mental limits. The experience blends body, mind, and character together, as it is deeply etched into a sense of self. Whenever people speak about the value of sports, it is this fundamental image that they principally have in mind. It is timeless, uplifting, and reaches into the core elements of one's being. But Coubertin took the image further by raising it to the grand vistas of nature, art, and music.

Imagine, Coubertin implored his audience, if all those emotions could be simultaneously felt by others at a level that is above and beyond the athlete's own experiences. Think about athletic contests entwined with the marvelous expanses of nature and the soaring raptures of music, bathed in sunlight, captured by creative flights of art, and tied together within a venerable frame. The fusion of mind, body, and character would reach into the highest realm of cultural expression and human fulfillment. Coubertin's dream was as expansive as his enthusiasm for selling it to a world that he believed needed a new direction. He tapped directly into an individual's personal experiences to guide the recollection of how athletic engagement should be remembered and then used that construction to lead the person through a carefully crafted script to a set of emotional conclusions.

The final element Coubertin introduced was classical antiquity—the glittering dream of ancient Olympism that, he assured his audience, inspired classical Europe for centuries. In a few short sentences, Coubertin set out the path he believed Europe had to follow—a return to the noble roots of ancient Greece, where the most remarkable civilization had achieved humanity's greatest intellectual, spiritual, and cultural accomplishments. Science, technology, and instrumental reason had no place in that world and, Coubertin implied, need not have a dominant role to play in the contemporary period either.

Anyone who had studied the ancient Olympic Games, Coubertin (2000) argued, would know that their significance rested on two key elements: beauty and reverence.

> If the modern Games are to exercise the influence I desire for them they must in their turn show beauty and inspire reverence—a beauty and a reverence infinitely surpassing anything hitherto realized in the most important athletic contests of our day. The grandeur and dignity of processions and attitudes, the impressive splendour of ceremonies, the concurrence of all the arts, popular emotion and generous sentiment, must all in some sort collaborate together. (p. 545)

Coubertin's dream was to use the inspiring reverence of the ancient Olympic Games to shape a unique athletic spectacle that would forge brothers-in-arms bonded by the experience of chivalrous competition to form Europe's new spiritual and political elite.

Although the modern Olympic Games are currently branded by *citius, altius, fortius*, it is the axiom *athletae proprium est se ipsum noscere, ducere et vincere* (it is the duty and the essence of the athlete to know, to lead and to conquer himself) that really captures Coubertin's belief that the muscular sphere could transform the moral sphere.

Modernity: Dominant, Resistant, and Emergent Forces

The basis for Coubertin's project was his concern over the impact that modernity was having on the quality of life in modern Europe and the future that lies ahead. He was not alone in holding such grave concerns; scholars, political leaders, public intellectuals, and members of the clergy had also reached similar conclusions. Despite their vast political and intellectual differences, Coubertin would have shared considerable agreement with Marx's assessment of modernity in the *Communist Manifesto*—a document that presents some of the most provocative imagery associated with the emergent, industrializing modernity of Western Europe and best conveys the tang and feel of modernity as it was constituted and reconstituted on an expanding scale in the mid-nineteenth century.

Wherever the bourgeoisie had gained the upper hand, Marx wrote, it "has put an end to all feudal, patriarchal, idyllic relations." The bourgeoisie had

> pitilessly torn asunder the motley feudal ties that bound man to his "natural superiors," and has left no other nexus between people than naked

self-interest, than callous "cash payment. . . ." It has resolved personal worth into exchange value, and in place of the numberless indefeasible chartered freedoms, has set up that single, unconscionable freedom—Free Trade. In one word, for exploitation, veiled by religious and political illusions, it has substituted naked, shameless, direct, brutal exploitation.

The bourgeoisie has stripped of its halo every occupation hitherto honored and looked up to with reverent awe. It has converted the physician, the lawyer, the priest, the poet, the man of science, into its paid wage laborers. (Marx and Engels, 1934, p. 12)

The modern era, Marx emphasized, was becoming vastly different from any that had preceded it; tradition, religion, and natural rights would no longer structure social relationships. The cash nexus and the ethos of progress through continuous development and perpetual change dominated production, interpersonal relations, and the social structure as a whole.

Marx fully acknowledged that the accomplishments of modernity were breathtaking—far surpassing the Egyptian pyramids, Roman aqueducts, or Gothic cathedrals. More importantly, however, was the speed and scale of change that modernity introduced. While previous eras were characterized by the conservation of the existing modes of production, modernity's insatiable drive for progress led to constant change, disruption, uncertainty and agitation. In one of the *Manifesto*'s most vivid images, Marx captured the essence of modernity:

All fixed, fast frozen relations, with their train of ancient and venerable prejudices and opinions, are swept away, all new-formed ones become antiquated before they can ossify. All that is solid melts into air, all that is holy is profaned, and man is at last compelled to face with sober senses his real condition of life and his relations with his kind. (Marx and Engels, 1934, pp. 12–3)

The period from 1789 through to the end of the Victorian era in England (1837–1901) was one of intense struggle and significant social transformation. It was a period of "convulsion," to use Williams' (1958) term, in which "numerous voices" were raised in support as well as condemnation of the "struggle for political democracy and the progress of the Industrial Revolution" (p. 3). The forces of emerging modernity and its associated interests in industrialization, individualism, and democratization were met by the resistance of a conservative tradition that wanted to re-establish the old order of Europe as well as radical, democratic interests that used imagery from the past to inspire a potentially emergent future that would realize the goals of the French Revolution along with the material gains of industrial production. As hard as it may be to imagine now, this period in European history had a fundamental impact on how steroid use in high-performance sports during the twenty-first century would be socially constructed.

To articulate their concerns with the emergent reality of modernity, Coubertin and others could draw from the very influential tradition of conservatism that began with Edmund Burke's (1793) *Reflections on the Revolution in France*, but as the *Manifesto* indicates, there were also radicals on the left who challenged the emerging power of industrial capital with its own image of the future. What is quite intriguing about the critique of the emergent modernist social formation was the extent to which conservatives and radicals drew upon particular constructions of medieval Europe to proffer remedies to the harsh realities of modernity in the nineteenth century.

By far the most coherent discourse of resistance—especially in the early part of the nineteenth century—came from the conservatives, drawing heavily from Burke. It was the conservative tradition that influenced Coubertin most profoundly.

Within France, the conservative tradition included the works of Joseph de Maistre, an avowed servant of the Roman Catholic Church and the French monarchy; Louis de Bonald, a key figure within the conservative tradition; Hugues Felicité de Lamennais, whose views were shaped by his devout Catholicism and experiences as a member of the priesthood; and François René de Chateaubriand, who emphasized that Roman Catholicism was more than just a creed and faith—it was the foundation for community (Nisbet, 1978).

The French conservatives had German counterparts. Included among them were Justus Möser, whose multivolume *Patriotic Discourses* (1774–1786) produced a relentless, systematic attack on individualism and rationalism while extolling the value and virtues of community, custom, and tradition. Those *Discourses* exerted a major influence on Burke's *Reflections*. Adam Müller was a disciple of Burke, while Friedrich Carl von Savigny emphasized Burke's notion that the historical spirit of a people was the only legitimate basis for law and government.

Within Britain, which industrialized ahead of France and Germany and where the impact of modernity was more obvious, resistance to the emergent forces of modernity came from conservatives and traditionalists as well as those who championed the interests of the newly created working class. During the Industrial Revolution, England—as Williams (1958) has demonstrated—was a study in contrasts: Burke the conservative versus William Cobbett, the first great advocate of the industrial proletariat, or Robert Southey in comparison with Robert Owen. But along with the contrasts, there was a well of common images and themes from which both the English conservatives and radicals drew.

Burke was an Englishman, and although he focused his essay on the French Revolution of 1789, the ideas he expressed held true for all conservatives resisting modernity's rise to dominance. The power of Burke's work stemmed from his ability to capture the immediacy of experience and embody it in a set of ideas that resisted challenge because of their appeal to the urgency of the moment. Burke's writing vividly captured people's lived experiences, giving his ideas greater impact and validity. By connecting those lived experiences to his own deeply imbedded values Burke was inspiring, leading Coubertin and others to emulate his resistance to modernity.

Acting as individuals, Burke maintained, humanity is prone to evil; the only guarantee of proper humanity was the historical community where the whole was placed above the individual and a value system that had stood the test of time was nurtured and passed on. The entire progress of humanity, according to Burke, depended on the eternal, inviolable contract of the community. Society is a contract, Burke (1793) argued:

> It is a partnership in all science; a partnership in all art; a partnership in every virtue, and in all perfection. As the ends of such a partnership cannot be obtained in many generations, it becomes a partnership not only between those who are living, but between those who are living, those who are dead, and those who are to be born. Each contract of each particular state is but a clause in the great primeval contract of eternal society, linking the lower with the higher natures, connecting the visible and invisible world, according to a fixed compact sanctioned by the inviolable oath which holds all physical and all moral natures, each in their appointed place. (p. 74)

The appeal to the past and the positive, integrative aspects of community was not confined to the conservative critique of modernity in industrializing England.

Cobbett represented the radical critique of modernity. He decried the impoverishment of his fellow countrymen forced off their lands into the satanic mills of industrial production and the absolute exploitation of workers by capitalist owners. Cobbett's solutions lay in two directions: education and the re-establishment of community. One gains a glimpse in Cobbett's work of how much conservatives and radicals shared in trying to think beyond modernity, where the pace and focus of life and human action were changing so dramatically, pushing aside traditional social life.

While Cobbett advocated strenuously for workers to control their own fates, he drew much of his inspiration—like the conservatives—from an idealized image of the middle ages. For Cobbett, the monastery was a key institution because the monasteries had provided an enduring source of stability and order tied to the cooperative spirit of Christianity during the chaos and decades of armed struggle over land following the fall of the Roman Empire (Bloch, 1961). The image of a functioning communal institution stood as an alternative to the individualist claims of modern capitalism.

The most important points to note are the following: the extent to which the dominant, residual, and emergent stood in struggle and flux with one another; that both the conservative and the radical critique of modernity drew from the same body of ideas emphasizing aspects of the past as points of resistance and opposition; and that the body of ideas from which the critique was made was widely discussed and familiar to people across the political spectrum. None of the ideas which Coubertin drew upon in constructing his Olympic project were minor or marginal thoughts during the nineteenth century; they were central to the political discourse of the late nineteenth century.

For Coubertin, the conservative tradition in France—because it was influenced by the English experience of industrialization—and the growing political power of the people in France were critical elements in shaping his visions of the future. What were the core of ideas that Coubertin drew upon?

Resisting Modernity: The Conservative Tradition

Robert Nisbet (1978) has indicated that there are six fundamental elements at the core of the conservative tradition, and each shaped Coubertin's worldview and the objectives he sought to achieve in the modern Olympic Games. The tenets began with Burke's fundamental conception that society was a "partnership" of the dead, the living, and the unborn and his belief that it was irrational and even immoral to try and organize a society on the basis of individual rights. As a result, the conservatives gave full priority to the social whole over the individual. Humanity does not create society, Bonald maintained; society creates humanity. Based on their intense repudiation of the Enlightenment and the French Revolution, Nisbet (1978) noted, the conservatives developed their anti-individualistic view of society in which the priority of the social was fundamental.

Although not all the conservatives thought that society was similar to a biological organism in which all its parts functioned smoothly together, many did; they all subscribed to the notion that all social elements are related to one another; and it was through the integration of society's many parts that stability and order were produced and maintained. This conception of society reinforced the conservatives' belief that history had determined the fundamental basis for social order, and any attempt by individuals to change the course of history or break away from tradition would have disastrous consequences; the French Revolution and the Reign of Terror were events that confirmed their worst fears.

If one of the defining characteristics of Enlightenment thinkers was their rejection of religion, then a defining feature of the conservatives was the importance they placed on it—Roman Catholicism in particular. The conservatives were particularly interested in the symbolic elements of Catholicism and the manner in which the church had served as the dominant integrating force throughout the feudal period. For Bonald, Lamennais, Chateaubriand, and others, no society could exist without the governing sense of the sacred, and that could only occur within a society saturated with tradition.

Committed to tradition, Roman Catholicism, social order, and the organizational structure of European society as it had evolved historically, the conservatives were staunch defenders of hierarchy. They drew upon scholastic theology's notion of "the great chain of being," which suggested that the Creator constructed the universe as a great, hierarchical chain where everything was linked together and arranged in rank order from the smallest, least significant organism up through the class structure of feudal Europe, to the king, pope, and, ultimately, God (Lovejoy, 1936). The great chain was *the* hierarchy of creation, and any attempt to change its rank order was against the will and grand design of God.

The commitment to hierarchy and tradition led to the fourth core element in conservative thought: the importance of intermediary associations within the social structure that bound the individual to the social whole. Medieval societies did not have a strong central state; they were comprised of a number of associations that included the patriarchal family, the village community, guilds, monasteries, various mutual aid organizations, and the king's court. Committed to conserving as much of the past as possible, the conservatives maintained that each of these associations fulfilled a valuable function in the maintenance of social life and the welfare of all. Indeed, it was through their belief and faith in the great chain of being that the conservatives felt so strongly about the importance of intermediary associations.

With respect to each of these four principles, the conservatives grounded their arguments and beliefs in the 1302 Papal Bull *Unam Sanctam* (One Holy Catholic and Apostolic Church). In the bull, Pope Boniface VIII proclaimed that all the existing institutions of society and their particular ranking were part of the divine order. "For, according to the Blessed Dionysius," the bull noted, "it is a law of the divinity that the lowest things reach the highest place by intermediaries. Then, according to the order of the universe, all things are not led back to order equally and immediately, but the lowest by the intermediary, and the inferior by the superior." Boniface continued: "Hence we must recognize the more clearly that spiritual power surpasses in dignity and in nobility any temporal power whatever, as spiritual things surpass the temporal." Boniface claimed that all this was clearly evident in the way the world was, in fact, ordered and governed. "For with truth as our witness," he proclaimed, "it belongs to spiritual power to establish the terrestrial power and to pass judgment if it has not been good." With the divine basis of order established, the manner in which the inferior must reach higher through their immediate superior as an intermediary, and the ranking of spiritual above temporal, Boniface could then confirm the absolute power of the pope: "Furthermore, we declare, we proclaim, we define that it is absolutely necessary for salvation that every human creature be subject to the Roman Pontiff" (Boniface, 1302). The bull confirmed the divine order of the great chain of being, justified the existing order and hierarchy, and put the Pope and Roman Catholic Church at the pinnacle of power on Earth.

Each of these elements leads to the fifth aspect of conservatism: the belief in and defense of "historicism." History was the main touchstone for the conservatives; the past was not celebrated as some abstraction but as the key force that had established the social order of the day. The veneration of the past and all the various institutional arrangements were central to the conservative tradition. The conservatives, like Coubertin, were committed to maintaining the traditions that history had established because it was on that foundation that one could fully understand the present and envision how the future should properly unfold.

Finally, the conservatives shared a deep, enduring fear of social disorganization. Following the French Revolution, all the conservatives could see were "uprooted kinship ties, dissolved communities, shattered classes and estates, and broken moral values, all without exception consequences of Enlightenment liberalism and Revolutionary democracy" (Nisbet, 1978, p. 103).

Relying heavily upon the conservative tradition, Coubertin feared that the growing market-based orientation of Europe and the spread of its commercial forces would slowly debase the great cultural achievements of Western civilization, push high culture to the margins, and replace it with a shallow, artificial culture that would be sold cheaply to mass consumers. While the athletic dimension of the Olympic Games was the critical centerpiece to Coubertin's defense of European culture, he wanted the Olympics to stimulate and be surrounded by other forms of art and high culture.

Coubertin's plan was to hold the Olympic Games alongside a massive exhibition of art, dance, and music. He founded the *Revue Olympique* to serve as a cultural manifesto that emphasized the way sports were tied to and inspired aesthetic concepts, such as the universality and autonomy of beauty. For Coubertin, sports, like dance, were particular forms of artistic physical movement and belonged within the realm of high culture. Through its practice and appropriate aesthetic celebration, sports provided significant insight into the human condition (Brown, 2001). As a result, even if the Olympic Games alone could not change the entire course of European history, they would at least add to Europe's rich cultural heritage and help facilitate the proper enculturation of Europe's future elite, guaranteeing the preservation of Europe's most treasured, long-standing values.

The Victorian Age, Transformation of Physical Pastimes, and Muscular Christianity

The Victorian age left three major legacies that shaped not only Coubertin's Olympic project but have continued to influence—profoundly in some cases—the social construction of sports in the current era and, as a result, contemporary understandings of steroid use in sports. One legacy involved the transformation of traditional pastimes undertaken by the gentry into specific, formalized sports forms that were more appropriate for an increasingly mobile, urbanizing society. The second concerned the code of conduct that characterized the Victorian upper class, the emulation of that code by members of the middle class attempting to gain entry to the upper class, and the extent to which—according to various, influential claims-makers—this particular code is intrinsically and irrevocably related to the very essence and meaning of sports. The third legacy arose within the British public school system in this period. During the latter part of the nineteenth century, the British public schools tried to bring together a specific system of student-run discipline and supervision, particular sporting activities, Christian values, and the legacy of the Victorian gentleman's code of conduct to demonstrate how the true "spirit of sports" could fill a significant educative role within the context of modernity. This particular approach to sports was clearly distinguished from professional, entertainment sports forms and held out the promise of a profound educational potential that could not be found in any other educational endeavor. Due to their continued relevance in certain social constructions of sports today, each of these legacies merits some examination.

The Victorian period in English history was one of dramatic but evolutionary change rather than revolutionary change. Over that 60-year period, the landed gentry were being progressively marginalized as an economic force, and industrial capitalism continued to consolidate the forces of modernity. However, at the same time, the nobles and squires of England remained an important social force—particularly in terms of defining, creating, and controlling culture. In many ways, as the forces of modernity became increasingly evident, there was a rising interest—fueled in part as a form of resistance—in the medieval period. Along with this growing attention to medieval life and the celebration of its customs—especially those centering on the knights and their code of conduct—there arose a profound sense of what constituted "the Victorian gentleman" (Gies, 1984). English literature, with Walter Scott's widely read and enormously influential novels serving as an example, emphasized knightly heroism, courtly manners, fair play, and chivalrous integrity. The heroic knights in Scott's novels created not only the character types that were "imitated in innumerable later novels," but they became models "for young men in real life" (Girouard, 1981, p. 37).

The unwritten code of the Victorian gentleman rested on an idealization of the chivalry of the medieval knights. It emphasized generosity, openheartedness, magnanimity, responsibility, leadership, disinterestedness, and an all-abiding courtesy to women—completely ignoring the fact that medieval knights were a ruthless "military technology" that allowed kings to rule by force and enjoy the spoils of territory taken from others (Mason, 1982). Nevertheless, the Victorian interpretation of medieval chivalry created a separation and distance—based on richer cultural experiences and a perceived sense of superiority—between the British nobles and squires on the one hand and those rising to power from within the upper level of the emerging middle class on the other. The social construction of the Victorian gentleman provided a cultural basis for the British upper class to maintain a feeling of security, stability, unity, and resistance to the modernist forces that were continuously undercutting and progressively eroding the gentry's power and authority throughout the Victorian period.

But the significance of the Victorian gentleman was more complex than the aforementioned suggests. First, the British experience differed from that in France and Germany insofar as those who rose to the upper levels of the middle class through entrepreneurial or industrial success were eager to merge into upper-class society rather than supplant it completely. Morford and McIntosh (1993) have emphasized that a unique feature of English life "lay in a whole class of men whose status was widely admired and whose behavior, morality, and manners were widely emulated even by those without the means to support the lifestyle and whose social existence was balanced between the two extremes of [upper and lower] social class" (p. 60).

A good deal of the lifestyle and associated status of the Victorian gentleman stemmed from the English gentry's ownership and control of vast tracts of land throughout rural England. As a result, the gentry engaged in a variety of field based pastimes that had endured for centuries. These activities—for which there were few if any written rules—were regulated by conventions and elaborate rituals. They involved long-standing traditions of dress, etiquette, and attendant terminology. The activities included horse racing, dressage, steeplechase, riding the hounds, a variety of forms of hunting, and coach racing. There were also certain team games, such as cricket and later equestrian polo, as well as various forms of individual competition between gentlemen that ranged from the fine art of fencing, to tennis, to the "sweet science" of pugilism.

Because the true nobleman derived all his wealth and status from the land through the work of others, he had the leisure to pursue the more refining aspects of life as well as cultivating and developing his physical skills and prowess. As a result, members of the English nobility could demonstrate some remarkable physical strengths through their mastery of horses and the hounds, love of the chase, determination as keen hunters, and a competitive drive and spirit that was refined by the principles of fairness, respect for the opponent (or prey), equanimity with the outcome, and greater pride in a game well played than the outcome. The true nobleman, like the medieval knight, tempered his physical strength and competitive intensity with a gentility that passed as substance rather than mere veneer.

Although there was tremendous social distance between the nobles and squires on the one hand and the lower classes on the other, the English gentry still had frequent, direct contact with those working for them or residing in the surrounding villages. Rather than undermining their status, such interaction reinforced it, as the gentry distinguished itself with its elaborate code of manners, particular sense of morality, distinct speech patterns and accent, and displays of physical skill and daring. All these markers demonstrated the gentry's superiority over others. Equally important, those social distinctions were recognized, respected, and even admired by many members of the lower classes.

As the Victorian period progressed and the forces of modernity became more dominant, two important changes took place that influenced the social construction of sports as well as the social perceptions of how they fit into the newly emergent social order. First, the center of English life moved from the rural estates to the growing urban centers. This had a dramatic impact in terms of space as well as the introduction of new conceptions of time. Both of these affected the pastimes of all Englishmen and women, including those in the upper class.

Whereas the traditional pastimes were embedded in rural life and allowed the gentry to demonstrate their status and significance by taking advantage of the vast tracts of land they owned, the urbanization of England forced sporting activities to adjust to the limitations of urban space and industrial life. Second, the industrialization of England had a dramatic impact upon the rhythms of daily life. While rural existence was dominated by the timetable of the seasons, industrial life was tied to mechanical clock time (Thompson, 1974). The beat of the hour, minute, and second hands ordered life, and the day was divided into work and nonwork time. Nonwork pastimes could no longer continue for days; they had to be brought into line with the new imperatives of industrialization (Kando, 1975). The increased urbanization and industrialization during the latter part of the Victorian period led to the development of formal, written rules, an increasing uniformity in sports forms, and adaptations to the physical and temporal constraints of the urban world (Dunning & Sheard, 2005).

The formalization of sports in response to the emerging forces of modernity was coupled with a powerful legacy from the Victorian era that would significantly influence how sports was socially constructed in the early twentieth century. That legacy would continue to fundamentally shape the perceptions and definitions of sports throughout the remainder of that century and into the first decade of the twenty-first century.

While the British upper class had traditionally educated their children through private tutoring at home, toward the second half of the eighteenth century, more and more members of the upper class sent their children to "public schools" for the basics in their education. These schools were open to the public as long as a student's parents could afford the tuition (making them "private schools" in today's terminology; publically funded education in Britain would come much later).

By the beginning of the nineteenth century, Morford and McIntosh (1993) noted, "it became increasingly fashionable among the upper echelons of English society to send their sons off to the top public schools" (p. 64). The public school experience was designed to accomplish more than simply teaching boys the essentials of reading, writing, and arithmetic. The British public schools were expected to instill the qualities of the Victorian gentleman in their charges. This goal also appealed to those who had, on the basis of commercial wealth, been able to move into the British upper class; their sons would directly experience the enculturation processes that would turn them into Victorian gentlemen alongside the traditional gentry.

On the basis of Thomas Hughes' popular novel *Tom Brown's Schooldays*, Thomas Arnold, the headmaster at Rugby School from 1828 to 1841, is usually credited as the first headmaster to successfully establish a sports-based educational program that transformed upper-class boys into Victorian gentlemen. But the educational programs that combined the traditional prefect-fagging system (senior boys overseeing, ordering, and controlling incoming students) with sports and a strong sense of Christian values to build boys' character and sense of duty and honor did not really come into existence until at least mid-century. Thus, it was really such headmasters as George Cotton at Marlborough College, Edward Thring at Uppingham School, Charles Vaughan at Harrow, and Hely Almond at Loretto School who developed the programs that established "muscular

Christianity" (Mangan, 1981). Charles Kingsley (1887), whose novels also epitomized the virtues of muscular Christianity, emphasized in a book of essays, *Health and Education,* the role sports played in the public schools:

> In the playing fields boys acquired virtues which no books can give them; not merely daring and endurance, but, better still, temper, self-restraint, fairness, honour, unenvious approbation of another's success, and all that "give and take" of life which stand a man in such good stead when he goes forth into the world, and without which, indeed, his success is always maimed and partial. (p. 86)

There were three significant outcomes from this. First, one can see how sports were transformed from their agrarian traditions to a more urban form as the social impact of modernity spread throughout England and the rest of Europe. Among the most important changes were the formal codification of rules, and the progressive elimination of local variations as the means of transportation improved and the possibility for intercity, interregional, and ultimately international competition expanded. Central to the formal codification of sports was the particular value system of the Victorian upper class. Even professional sports that appealed directly to the working class—boxing, for example—were influenced by a rule structure that reflected upper-class attitudes to sports (e.g., Queensbury's rules).

Second, within the modernization process, it became apparent that sports could serve as vehicles for educational purposes. As a result, two very different orientations to sports began to evolve: One form involved professionals and was for entertainment, and the other was wholly educational in its orientation and was aimed at schoolboys and then carried on by amateurs who played for the intrinsic values of sports rather than any extrinsic rewards. While the former was subverted and debased by the power of the market and the realities of the cash nexus, the latter was held forth as the "true" embodiment of sports.

Finally, the educational, intrinsically rewarding form of sports was associated with a specific code of conduct, and that code continued to constitute and reconstitute the values and worldview of the Victorian gentleman well beyond the period in which those values and that perspective developed. In other words, during the period in English history when the rural pastimes of the landed gentry were being replaced by formally codified and regulated sports forms—adapted to the spatial limitations of urban life and the confines of clock time—a specific set of values and attitudes toward how one would best gain from sporting experiences also rose to a position of dominance. During the late Victorian period, the coincidental unification of sports with the legacies of the Victorian gentleman's code of conduct and the precepts of muscular Christianity in the public schools became an ongoing reference point for the definition of "sports" (and all its potential) that has endured right up to the present.

Almost lost in these developments is the fact that the social foundation that gave rise to and sustained the Victorian gentleman and the educational ethos that sports was supposed to play in the British public schools was being quickly transformed by the forces of modernity, democratization, and industrialization. By the end of the nineteenth century, the code of conduct appropriate to the Victorian gentleman had become little more than a cultural artifact cut largely adrift from the social conditions of existence that had created, nurtured, and supported it. The ongoing constitution of life in the post-Victorian world involved values, orientations, and actions that increasingly diverged from the Victorian code, but amateur sports leaders would continue to invoke that code despite its increasing obsolescence. That code would be a constant source of inspiration for all who wanted to resist the impact of modernity on sports.

Coubertin's Dream versus Modernity's Reality

Despite Coubertin's well-laid plans and noble intentions, his dream of transforming the world through a sacred Olympic spectacle ran into two major obstacles right at the outset—social realities that are central forces within modernity and which have continued to shape the Olympic Games and move them further and further from Coubertin's original goals right up to the present point in time. The first reality confronting Coubertin's project was one of the forces that he most wanted to overturn through the Olympic Games: the commercial marketplace.

From the very outset, Coubertin and the International Olympic Committee (IOC) were at the mercy of the market forces of modernity. To host the Olympic Games in their appropriate splendor and close to their origins, the IOC selected Athens as the first host city for the modern Olympics. Although the magnificent marble Panathenaic Stadium had already been refurbished to stage international games in 1870 and 1875, by the end of the century, it required further renovations. It was only due to the public-minded philanthropy of the wealthy Greek businessman George Averoff—at the behest of Crown Prince Constantine—that Athens and the IOC were able to complete the needed restoration to host the first modern Olympic Games in 1896 (Guttmann, 2002).

"No matter what the intentions of the founders of the modern Olympics," Richard Gruneau and Hart Cantelon (1998) have emphasized, "the actual possibilities open to them were limited by the nature of the economic system as a whole and the network of social institutions associated with it" (p. 352). From the first Olympic Games onward, organizers needed to have access to land, facilities, and more and more money. Instead of combating the crass, material interests of the market, the Olympic Games were quickly intimately linked to the flow of capital, speculative investment for profit, and the production of a new entertainment spectacle for sale to a growing consumer public.

The expenses for organizing the Olympic Games were the responsibility of the host city; as those costs rose, organizers began looking for innovative ways to generate enough money to hold such a major international event. By 1928, despite vehement protest by the IOC, the Amsterdam organizing committee sold advertising rights to different commercial interests, which gave them the right to advertise their wares around the Olympic venues and directly within the stadium itself (Barney, Wenn, & Martyn, 2002). It was at the Amsterdam Games that Coca-Cola made its first appearance as an official sponsor at the Olympics—a relationship that continues through, with some fanfare on the part of Coke, to today. Far from Coubertin's lofty goals, the sale of exclusive advertising rights quickly turned the Olympic Games into another location for giant billboards to push products and keep commercial interests alive and thriving.

Similarly, after the inaugural Olympic Games in Athens, the IOC had difficulty finding hosts who had access to the necessary facilities and would undertake the enormous effort and expense entailed in organizing a major international event. To keep the Olympic Games going, the IOC ended up holding the Paris (1900), St. Louis (1904), and London (1908) Olympics in conjunction with the international world's fair, which celebrated science, technology, industrial capitalism, and the modern world in general. The Olympic Games were a mere sideshow to the spectacle of scientific and technological innovation from around the world. By the end of the IV Olympiad, it was already becoming abundantly clear that rather than resisting—let alone overturning—the forces of the marketplace, the Olympics had been easily co-opted and quickly integrated into one of the central driving forces of modernity: the capitalist market.

The second modernist force Coubertin encountered was the presence of the nation-state and all that this particular social entity entailed. Although a good deal has been written about the politicization of the modern Olympic

Games, no one has explicitly tied that politicization to the existence of the modern nation-state—a key distinguishing feature of modernity.

Throughout his work, Giddens (1971; 1984; 1987; 1990) has developed and been an advocate for a "discontinuist" approach to the study of social formations. Thus, in contrast to the largely evolutionary theories and discussions one finds in most sociological analyses regarding the transformation from early agrarian to feudal to capitalist and then industrial and postindustrial (or modern and then postmodern) societies, Giddens has argued that there are important distinguishing features that separate traditional social formations from those of modernity. More to the point, Giddens (1990) has maintained that modernity has been inadequately grasped within the social sciences. Sociologists have not paid sufficient attention to the manner in which modern social institutions are fundamentally different from those found in traditional societies. Among those distinct features is the nation-state (which began to emerge in Western Europe during the seventeen century). In contrast to traditional societies, Giddens (1985) wrote, modern societies "are nation-states, existing within a nation-state system" (p. 1).

The nation-state, Giddens (1985) has maintained, is very different from traditional societies in its internal characteristics, its orientation to its citizens, and its external relations. While the emergence and growth of capitalism was one of the great institutional transformations that enabled and then accelerated the rise of modernity, the nation-state was the other:

> Nation-states and the nation-state system, cannot be explained in terms of the rise of capitalistic enterprise, however convergent the interests of states and capitalistic prosperity have been. The nation-state system was forged by a myriad of contingent events from the loosely scattered order of post-feudal kingdoms and principalities whose existence distinguished Europe from centralised agrarian empires. . . . Nation-states concentrated administrative power far more effectively than traditional states were able to do, and consequently even quite small states could mobilise social and economic resources beyond those available to pre-modern systems. (p. 1)

The importance of the nation-state has also been noted by Foucault (2007), who used the 1648 Treaty of Westphalia as a useful demarcation point in European history between traditional social arrangements and the consolidation of the modern nation-state. To a significant extent, Foucault argued, the Treaty of Westphalia represented the end of the Roman Empire's enduring legacy of imperial ambition. By 1648, it was clear that conflict between or among independent nation-states in Central and Western Europe would only result in protracted wars if the leaders of those nation-states could not reach mutual agreements through negotiation and diplomacy. The quest for empire—a single territorial and political *imperium*—was no longer a feasible objective or rational ambition for nations and their leaders. The Treaty of Westphalia, Foucault emphasized, represented the symbolic moment in European history where it became a continent of multiple nation-states, and the emphasis shifted from the creation of an *imperium* (or Roman-styled empire) to one of independent nations.

The Treaty of Westphalia demonstrated the birth of the nation-state and the Roman Catholic Church's declining influence—a process that had begun with the Reformation during the sixteenth century. One of the conditions of the 1648 treaty was that each state would determine its own national religion. At the same time, despite the religious differences that existed among the various nation-states, the signing of the treaty indicated that diplomacy and negotiation were possible among the various nation-states of Western Europe despite their fundamental religious differences and growing nationalist interests. The treaty showed that independent nation-states would no longer have to form alliances based on a shared religious outlook or seek to be part of a movement toward one single empire. The new independent nation-states, Foucault (2007) argued, sought to assert themselves "in a space of commercial competition and domination, in a space of monetary circulation, colonial conquest, and control of the seas, and all this gives each state's self-assertion not just the form of each being its own end ... but also this new form of competition" (p. 291).

The rise of the nation-state created a new approach to governance—strategies that Foucault termed *raison d'état* and "governmentality" and Giddens linked to the new institutional arrangements that constituted the nation-state. Under the new *raison d'état*, the nation-state became focused on its own essence as an independent entity. This required more than "a good constitution, good laws, and virtuous magistrates," Foucault (2007) noted; it also involved "an art of government, and so a sort of skill, at any rate *a rationality* in the means employed to govern" (pp. 288–9). Part of this new art of government—the new rationality—involved the development of nationalist sentiment and attachment to the nation-state rather than one's ancestry or religion. The existence of independent nation-states created a profound set of social forces that fundamentally opposed support for any genuinely internationalist projects, despite lip service to the contrary. In other words, the interests of the nation-state were at odds with the professed internationalist objectives of the modern Olympic Games. By 1894, the power of nationalist sentiment within a single nation-state had become the dominant sense of attachment felt by most Europeans. Coubertin's internationalist ambitions were already forced into the position of resisting a well-entrenched orientation to life.

Thus, although Coubertin wanted the Olympics to be an international celebration in which all participants became chivalrous brothers-in-arms through the rigors of athletic competition, some nation-states and their National Olympic Committees (NOCs) approached the Olympic Games as an opportunity to demonstrate—and thereby further—national strength and vitality. As a result, even before the inaugural Olympic Games in Athens, officials from the Russian, British, German, American, and French delegations all quarreled over the type of athlete who would be admitted into the Olympic Games. For some IOC delegates, the issue was clear: To demonstrate a nation's strength and vigor and to make the Olympic Games a true spectacle, the best athletes from each nation-state should compete. For others, Coubertin's internationalist aspirations had to take precedence over the interests of separate nation-states—the Olympic Games should be restricted to only those athletes who would genuinely engage with Coubertin's project and could potentially become part of the new European elite that he envisioned.

At the end of the nineteenth century and at the turn of the twentieth century, the only athletes who seemed capable of embodying, displaying, and developing the characteristics Coubertin sought were those who met the strict criteria stipulated in the prevailing amateur codes regulating sports. In the 1902 edition of the *Revue Olympique*, under the title "The Charter of Amateurism," Coubertin reproduced the portion of the IOC's general report of 1894 that contained the resolution on amateurism as well as excerpts from other major international athletic federations. The resolution noted that the following would define an amateur athlete:

> Any individual who has never participated in a competition open to all comers, nor competed for a cash prize, or for a prize of any amount of money regardless of its source, specifically from admissions to the field—or with professionals—and who has never been, at any time in his life, a teacher or paid instructor in physical exercise. (Coubertin, 2000, p. 636)

The report also indicated that such a definition was consistent with those found among all the major international sports federations.

The amateur athlete engaged in athletic competition for the intrinsic satisfaction and character-building experience that it entailed. With good reason, the members of the IOC felt that Olympic Games restricted solely to amateur athletes would embody Coubertin's goals and objectives.

All the criteria that designated an athlete as amateur stemmed from the legacy of the Victorian gentleman, even though the "gentlemanly amateur athlete" was, by the end of the nineteenth century, merely a cultural construction that was artificially sustained by regulations and fiat. It had little connection with the social conditions prevailing at the turn of the twentieth century.

Surprisingly perhaps, Coubertin (2000) was never adamant about the importance of the amateur athlete to his project. Although the resolution at the 1894 congress seemed to resolve the amateur question, that was far from being the case. Following the 1908 Olympic Games in which the British hosts attempted to enforce the amateur code, Coubertin published a survey in the May 1909 issue of the *Revue*. In the preamble, Coubertin (2000) noted that although there was considerable British support for a formalized definition of amateurism, other NOCs were concerned that the regulation would impose a final solution to a long-standing issue that had not yet been fully resolved. About a year later, Coubertin (2000) explored the complexities involved in arriving at a single universally accepted definition of the amateur in a piece entitled "The Possible Unification of the Amateur Definition."

In his memoirs, Coubertin (2000) candidly remarked that his conception of sports had always differed from the majority. For him, sports were religions with their own dogmas. More importantly, sports involved religious feelings, and it seemed churlish to exclude an athlete because at one point in time he had received money. Honor, rather than amateur status, was the real criterion that Coubertin valued most in determining who should participate in the Olympics. To confirm the Olympic Games' integrity and ensure that each competitor was committed to the spirit of Olympism, Coubertin argued strongly for the IOC to introduce a ceremonial oath that each athlete would swear.

Irrespective of Coubertin's particular position, when Britain became the host for the 1908 Olympic Games, it instituted several new regulations, including the 1894 definition of amateurism (Senn, 1999). On the surface, the resolution's implementation seemed straightforward, but there were disputes from the outset. The British felt that although the American NOC had approved their athletes for competition, the American participants failed to live up to the spirit of amateurism through their overly competitive zeal for victory and the time and money the Americans had invested in preparing athletes for the Olympic Games. The Americans responded with complaints about biased officiating and were particularly outraged when "British officials, in violation of the rules, helped an Italian, Dorando Pietri, over the finish line ahead of an American, Johnny Hayes" (Senn, 1999, p. 29). Coubertin sided with the British, as he found the American drive for "athletic supremacy of the world" completely contrary to the spirit of the Olympic Games (even though it was fully consistent with the aspirations of nation-states at the Olympic Games and the ethos of modernity) (cited in Senn, 1999, p. 30).

There were complaints prior to the 1912 Olympic Games in Stockholm that the Swedish athletes had violated the amateur code through the systematic training regimes that they followed in preparation for that Olympiad. Australian swimmer Frank Beaurepaire was not permitted to compete because he was a physical education teacher, and that was a violation of the 1894 definition of amateurism.

The most controversial breach of the amateur code involved Jim Thorpe, an athlete with Native American ancestry who had won gold medals in the decathlon and traditional pentathlon. Thorpe was disqualified when a member of the American Athletic Union (AAU) revealed that Thorpe had played semiprofessional baseball for two years prior to the Olympic Games. Even though Sigfrid Edström, the president of the newly created International Amateur Athletic Federation (IAAF) was hesitant to act, continuing pressure from the AAU forced his hand.

Writing in the *Revue Olympique* just before the IOC was to officially rule on Thorpe's disqualification, Coubertin (2000) emphasized that amateurism was, above all else, a state of mind. He noted that the amateur regulation was fraught with contradictions, allowing athletes who were actually professional to compete while excluding so-called professionals who genuinely embraced the spirit of the Olympic Games. The Thorpe affair, he continued, will have provided a valuable service if it convinces people to change the requirements for participation in the Olympic Games. In 1982, 30 years after Thorpe's death, the IOC overturned his disqualification and returned his medals to his family (Gutmann, 1984).

Coubertin used the opportunity to once again advocate for the institution of an athlete's oath. Swearing to the flag of one's country, Coubertin believed, was the strongest test of one's attitude to the Olympic Games and personal honor.

When the 1916 Olympic Games were awarded to Germany, Carl Diem—who became one of Germany's most long-standing members in the Olympic movement and was a significant historian of the Olympic Games and all its traditions as well as a controversial figure following his close involvement with the Nazi regime from its rise to power until its ultimate defeat—indicated how complex the amateurism question was becoming as he began to mobilize the resources of the German nation-state to import American coaches and institute American-styled training and preparation for the German contingent. Diem was a staunch supporter of the Olympic movement and traditions, but he also believed that nationalist interests were important. Diem wanted to match or even surpass Sweden's success when it hosted the 1912 Olympic Games, where they captured the most medals and only missed the American gold medal total by one. Although some would feel that Diem's systematic approach to developing athletes for the Olympic Games pushed the boundaries on what the IOC might accept, Coubertin was impressed by the broad-based athletic program Diem had established across Germany (Senn, 1999). Diem's program was never tested because World War I forced the cancellation of the VI Olympiad.

By 1930, the amateurism question still plagued the Olympic Games. The international football association (FIFA) was approached by the IOC to introduce soccer to the Olympic Games but soccer was already thoroughly professionalized. As a compromise, FIFA suggested that players who went to play in the Olympics should be able to receive payment for lost wages while at the Olympic Games. The now powerful and ultraconservative IAAF opposed the "broken-time-payments" proposal, and the IOC was pressured by the IAAF to reject FIFA's proposal. The outcome was FIFA's decision to organize its own world festival, launching its first World Cup in 1930.

Complaints over systematic training and too great an interest in winning continued. At the 1936 Berlin Games, building on the infrastructure that Diem had constructed 20 years earlier, British sports administrator Jack Crump complained that the athletes from outside Germany "had the impression that we were competing against a scientifically organized machine." After each event, he noted, the German athletes were taken into a room, where their blood pressure was measured and other tests undertaken. "It was all very serious and highly planned and to my mind the antithesis of amateur sport" (cited in Senn, 1999, p. 61).

Born as a project that would resist—if not overturn—the emerging dominance of modernity, Coubertin's Olympic Games were quickly engulfed in a variety of contradictions and tensions. The Olympic Games would not be able to resist the forces modernizing Europe, but the nobility of his project, the image of sports and what it could accomplish, and the links Coubertin made between the legacy of Victorian England and the values he wanted to promote through sports left an enduring mark on the interpretation of high-performance sports throughout the twentieth century. Indeed, the struggle over the growing performance orientation to sports and the use of performance-enhancing substances, such as steroids, would lie at the center of the Olympic Games' most significant tensions and controversies throughout the remainder of the century.

Chapter 2

Sports, Spectacles, and the Nation-State: The Nazi Olympics

The Olympic Games of the XI Olympiad were critical for the Olympic movement as a whole as well as serving as an important chapter in the history of steroid use in sports. Nazi Germany hosted the Summer and Winter Games of 1936, but it was the Berlin Summer Games that received the greatest attention and served as a significant watershed in Olympic history. Not only were the Berlin Games the last Olympics before WWII, but they brought out some of the most powerful and salient contradictions that existed within Coubertin's project as it matured within the context of an increasingly encompassing modernity.

From the day he announced his project in the hallowed halls of the Sorbonne, Coubertin wanted to link the powerful symbolic power of sports to a magnificent, inspiring international spectacle that would be without rival. In the minds of many (including Coubertin), the Berlin Games would achieve that goal, although the ends for which that symbolism was used caused grave concerns. Coubertin and the IOC had also wanted the modern Olympic Games to inspire a return to Europe's traditional values within the context of an open, embracing internationalism. The Nazi leadership would use the internationalist aspirations of the Olympics to project a very specific image of internationalism—one that resonated with the imperial worldview of Nazi Germany. The Berlin Games were a mere prelude to the Nazi ambitions that resulted in WWII and the complete restructuring of the world order in the post-WWII period. Finally, the 1936 Olympics spectacle—shaped and controlled by a dictatorship—the atrocities committed in Eastern Europe, and steroids were all woven together in the postwar period, producing one of the most demonizing social constructions of steroids that still remains today. Each of these aspects of the 1936 Olympic Games merits examination.

In the aftermath of WWI—after he joined the National Socialist German Workers' Party and began to rise in its ranks—Hitler tramped through the beer halls of Bavaria to drum away at three simple themes. He argued that a group of weak, political traitors had stabbed the German army—the German nation—in the back by surrendering to the allied forces and signing the Treaty of Versailles in 1919.

Second, Hitler continually maintained that the true strength of the German nation rested in its history, racial unity, purity, and superiority as well as its military traditions. Germany's future lies in recovering its illustrious past.

Finally, Hitler argued that only a single great Führer could lead Germany back to its former glory. Power, pride, racial purity, struggle, continuity with the past, and a renewed quest for empire constituted the central core of Nazi ideology (Hitler, 1939).

The highly orchestrated, torchlight parade celebrating Hitler's appointment as Reich Chancellor signaled that this was not an ordinary change of government (Evans, 2004). A pro-Nazi newspaper estimated the crowd at 700,000, although more plausible figures were 18,000 Storm Troopers, 3,000 veterans and elite forces, and 40,000 nonuniformed civilians (Evans, 2004). The numbers seemed so overwhelming because Joseph Goebbels managed the event perfectly. He had the soldiers follow a large, circular route, exchanging old torches for new ones well away from the Reich Chancellery, making the 60,000 marchers passing by the chancellery appear and feel like hundreds of thousands of ardent, ecstatic supporters witnessing "the dawn of a new era" (Kershaw, 1987, p. 48).

Hitler was keenly aware of the power of propaganda—how a charismatic leader could sweep up a mass population and shape its dreams with the appropriate message and symbols. From as early as April 1930, Hitler had centralized the Nazi party's propaganda machine under Goebbels, and the Hitler image was "shaped with increasing skill and direction":

Campaign slogans, themes, speakers and publicity were centrally orchestrated, but with attention to local or regional emphases. New, striking techniques were deployed, as in the second presidential campaign in spring 1932 when an aeroplane was chartered to carry Hitler to his election rallies under the slogan "the Führer over Germany." The image was suggestive of a modern, technological world, though one in which true German values would be restored and would dominate. Above all, the image that Nazi propaganda ceaselessly portrayed was that of power, strength, dynamism and youth—an inexorable march to triumph, a future to be won by belief in the Führer. (Kershaw, 1991, p. 53)

Despite an initial reluctance to host the XI Olympiad, Hitler soon recognized that the 1936 Olympics were a unique opportunity to project indelible images of Nazi power and discipline to domestic and international audiences (Mandell, 1987; Murray, 1992; Krüger, 2003). In election rallies leading up to 1933, the Nazis had refined their ability to exploit various mass media to convey specific messages and images to a mass public.

The Nazis used the massive 1934 Nuremberg Party Congress as their first opportunity to project the power and vision of the Führer and as a testing ground for the 1936 Olympic Games. At Nuremberg, Goebbels orchestrated a genuine Wagnerian *Gesamtkunstwerk*—a total work of art—where thousands of troops performed precisely choreographed movements en masse on a gigantic parade square within an imposing neoclassical stadium. The disciplined mass movements, coordinated by the rising and falling crescendos of hundreds of drummers, spread along the field created a captivating, exhilarating, and emotionally draining experience (Clark, 1997; Speer, 1969).

For the closing ceremony at the 1934 Congress, Albert Speer placed anti-aircraft searchlights around the perimeter of the stadium. As dusk gave way to darkness, the searchlights projected powerful beams of light up into the night sky, creating a "cathedral of light."

As carefully orchestrated and scripted as the Congress had been, Hitler had selected Leni Riefenstahl, one of the most innovative filmmakers of the period, to produce a film that Hitler himself entitled *Triumph of the Will*. The film concentrated almost exclusively on Hitler, carrying the unmistakable message of strength, unity, and loyalty to the Führer. Based on the success of the 1934 Congress, the Nazis went further at the Berlin Games.

The primary significance of the 1936 Olympic Games for the contemporary social construction of steroids is how Nazi Germany capitalized on the powerful symbolic potential of the Olympic Games and showed how Olympics symbols could be manipulated by a dictator for political ends (Krüger, 2003; Teichler, 1982).

The Nazis began to invoke the powerful symbols of the Olympic movement before the Olympic Games began. While at an Olympic conference in Greece in 1934, Carl Diem (the secretary general of the German Committee for Physical Education) and Theodor Lewald (the chairman of the German Olympic Committee) realized they could forge a symbolic connection between classical Greece and Nazi Germany—part of the Nazis' race theory suggested that Aryan superiority descended from the great achievements of ancient Greece—through a torch relay. The relay became an elaborately constructed, painstakingly coordinated pageant of ceremony and unmistakable symbolism.

Using a concave mirror to focus the light of the sun at Olympia, the original site of the ancient Olympic Games, a high priestess kindled a flame. The flame was carried to the Acropolis in Athens to receive a special invocation before beginning its journey from the heroic cradle of European civilization to the new birthplace of all future civilization: the "Thousand-Year Reich" of Nazi Germany. Carrying the torch for one kilometer each, 3,422 runners—carefully selected for their "Aryan features"—carried the torch from Olympia to Hitler's Berlin. Riefenstahl (2006) later incorporated the torch relay into the prologue to *Olympia.*

Goebbels had no trouble embedding the dominant ethos of German fascism within the Olympic Games themselves. Coubertin (2000) had established the Olympics to inspire awe and reverence; they centered on ceremony and spectacle, emphasizing the health and vigor of youth and the virtues of chivalry within competition. All the dominant Olympic imagery and symbolism complemented the central themes of German fascism and the Hitler cult Goebbels was fostering.

Fascism was a male-based cult that glorified youth, strength, dynamism, and conquest. It drew upon the heroic traditions of medieval Europe—a controlled, disciplined, and total commitment to the cause and a willingness to endure personal sacrifice for the greater whole (Baird, 1990). From the 1930s onward, with greater intensity and far more resources after 1933, Goebbels had continuously built the Hitler myth and consolidated the central themes of Nazi ideology. Within that well-developed ideological context and in the absence of alternative worldviews, the themes of the Olympic Games were easily overwhelmed and engulfed within those of Nazi Germany.

The climax of the closing ceremonies came directly from the 1934 Party Congress—the cathedral of light. "At first the columns of light were straight up," Richard Mandell (1987, p. 312) wrote of his experiences in the stadium, "but then the infinitely distant tops of the shafts gradually converged to enclose the darkened stadium in a temple composed entirely of glowing spirit." The darkness as the ceremony came to a close signaled the end of the Olympics, but the unlimited power and majesty of the Thousand-Year Reich would illuminate the path forward and begin a new era in human history.

While some believed that Jesse Owens' four gold medals undermined Hitler's political objectives, amid all the careful orchestration and symbolism, the German total of 33 gold, 26 silver, and 30 bronze medals easily topped the Americans' 24, 20 and 12, respectively. The medal count itself ensured that the Führer's message was not lost on the sympathetic or undecided German viewer.

Internationally, Hitler also enjoyed an enormous propaganda victory. William Shirer, an American news correspondent stationed in Berlin covering the Olympic Games, noted in his diary:

> I'm afraid the Nazis have succeeded in their propaganda. First, the Nazis have run the games on a lavish scale never before experienced, and this has appealed to the athletes. Second, the Nazis have put up a very good front for the general visitors, especially the big businessmen. . . . They said frankly they were favorably impressed by the Nazi "set-up." (Shirer, 1961, p. 53)

In *The Rise and Fall of the Third Reich*, Shirer (1959) made a similar assessment: "The visitors, especially those from England and the United States, were greatly impressed by what they saw: apparently a happy, healthy, friendly people united under Hitler—a far different picture than they had got from reading newspaper dispatches from Berlin" (p. 233).

Victor Klemperer, living in Dresden, reached a similar conclusion. His diary entry of August 13, 1936, noted that the Berlin Games were far more about politics than sports. "'German renaissance through Hitler' I read recently. It's constantly being drummed into the country and into foreigners that here one is witnessing the revival, the flowering, the new spirit, the unity, steadfastness and magnificence, pacific too, of course, spirit of the Third Reich, which lovingly embraces the whole world" (Klemperer, 1999, p. 182). But it was all for show, as street demonstrations, repression of Jews, and the slogan chanting in the streets were merely suspended until after the Olympic Games.

In France, there were several critics of the Berlin Games, but it was Jacques Goddet's front page editorial in one of Europe's foremost sports journals that drew the most attention. Goddet said the Olympic Games were disfigured. Coubertin (2000) categorically rejected Goddet's assessment, claiming that the 1936 Olympic Games had served the Olympic ideal magnificently (see also Murray, 1992; Teichler, 1982).

As successful as the Olympic Games were live, Hitler had once again relied on Riefenstahl's (2006) talents to convey his message. Like *Triumph of the Will*, *Olympia* appeared on the surface to be a lengthy, technologically innovative documentary. But it was far more.

To begin with, *Olympia* was created and shown within a powerful, pre-existing ideological context—one that filtered the central themes of the Olympic Games through the lens of Nazi ideology. This was a conscious strategy. Rather than presenting a steady stream of overt propaganda films, Goebbels approved a large number of "*Tendenzfilme*" that portrayed Nazi tendencies instead of the standard propaganda fodder (Welch, 1993).

Because the Olympic Games were staged and orchestrated as a particular Nazi *Gesamtkunstwerk*, Riefenstahl's contributions came through her film techniques, editing, and the use of music to romanticize the event even further. *Olympia* became a mythical representation of the Olympic Games that linked itself easily to Nazi ideology (Baird, 1990). Thus, for example, Klaus Kreimeier (1996) has argued that Riefenstahl created a "pictorial architecture" that synthesized the actual with the abstract and moved—often without the viewer's awareness—from shots of the real to abstract themes and ideas. The classic example is the dissolve from Myron's famous statue *Discobolus*—the discus thrower—to the living decathlete Erwin Hubner. It is hard to imagine a more ingenious, awe-inspiring, and aesthetically effective way of signifying how the power, strength, and dynamism of Nazi Germany would bring the graceful youth and magnificence of classical Greece back to life and carry on as the rightful heir of that ancient and venerable civilization.

One of the dominant themes in Nazi race theory and aesthetics was the celebration of the "Aryan body," which was starkly contrasted to any abstract, "degenerate art" forms (Barron, 1991). Despite its otherwise extreme prudishness, official Nazi art celebrated the "perfectly proportioned" nude. During the Olympic Games, Riefenstahl became enamored with a series of nudes entitled "The American Champions," which Hubert Stowitts had painted. The U.S. Olympic Committee had denied Stowitts' request to show the paintings in the art exhibit associated with the Olympic Games because they shocked the committee's sensibilities (Graham, 1986). Stowitts paid to have the paintings exhibited himself, but because the series included Jewish and African American athletes, it was ultimately removed from the exhibit.

While editing *Olympia*, Riefenstahl expressed a desire to include them in the movie's prologue, but she changed her mind and considered using a series of figure studies of prominent German athletes instead. The Nazi aesthetic gained greater prominence within the prologue, as Riefenstahl modified the idea still further to ensure that the most perfect Aryan bodies possible were given central prominence in *Olympia*.

Riefenstahl instructed Willy Zielke, an established photographer and film producer, to go to the three best dance and gymnastics schools in Germany—the Bode, Laban, and Wigman schools—to select "the best female bodies in Germany to photograph" (Graham, 1986, p. 138). As an assignment from the Führer, supported by Goebbels, Zielke had no problem getting the schools' or the young women's permission to conduct his peculiar audition. The women chosen were taken to Kurischer Nehrung, a narrow spit of land on the Baltic coast that is comprised of perfectly white sand dunes, where Riefenstahl filmed the scene for the prologue of the female temple dancers invoking the Olympic flame.

Whether Riefenstahl believed that she was merely showing "the beauty of movement coming into its own" and expounding a visual form of "the Olympic idea of the ancients," as she claimed in an interview with the *Preussiche Zeitung* (cited in Graham, 1986, p. 142), or fully recognized but avoided the fact that her "imagistic language" was celebrating the Aryan body and Nazi race theory will remain the subject of debate. But in the same manner that Goebbels and Speer were able to frame the Olympic ideals within a *Gesamtkunstwerk* that celebrated Nazi ideals and achieved their desired propaganda objectives, *Olympia*'s prologue, which framed the entire movie to follow, blended concrete and abstract in a manner that conveyed powerful Nazi messages—especially for its German viewers.

By drawing on the work of Eric Rentschler and Kreimeier, one can see ideological themes at an even deeper level. The concrete images in *Olympia*—already being viewed within a particular ideological context—slide into abstractions that complemented the dominant ideology of the time. Rentschler's (1996) discussion of *Olympia* underscores this point made by Kreimeier:

Riefenstahl's *Olympia* treats athletes as raw material and transforms their bodies into abstract shapes and mass ornaments. This formalizing process climaxes in the famous diving sequence in which well-known figures become faceless and nameless entities who perform in an unreal space. We see the sublime forms of divers in mesmerizing slow motion as they descend through the heavens and drop like bombs. These apparitions of life are ideal and definitely not of this earth. Fascist artworks exercise a powerful and persuasive effect; they present seductive intimations of oblivion with visual beauty and operatic glory. Well-proportioned bodies, divorced from physical reality and raised to ethereal heights, provide aesthetic pleasure of the first order. "Fascist art," in [Susan] Sontag's often-quoted formulation, "glorifies surrender, it exalts mindlessness, it glamorizes death." (p. 22)

In addition to its propaganda potential, there is another dimension of *Olympia* that is significant for the contemporary social construction of sports. Whether or not one agrees with Michael Real (1996) regarding the postmodern gods, the main point in his assessment of Riefenstahl's *Olympia* is an important one:

> In 1936, Leni Riefenstahl is the first to segue from the classical Greek statue "The Discus Thrower" into a contemporary athlete unleashing the spiraled energy into full athletic movement captured on film. In doing so, she ushers in a new era in which technological recreations of Olympic success become better than the original experience, through close-up, slow motion, powerful music, voice-of-god narration, and brilliantly emotional editing. Olga Korbut, the Dream Team, Tomba—what postmodern gods hath media wrought? (p. 9)

The *Gesamtkunstwerk* of the Berlin Games had realized, as no others before them, the full symbolic potential of the Olympics. Riefenstahl's *Olympia* had taken the live spectacle even further by demonstrating how technology could accentuate the symbolic power of Coubertin's project. Beauty, strength, grace, determination, joy, power—every aspect of competitive sports could be sharpened by the lens of a camera. But to fully capitalize on the symbolic potential that the Nazis had shown was possible within the context of modernity, it did not matter how hard a nation-state's athletes struggled—they had to win. Performance and performance-enhancing practices and substances would dominate Olympic sports in the postwar era.

The Myth of Nazi Steroids

The final aspect of the Berlin Games that has continued to resonate with contemporary social constructions of steroids concerns the myth of "Nazi steroids." Whether it is Internet articles ranging from the Association Against Steroid Abuse (2010) through to the World Steroid Review (2010), popular accounts of sports and steroids (e.g., Surtees, 1989; Taylor, 2002; Ungerleider, 2001), various medical reports on steroid use in sports (e.g., Cowart, 1987; Haupt & Rovere, 1984; Wade, 1972), scholarly studies (Todd, 1987), or even the transcripts or reports of government hearings and commissions of inquiry (e.g., Dubin, 1990), there is constant reference to the use of steroids by Nazi troops on the Eastern Front during WWII. How else, it seems, could one explain the atrocities that took place in the sieges of Soviet cities, the wanton destruction of Eastern Europe, and the capacity for normal human beings to conduct the horrors and systematic murder of the Holocaust?

One key reference to the alleged use of steroids by Nazi soldiers that is either cited or simply used without reference is Nicholas Wade's commentary in the early 1970s just as steroid use was being defined as a problematic issue in sports. Without citing any source or supplying supporting evidence, Wade (1972) wrote that the first use of steroids "to improve performance is said to have been in World War II when German troops took them before battle to enhance aggressiveness." "After the war," he continued,

> steroids were given to the survivors of German concentration camps to rebuild body weight. The first use in athletics seems to have been by the Russians in 1954 [*sic*; American weightlifting coach Bob Hoffman and team physician John Ziegler maintained that Soviet athletes at the 1952 Olympic Games had trained with steroids. They confirmed their suspicions at the 1954 World Weightlifting Championships.]. John D. Ziegler, a Maryland physician who was the U.S. team physician to the weightlifting championships in Vienna that year, told *Science* that Soviet weight lifters were receiving doses of testosterone, a male sex hormone. The Russians were also using it on some of their women athletes, Ziegler said.
>
> Besides its growth-promoting effect, testosterone induces male sexual development such as deepening of the voice and hirsuteness, which might account for the manifestation of such traits in Soviet women athletes during the 1950s. (p. 1400)

In five sentences, Wade brought together notions of ruthlessness totalitarianism, Nazi military aggression, concentration camp horror, unconstrained Soviet ambition, medical knowledge, and the hormone-induced masculinization of female athletes in the Soviet Union. What is remarkable is the extent to which those images and even Wade's exact language appear in so many ensuing discussions of steroids.

In a very sound and extensive review of steroids and athletics, James Wright (1980) cites Wade to indicate that "the medical community has categorically condemned the use of anabolic steroids as not only hazardous but ineffective," although—unlike many others—he does not refer to their alleged Nazi use. In a review four years later for *The American Journal of Sports Medicine*, citing Wade as their source, Herbert Haupt and George

Rovere (1984) wrote: "Anabolic steroids were reportedly first used during World War II when they were given to German troops to enhance their aggressiveness" (p. 469). Continuing to draw from Wade, they also noted that: "Their first use in athletics was reportedly by the Russians in 1954 [*sic*]" and attribute the discovery to a "team physician from the United States."

That same year, Robert Goldman (1984), a former steroid user turned steroid opponent and protégé of Ziegler, wrote:

> The first reported use of steroids in a non-clinical setting was during WWII when German troops took them to enhance aggressiveness. It was only a small step to recognize that enhanced aggressiveness might be desirable in athletic competition, and the Russians took that step in the early 1950s. (p. 423)

To show how convoluted and internally referenced the myth has become, in a 1988 review of anabolic steroids for *Postgraduate Medicine*, Windsor and Dumitru cited Wade (1972) as well as Goldman (1984), Haupt and Rovere (1984), Mellion (1984), and Wright (1980)—all of whom had drawn from Wade when repeating the claim of Nazi steroids.

William Taylor's publications on steroids present an interesting case. In the first edition of *Anabolic Steroids and the Athlete*, Taylor's (1982) intention was to present an accurate picture of what was medically known about steroids and their use by athletes. He noted in the introduction that the book was directed to men and women using steroids without proper knowledge or medical attention. As a physician, he felt it was his responsibility to educate athletes so they could make properly informed decisions. In a one-paragraph summary of the book, Taylor (1982) wrote:

> Briefly, anabolic steroids have been shown to enhance muscular strength and body size while reducing the percentage of body fat in weight-trained athletes concurrently ingesting adequate dietary protein and calories and undergoing intensive weight training. The short-term adverse effects of anabolic steroids are rare, mild in nature, and are reversible (according to current knowledge). The long-term adverse effects of both short-term use and the prolonged use are uncertain, and there seems to be a relatively loose association with prolonged use of anabolic steroids with the occurrence of hepatocellular carcinoma and other liver abnormalities. (p. 3)

It seems from the introduction that Taylor's interest was to overcome the American College of Sports Medicine's and other sporting officials' obstruction of "further scientific investigation to determine the necessary facts concerning the entire anabolic steroid picture" (p. 3).

Rather than concentrating so much on what he termed "noncompliant patients" who chronically abused their bodies and the health care system, Taylor felt it was important to provide accurate information to those who were working hard to train their bodies and keep them healthy. "It can be shown," he continued, "that prescribing anabolic steroids to athletes in a controlled fashion with regular physician follow-up visits is less dangerous than prescribing many—if not most—of the medications currently available." Steroid use, he argued, should be like elective surgery, where there is informed consent following an explanation of the risks. In view of his position in 1982, Taylor did not demonize steroids or mention the Nazi steroids myth.

By the time Taylor (1985) wrote *Hormonal Manipulation: A New Era of Monstrous Athletes*, Taylor's position seems to have changed considerably. In *Anabolic Steroids and the Athlete*, within a section entitled "Minor Abnormalities Possibly Associated With Anabolic Steroids," Taylor (1982) noted that "many of the possible side effects are no different from those reported for almost any medication" (p. 66). Among 20 "common adverse effects *associated* with the usage of anabolic steroids," "psychological disturbances" was limited to one paragraph, which noted that they "usually take the form of aggressiveness, changes in mood (elevations and depressions), and, rarely, actual psychotic illness" (pp. 66–7, emphasis in the original).

In *Hormonal Manipulation*, one of Taylor's (1985) major concerns was the impact that steroids might have on athletes' psychological outlook. Steroids led to "The Steroid Spiral," which began with low doses of steroids in a series of on-again, off-again cycles, leading to larger dosages and causing greater mood swings, erratic behavior, and an altered lifestyle, followed by divorce, violent crime, violent marriages, violent sexual crimes, and early death (p. 19). Consistent with his changed position, Taylor (1985) wanted to eliminate "the widespread use of athletic performance-enhancing drugs, especially anabolic steroids and hormones" (p. 126).

In contrast to his 1982 book, without citing Wade, Taylor (1985) wrote this in *Hormonal Manipulation*:

Anabolic steroids were apparently first used in World War II; steroids were said to have been administered to Nazi SS troups [*sic*] in order to make them more aggressive and less fearful of violence. It has been speculated that these early anabolic steroids were used by Hitler and his entire military staff, which may have accounted for, in part, the "driven," aggressive and violent acts committed by the German military.

Shortly after World War II, anabolic steroids were administered to survivors of concentration camps for their potential protein and muscle-building properties. (p. 33)

By the time Taylor (1991) wrote *Macho Medicine: A History of the Anabolic Steroid Epidemic,* his commentary was much more elaborate, mixing some truths with numerous allegations that seem to gain credence within the context of the accurate statements. The section has only one reference:

In the records of World War II are numerous accounts of hormonal manipulation and experimentation with human prisoners by Nazi scientists. After all, a group of German scientists pioneered the synthesis of testosterone and other hormones to follow. Several publications also suggest that testosterone and its analog, anabolic steroids, were given to Nazi troops to make them more aggressive in battle. But perhaps one of the first and certainly the most famous steroid user was Adolf Hitler. From the records of Hitler's personal physician, it was reported that Hitler was given injections of the "derivatives of testosterone" for a variety of presumed mental and physical ailments [(Breo, 1985)]. In fact, besides the "derivatives of testosterone" (anabolic steroids), Hitler's physician reported that Hitler took methamphetamines and several other drugs now considered narcotics during the last few years of life. Who will ever know how much these psychoactive steroids and other narcotics affected Hitler's judgments and dehumanizing tactics? (pp. 8–9)

The question is, of course, intended to be rhetorical, although it is actually one that would require some empirical substantiation to make Taylor's flourish anything more than speculation.

The sole reference in Taylor's argument is to Dennis Breo's interview with Ernst Gunther Schenck, the only surviving physician who was in the Berlin bunker when Hitler committed suicide and who studied Dr. Theodor Morell's extensive diaries. Aside from the fact that it was Morell and not Schenck who was Hitler's personal physician, neither Breo's article nor Morell's (1983) diaries support Taylor's claims. Although Breo's (1985) article indicates that Morell "used the standard medication, belladonna drops, to quiet the tremors [of Parkinson's disease], and he also used a testosterone derivative," there is no recollection of testosterone-based mood swings (p. 40). The diaries themselves show that Morell (1983) gave Hitler orchikrin—"a combination of all hormones of males"—once to combat fatigue and depression and prostakrimum—"an extract of seminal vesicles and prostate"—for a short period of time in 1943 to prevent depressive moods, but once again, there is no discussion in Morell's diaries of mood swings or aggression due to testosterone use (p. 162).

By 2002, Taylor had published a second edition of *Anabolic Steroids and the Athlete*, but it had a very different agenda than the first edition. While the first, as phrased by Taylor (2002) in the second edition, was "intended to strike a balance between the athlete's use and the physician's knowledge" of steroids, "[d]escribing both the medical applications and the athletic abuse [of steroids] is one of the major goals of this book; distinguishing between the two is another" (p. 1). The new introduction shows that in 2002, Taylor wanted steroids to remain a controlled substance: He continued to advocate for steroid use in legitimate medical treatments and wanted to eliminate steroid use by athletes and youths in general. Too few, he argued, recognize "the potential addiction, denial of such addiction, violent behavior, hostility, aggression, likelihood of promoting narcotic abuse, suicidal behavior, premature death, and the heightened sexual appetite that the abuse of anabolic steroids can cause" (p. 7). "Fewer still," he continued, "comprehend the multifaceted degree of anabolic steroid abuse or *anabolic steroid charisma* that has captured a significant portion of Americans." In view of that perspective, although Taylor used almost the same language in presenting the myth of Nazi steroids, the following italicized portions show insertions that make the myth more demonizing than before, although no new sources of evidence were cited (the lines through some text indicate deletions):

> In the records of ~~World War II~~ *this war* are numerous accounts of hormonal manipulation and experimentation with human prisoners by Nazi scientists [(Taylor, 1991)]. After all, a group of German scientists pioneered the synthesis of testosterone and other hormones. *They were awarded the Nobel Prize in medicine for it. Several anecdotal accounts have been published* suggesting that testosterone and its analog, anabolic steroids, were given to *Nazi Gestapo and* Nazi troops to make them more *muscular, sexually aggressive, and mean fighters* ~~aggressive~~ in battle. ~~But perhaps one~~ *One* of the first and certainly most famous *anabolic* steroid use*rs* was Adolf Hitler. From the records of Hitler's personal physician, it was reported that Hitler was given injections of the "derivatives of testosterone" for a variety of presumed mental and physical ailments [(Breo, 1985)]. *Hitler may have been best described as a drug addict in the last years of his life.* ~~In fact, besides the~~

"~~derivatives of testosterone" (anabolic steroids),~~ Hitler's *personal* physician reported that Hitler took methamphetamines and several other drugs *that are* now considered narcotics ~~during the last few years of life~~. Who will ever know how much these psychoactive steroids, *"speed"* and other ~~narcotics~~ *drugs* affected Hitler's *irrational* judgments and dehumanizing tactics? *Today, the drugs Adolf Hitler used are commonplace and are used among anabolic steroid-using strength athletes and bodybuilders who train in gyms and health clubs across America. The abnormal mental health conditions of heavy anabolic steroid users, such as mania, acute paranoid psychoses, overly aggressive and violent behavior, withdrawal depression, withdrawal suicide, and so forth, describe the documented behaviors of Adolf Hitler.* (pp. 180–1)

The myth of Nazi steroids may be found in some scholarly literature. For example, Todd (1987) perpetuated the Wade myth by citing Taylor (1986):

Much of the research involving testosterone and human subjects was done in Germany, before World War II. Heinz Arandt recorded 17 case studies of testosterone use, all of which showed positive results. There is also evidence that the Germans continued their experimentation during the war, and even administered testosterone to some storm troopers to increase their aggressiveness. Dr. William Taylor has speculated that since Hitler had used the drug, it might have accounted for some of the mood swings and aggressiveness of the German fuhrer [*sic*]. (p. 93)

In a "Medical News and Perspectives" piece, Virginia Cowart (1987) noted that Taylor, "who has been writing on steroids for a number of years," had indicated in *Hormonal Manipulation* that "there is likely to be a connection between increased use of anabolic steroids in sports and increasingly violent personalities of athletes" (p. 421). Cowart also indicated that Taylor had suggested that "there is a psychological shift in men taking steroids that causes the normal mixture of psychological behavior to become polarized in a more hostile, aggressive, and assertive nature." However, without any particular reference, Cowart (1987) echoed Wade and Taylor directly:

The first reported use of steroids in a nonclinical setting was during World War II when German troops took them to enhance aggressiveness. It was only a small step to recognize that enhanced aggressiveness might be desirable in athletic competition, and the Russians took that step in the early 1950s. As television coverage of the Olympic Games became available, US viewers of the 1960s became accustomed to seeing European competitors whose gender needed to be announced. (p. 423)

In her extensive critique of steroid use in East Germany, Brigitte Berendonk (1991) also attributed steroid use to the Nazis. "In many general review articles," she wrote, "it was noted that during the Second World War, German storm troopers had been doped with psychotropic testosterone just a few years after the first chemical identification, synthesis, and structural description of these compounds" (p. 227). The references she supplied for this statement refer to studies about the chemical identification and synthesis of testosterone, but they do not refer to the Nazis' use of the drugs. In a similar manner, Steven Ungerleider (2001) gave the following unreferenced account in *Faust's Gold: Inside the East German Doping Machine*:

> During World War II, Hitler issued vast quantities of steroids to the SS and the Wehrmacht so that his troops would better resist combat fatigue and be more ruthless in following any order. As early as 1941, Soviet Red Army observers had noted an unusually passionate fighting spirit among German soldiers, who often seemed eager to die for the glory of the Third Reich. (p. 45)

Despite the pervasiveness of the myth of Nazi steroids, the two leading North American scholars in the history of steroid use—Hoberman (1992a, 1992b) and Yesalis (Yesalis and Bahrke, 2002)—concur that the use of steroids by Nazi troops in any theater of war was a myth. Commenting directly on Wade's (1972) claim that German soldiers "took steroids before battle to enhance aggressiveness," Yesalis and Bahrke (2002) wrote that the "assertion, although often cited, has yet to be documented, in spite of efforts in this regard" (p. 48).

Aside from producing ample evidence demonstrating that no connection between the Nazis and the use of steroids by their troops has ever been established, Hoberman (1992b) targets one explanation for the emergence and perpetuation of the myth:

> It seems improbable that the enormous achievements of German science over the past two centuries did not culminate in scientific experiments aimed at producing the super-race of which the Nazis boasted, including superhuman athletes. Our eagerness to believe that the Nazis did carry out such a project suggests that the world outside Germany has projected its own experimental impulses onto this ultimate gangster regime and assumed that on morally alien territory these forbidden wishes would be fulfilled. (p. 213)

Combining long-standing stereotypes of an authoritarianism, hypermasculinity, and total compliance with a superior's orders provides very fertile ground for the Nazi steroid myth.

The fact that this myth has no empirical basis is not of particular importance—other than indicating that it is indeed a myth. However, what is important is that such opinion leaders as physicians, scientific researchers, policymakers, and journalists have believed the myth was true. When it was confirmed by more than Ziegler that the Soviet athletes were using steroids, the Nazi myth instilled fear among many sports leaders in the West because so many felt there was little to distinguish between Nazi and Soviet totalitarianism. Because the Soviets, like the Americans, had conscripted German scientists to work in the USSR, the myth of Nazi steroids took on a greater urgency as sports leaders in the West feared that German scientists, committed to communism, working for Stalin's totalitarian regime would tip the balance of athletic power decidedly in the direction of the Soviets. As a result, in the postwar period, steroids quickly became more than a Nazi drug. The secret research program involving steroid development and use in the German Democratic Republic (GDR)—*Staatsplanthema 14.25*—became, in Berendonk's (1991) words, "the Manhattan Project in sport" (p. 91). Steroids would be viewed as the "atomic bomb" of Cold War sports.

Chapter 3

The Olympic Games' Fundamental Principle: The Spirit of Olympism

The modern Olympic Games have always been faced with the divisive tension between the logic of athletic conquest and the imperatives entailed in the Olympic Games' lofty, noble aspirations—between the cult of victory and the ideal of moral enhancement. Even in the pre-WWII period, as the Olympic Games grew in stature, countries increasingly viewed them as a symbol of national vitality. The Nazi Games of 1936 had confirmed the extent to which a nation-state could exploit the symbolic power of the Olympics to its advantage. In the post-WWII period, the central tension of the Olympic Games was intensified even further as several factors coalesced around their development, and the impact of each would increase throughout the second half of the twentieth century.

While it is difficult to determine which factor was the most important because they are all thoroughly intertwined, the best starting point would be the Cold War, which pitted East against West—the USSR against the United States. The Cold War heightened nation-states' interests in using the Olympic Games to convey their strength and vitality and thereby raise their international prestige. At the same time, the growth of television and the full impact of the consumers' republic brought a number of commercial forces directly into the dynamics of the Olympic Games. World-class athletic competition was good television, attracting large audiences; the political dimension of the Olympic Games was an added bonus.

The interests of nation-states and the growth of the consumers' republic became major forces in the quest to enhance athletic performance leading to the increasingly systematic study of how to enhance athletic performance. Science and technology became critical elements in the preparation of athletes for Olympic competition. All three factors had a direct impact on the type of athlete who would participate in the Olympic Games during the post-WWII period and the role of performance-enhancing substances, including steroids.

The following discussion will build around a focus on the type of athletes taking part in the Olympic Games after 1945 and how performance expectations placed upon those athletes fundamentally changed the nature of the Olympics, particularly after 1974, when the IOC abandoned Coubertin's fundamental principle for the modern Olympic Games. The 1974 decision has significant implications for the ban on performance-enhancing substances in the Olympics.

As the IOC began to prepare for the first post-WWII Olympic Games, Swedish delegate Bo Ekelund argued that the amateur/professional athlete distinction should be abandoned. Ekelund believed that it was time for the Olympics to feature the best athletes in the world. The American IOC delegate, Avery Brundage, defended Coubertin's Olympic ideals by criticizing the excesses of sports and the crass material interests to which they were becoming beholden (Killanin, 1976).

One year later, as chair of the Amateur Commission, Brundage argued that the IOC should clearly define the term *amateur athlete*, enshrine it in the *Olympic Charter*, and restrict participation solely to amateur athletes. Brundage's proposal combined Coubertin's belief in the importance of an oath and the ultimate significance of an athlete's honor and intentions with respect to the Olympic Games with some specific, objective criteria that the IOC could monitor. The agreement reached in Stockholm noted that an amateur athlete "is one whose connection with sport is and always has been solely for pleasure and for the physical, mental or social benefits he derives there from and to whom sport is nothing more than recreation without material gain of any kind, direct or indirect" (cited in Killanin, 1976, p. 150). The national association governing an athlete's sport had to certify that he or she was an amateur and the declaration countersigned by the athlete's NOC. The competitor had to sign the following statement:

> I, the undersigned, declare on my honour that I am an amateur according to the rules of the International Federation governing my sport, that I have never knowingly transgressed such rules, that I have participated in sport solely for pleasure and for the physical, mental or social benefits I derive therefrom; that sport to me is nothing more than a recreation without material gain of any kind, direct or indirect, and that I am eligible in all respects for participation in the Olympic Games. (Canadian Olympic Association, 1988, p. 15)

Brundage believed that by including the appropriate definition of an amateur athlete in the *Olympic Charter*, the IOC could insulate the movement from the growing pressures of modernity, preserve the central meaning of "sports" as he understood it, and continue the pursuit of Coubertin's original lofty ideals. However, the struggle over the fundamental principles of the Olympic Games was just beginning.

Following the defeat of Nazi Germany, Stalin began to rebuild the Soviet Union. His goal was to surpass the advanced industrial powers of the West in every realm, including sports (Keys, 2003). This goal was consistent with a policy change on sports within the Soviet Union that took place in the late 1930s. To appreciate the nature of the USSR's interest in sports and its decision after WWII to seek entry into the Olympic Games, it is important to quickly review the very instrumental approach to sports that Soviet leaders had always followed.

During the first four years following the Russian Revolution of 1917, there was no single coordinated sports policy in the Soviet Union. The Communist Youth Movement organized sporting events, while the Hygienists and Proletkultists rejected formal sports in favor of a radically new approach to education and physical culture. In 1921, Soviet leaders decided to take control of sports and use them to advance the USSR's own political agenda making it, clear that the Communist Party always had the final word.

As a result, as part of its sponsorship of the Communist International (or Comintern), the Soviet Union initiated the Red Sport International (or Sportintern) in 1921. The Sportintern featured athletic competitions, demonstrations of physical skill and physical culture, parades, political demonstrations, and meetings—all of which were designed to support the Comintern's particular, Soviet-controlled, revolutionary agenda. Although the Sportintern was designed to appeal to workers who were not part of the socialist or communist movement, its primary target were workers who were already committed to communism and were affiliated with communist organizations outside the Comintern. As a result, the Sportintern competed against the larger and more successful Socialist Workers' Sport International (founded in 1920) and the existing workers' sports movement. Although the Sportintern drew members from Europe, Latin America, and North America, its numbers outside the USSR were never more than a few hundred thousand (Keys, 2003). In other words, it failed to bring workers under the Soviet umbrella.

The year 1934 was an important turning point in Soviet history, as Stalin consolidated his position as the supreme leader of the USSR. Stalin now made or oversaw all major decisions. There was an abrupt "right turn" in Soviet foreign policy, as Stalin ended the rhetoric of a world communist revolution, formed coalitions with various socialist parties in Europe to oppose the rise of fascism in Germany and Italy, and joined the League of Nations.

Changes within the Soviet Union were equally as dramatic. In place of the rhetoric of the USSR as an egalitarian, communist society, Stalin established programs and structures that legitimated hierarchy and inequality while actively encouraging Soviet citizens to seek personal advancement at the expense of others. The most important symbol of this change was the Stakhanovite movement—a program named after the coal miner Alexi Stakhanov, whose capacity to exceed productivity quotas was legendary and became widely celebrated by the Soviet leadership. In truth, the Stakhanovite movement was largely an ideological fiction that was closely patterned on the incentive-based system advocated by Frederick Winslow Taylor's (1911) *The Principles of Scientific Management,* and whether Soviet workers who exceed production norms received greater compensation is disputed. Nevertheless, by improving technology, rationalizing production, and providing a rhetorical impetus to increase production, the Stakhanovite movement represented a significant shift in Soviet ideology.

From the introduction of Taylorism in the workplace and the emphasis on production quotas and comparisons between individuals, it was a short step to justifying changes in sports. As a result, after 1934, the Soviets focused on the bourgeois, competitive, high-performance forms of sports, with the goal of also outperforming the capitalist world in this arena. But the shift in Soviet policy also had a more profound aspect.

In a "deeper sense," Keys (2003) has emphasized, the shift was "a reflection of the ways the Soviet Union was caught up in broader modernizing processes that affected all of Europe in this period" (p. 415). "In an era obsessed with quantification and comparison," Keys continued, "competition in international sports seemed to offer an equitable basis for quantifiable comparisons of national success in harnessing population resources, a political lure that proved irresistible even to a Stalinist mentality deeply hostile to capitalist forms of internationalism" (pp. 415–6).

Participation in the contests run by international federations was, according to Keys (2003), "increasingly considered an essential feature of a modern state"—precisely because the uniformity of its rules and the claim that sports were universal forms of activity that offered "a uniquely objective and quantifiable marker of national success." "Thus," Keys continued, "nationalist motives and cultural internationalism served to reinforce each other" (p. 433).

Within the Soviet Union, the goal of surpassing capitalist sports first appeared in late 1933, and the official commitment to catching and surpassing bourgeois sports records was implemented in 1934. By 1937, the Sportintern was dissolved and replaced by the Physical Culture Council, which celebrated the traditions of modern sports. To ensure success, the Soviets introduced a centralized, hierarchical structure for the development of Soviet athletes who would now represent the nation-state in head-to-head competition with athletes from the capitalist nations of the West.

In the postwar period, the Soviet Union continued to develop its centralized sports system, complete with a financial reward system that was a powerful incentive for athletes to break European and world records. As Stalin focused on entry into the Olympic Games, the Physical Culture Council began to refine its athlete development system by including housing and training facilities, where top-level athletes could concentrate on systematically planned programs to enhance their performances (Senn, 1999). The system was not consistent with the IOC's or most international sports federations' (ISFs) regulations, but despite exchanges between the Soviets and Brundage and IAAF president Sigfrid Edstrøm, Soviet sports officials changed very little in their athlete development system.

The Soviet strategy was to wear down the IOC and the various ISFs. Despite the fact that the USSR had not met any eligibility requirements and frequently was not even a sanctioned member of an IF, the Soviets simply sent athletes to various sanctioned competitions. Each time an IF granted the Soviet delegation permission to participate, it gave tacit legitimacy to the Soviet system.

Although Soviet leaders had expressed a strong interest in taking part in the first postwar Olympic Games in London, distrust in the Soviet's tactics during the prewar period prevented the IOC from admitting the USSR to the 1948 Olympic Games. By April 1951, the Soviet Union had met enough of the IOC's conditions to gain admission to the 1952 Olympic Games.

This short overview of Soviet sports from the 1920s to the USSR's entry into the Olympics underlines four specific points. First, throughout its short history, Soviet leaders tried to use sports and physical culture to achieve particular political objectives. Second, Soviet leaders determined how sports would be used and how those goals would be reached. Third, the USSR was deeply influenced by the same modernist forces that affected the West throughout the twentieth century. Finally, those modernist forces were a key influence in the Soviet leadership's decision to compete head-to-head with the bourgeois nations of the West, and they determined the approach the Soviets took to competing against the West in the sports world. In short, the forces of modernity and the development of the Soviet sports system were intimately related.

For four very different but interrelated reasons, the Helsinki Games were a momentous transition point in the history of the Olympic movement and the use of steroids in sports. First, in 1952, Brundage began a 20-year term as IOC president. Of all its leaders, Brundage was the most committed to Coubertin's Olympic ideal. Second, the Olympic Games promised a gripping drama, as the USSR and United States would directly confront each other in a critical, symbolic test of national strength. Third, the Helsinki Games were the first Olympics in which athletes who had trained with steroids took part. Finally, the IOC admitted a new nation-state to the Olympic movement: West Germany. Because Western powers had refused to acknowledge the German Democratic Republic (GDR; East Germany) as a legitimate nation-state and each member of the Olympic movement could have only one NOC, the IOC would not recognize an NOC from the GDR. The "German team" would be comprised of athletes from the Federal Republic of Germany (FRG; West Germany) and the GDR. Each of those four factors had long-term implications for the Olympic movement and the IOC's policies on steroids.

The Soviets jumped to an early, almost insurmountable lead in the opening days of the 1952 Summer Games, but the Americans overtook them on the last day of competition. While the East/West confrontation brought tremendous excitement to the Olympics, it also initiated the most formidable challenge to Coubertin's founding principles. The cold, calculated pursuit of victory emerged as a dominating principle from the Helsinki Games onward. Perhaps nothing symbolized that commitment to victory more than the three gold, three silver, and one bronze won by the Soviet weightlifters.

After the competition, American weightlifting coach Bob Hoffman alleged that the Soviets were using hormones to build strength (Todd, 1987). At the 1954 World Weightlifting Championships, Hoffman and American team physician John Ziegler satisfied themselves that Soviets were using synthetic testosterone to enhance their athletes' muscle-building capacities.

The standard story in most discussions of steroids in sports—propagated initially by Ziegler—indicates that Ziegler returned from the 1954 championships and duplicated the Soviet example (Ziegler, 1984; see also Goldman, 1984; Ryan, 1976; Todd, 1983; Waddington, 1996). Through the Ciba Pharmaceutical Company, Ziegler developed the synthetic steroid methandienone (Dianabol), which he distributed to weightlifters at the York Barbell Club in Pennsylvania. "The news of anabolic steroids spread through the athletic community like wildfire," former steroid user Bob Goldman (1984) noted, "and soon drugs and stories of drugs became the chief topic of conversation at training camps and the subject of articles in all of the sports magazines" (p. 94).

Although that scenario seems plausible based on a detailed history of steroid use in sports, Paul Dimeo (2007) is skeptical; the story is too neat and convenient. The account allows Ziegler to use patriotism to exonerate himself from the responsibility of introducing steroids to athletes in the United States and places the ultimate responsibility for their presence with the Soviet Union.

Dimeo has argued that the successful use of steroids did not simply spring up in 1952. Steroid use in sports was the result of a lengthy, complex process that involved refining the synthetic hormone, convincing weightlifters to use it, and developing training programs that would produce significant results (Fair, 1993). Steroid use certainly became part of the high stakes East/West competition for nations to gain an edge in the early Cold War period, but it was pursued in largely clandestine settings—away from the glare of gold medals and public scrutiny—by committed (perhaps patriotic) researchers, physicians, administrators, coaches, and athletes on both sides of the Cold War divide.

Irrespective of how steroids first entered sports, as their performance-enhancing properties became increasingly evident in the 1950s and early 1960s, synthetic steroids were incorporated into a widening array of training programs for athletes in the strength and power events. Although documented evidence of steroid use by East and West bloc athletes is uneven, it is clear that by the early 1960s, steroids were commonplace in strength sports (see Dimeo, 2007; Dubin, 1990; Franke & Berendonk, 1997; Todd & Todd, 2001; Yesalis & Bahrke, 2002).

Rule 26 of the *Olympic Charter* and the Struggle Over Coubertin's Founding Principles

While steroids—or rumors of steroid use—were one of the most significant phenomena in the first East/West confrontation, they hardly registered in public commentary at the time and remained low profile throughout the 1950s. The IOC's major concern was the growing win-at-all-costs approach to high-performance sports that the confrontation between the world's two superpowers was fostering and the increasing professionalization of athletes on both sides of the Cold War divide.

As the newly appointed IOC president, Brundage fiercely defended the movement's central principles while also emphasizing the role they could play in improving international relations. "Sport," Brundage noted at the end of several speeches at the time,

> which still keeps the flag of idealism flying, is perhaps the most saving grace in the world at the moment, with its spirit of rules kept, and regard for the adversary, whether the fight is going for or against. When, if ever, the spirit of sport, which is the spirit of fair play, reigns over international affairs, the cat force, which rules there now, will slink away, and human life emerge for the first time from the jungle. (cited in Guttmann, 1984, pp. 115–6)

Although steroids would become the most sinister performance-enhancing substance, the death of Danish cyclist Knud Jensen, allegedly from a nicotinyl titrate and amphetamine cocktail at the 1960 Summer Games, brought the movement's fundamental principles back to center stage. Moreover, even though the cause of Jensen's death was due to extreme dehydration resulting from Jensen's unwavering commitment to his and his time trial teammates' single-minded pursuit of victory in a race held in 100+ Fahrenheit temperatures (and not an amphetamine overdose), the instant spread of the rumor and immediate jump to judgment demonstrated how sensitive performance-enhancing substances had already become (Møller, 2005). Jensen, his teammates, and other cyclists' embrace of an unqualified commitment to victory for personal and nationalist reasons—not substance use—threatened to bring down the ancient pillars on which Coubertin—and now Brundage—based the Olympic movement. The forces of modernity had cut deeply into sports by the end of the Rome Olympics.

Jensen's death reinforced Brundage's commitment to end what he believed was the real problem facing the IOC: the growing professionalized attitude toward sports and the all-out pursuit of victory.

Following Jensen's death, the IOC moved quickly to reassert the Olympic Games' central principles. Brundage believed that if the IOC could formally control the types of athletes taking part in the Olympic Games, then the Olympics could once again embody Coubertin's principles. At the

1962 meetings in Moscow, Brundage achieved a goal that he had articulated a decade and a half earlier: enshrining "The Amateurism Code" as Rule 26 in the *Olympic Charter*. Rule 26 stated:

An amateur is one who participates and always has participated in sport without material gain. To qualify as an amateur, it is necessary to comply with the following conditions:

a) Have a normal occupation destined to ensure his present and future livelihood.
b) Never have received any payment for taking part in any sports competitions.
c) Comply with the rules of the International Federation concerned.
d) Comply with the official interpretations of this regulation. (cited in Killanin, 1976, p. 150)

While Rule 26 was important, Brundage recognized that the spread of performance-enhancing substances on both sides of the East/West divide still left the ghoulish image of victory-at-any-cost untouched. The Olympics had to be drug-free. To keep the pressure on athletes engaged in the all-out pursuit of victory and recognizing that performance-enhancing substances could become a significant problem for the Olympic Games, Brundage turned to Arthur Porritt, the chair of the British Association of Sports Medicine (BASM) (Dimeo, 2007). Porritt shared Brundage's views on amateurism and drug use and quickly became one of several influential British physicians and researchers who would help shape IOC policy.

In leading the attack on drugs in sports, Porritt was able to link his position with concerns that mounted throughout the 1960s over the growing use of recreational drugs in the public at large. Appointed by Brundage in 1962 to head the IOC's antidoping commission, Porritt and his committee acted quickly. In 1964, they recommended that the IOC condemn drug use, introduce testing, have athletes sign a pledge that they were drug-free, and sanction individuals and National Sports Organizations (NSOs) implicated in drug use (Todd & Todd, 2001). In conjunction with the BASM, Porritt hosted the first major international conference on drugs in sports—an issue given added urgency by British cyclist Tommy Simpson's death in the 1967 Tour de France (Dimeo, 2007).

The conference provided an international stage for Porritt and others to press for the strict control of pharmaceuticals in sports. "Doping is an evil—it is morally wrong, physically dangerous, socially degenerate and legally indefensible," Porritt argued in 1965 (cited in Dimeo, 2007, p. 108).

Drug use, he continued, reflected a "weakness of character" and was a "temptation in this fast-moving dynamic and somewhat amoral world" and had to be controlled. At the BASM conference, Porritt maintained that drug use had significant moral implications related to sportsmanship and fair play.

Although sentiment at the conference was overwhelmingly in support of Porritt's position, there were dissenting voices. For example, M. Hollyhock argued that amphetamines or steroid use for limited periods—and under strict supervision—would not harm a physically and psychologically normal person (Dimeo, 2007). Hollyhock rejected the notion that drugs contravened the principles of fair play because the existing inequalities in coaching and facilities precluded a level playing field in the first place. He also argued that in times of peace, patriotic fervor is focused on sports and performance receives greater emphasis than sports' simple enjoyment, and performance-enhancing substance use stems directly from the intensified focus on victory. Hollyhock suggested that the real problem was international sports and not simply substance use.

Based on his analysis of the IOC's deliberations over performance-enhancing substances, Dimeo (2007) has emphasized that its policy was not simply a response to the use of drugs in sports but the product of a particular time and place. The key individuals who drafted the policy, brought it forward to the IOC, presented it, and defended it against any criticisms had all grown up in an environment where the ideals of the gentlemanly amateur sportsman had exercised considerable influence. No matter how much the world had changed from 1920 to 1960, the decision-makers continued to employ that traditional image. At the same time, policymakers viewed performance-enhancing substance use as part of the larger drug problems of the turbulent 1960s. As a result, Dimeo (2007) noted, the IOC policy went "far beyond the narrow question of drugs in sport" (p. 14). The policy was framed more by entrenched beliefs, peer and social pressures, and personal, emotional responses to issues of "drug use" in the late 1960s than it was by carefully considered, rational argument and dispassionate decision making.

At the 1967 Tehran meetings, the IOC defined "doping," drafted the first list of banned substances—ranging from cocaine, pep pills, and vaso-dilators to alcohol, opiates, and hashish—adopted the principle of testing athletes for banned drugs, and enshrined it all in Rule 28, the "Medical Protocol," of the *Olympic Charter*. The new rule stated that "the use of substances or techniques in any form or quantity alien or unnatural to the body with the exclusive aim of obtaining an artificial or unfair increase of performance in competition" was forbidden (cited in Todd & Todd, 2001, p. 68). The dominant, public justification for Rule 28 was—and remains—the moral and ethical rationale that underlies what the IOC and World Anti-Doping Association (WADA) refer to as "the spirit of sport."

It is important to emphasize that although Rule 28 represented a decisive step in the proscription of certain substances, it did not meet Porritt's objectives fully. Porritt recognized that a ban alone would not solve the problem. He contended that a long-term education policy that stressed the physical dangers and moral aspects of drug use would stop athletes from using performance-enhancing substances (Todd & Todd, 2001). Educating athletes about the potential physical harm associated with performance-enhancing substances probably seemed unnecessary in the wake of Jensen's and Simpson's highly visible and widely discussed deaths, but without a full and open discussion about the substances themselves and the reasons athletes took them, it was unlikely that a policy of proscription alone would succeed. The members of the IOC—Porritt's views notwithstanding—seemed to believe that if performance-enhancing substances were forbidden and the athletes were compelled to comply with the ban, then the problem would be solved.

The moral aspect to the ban on performance-enhancing substances was grounded in Coubertin's original founding principles. The morally sound Olympic athlete competed in the spirit of chivalry and fair play so competitors could form an enduring bond and build their character. The overly competitive zeal that led to the use of performance-enhancing substances was not part of the movement's moral code. This was the fundamental message Porritt wanted the IOC to impress upon athletes.

Rule 28 also signified the IOC's opposition to the growing reliance on scientifically assisted performance enhancement in general. Sports science and the cult of victory were two sides of the same coin, and neither had any place in Coubertin's vision of the Olympic Games. Rule 28's legitimacy and the IOC's opposition to the material forces of world-class sports rested in the movement's continuing commitment to Coubertin's heritage—his philosophy of Olympism and its fundamental principles.

While there was little resistance to the incorporation of Rule 28 into the *Olympic Charter*, Soviet delegate Constantin Andrianov returned to Rule 26. The IOC, he noted, had argued about a clear, precise definition of amateurism for more than half a century. "The IOC," Andrianov maintained, endeavours to prove to the world its own point of view without taking into account the requirements of life and conditions in which modern sport is developing. This is one of the most knotty questions and it seems necessary to find a new approach to this problem, renouncing antiquated formulas of amateur status, formulated at the end of the nineteenth century.... We should be able ... in the face of modern requirements, to determine the new rules of amateur status, and not to cling to the former ones, which ... are very often violated.... It is proposed that the IOC should work out new eligibility rules for the Olympic Games. (cited in Killanin, 1976, p. 151)

Brundage knew that the movement's fundamental principles were invested in the type of athlete who was admitted to the Olympic Games, and he held firm. Even after a joint IOC/NOC commission reviewed the "eligibility question" in 1969 and 1970 and proposed to rename Rule 26 the "eligibility code," Brundage barely wavered. In an apparent compromise, he renamed Rule 26, but he did not concede any ground on the movement's principles. The criteria contained in the new eligibility code were as restrictive as any previously employed by the IOC. For example, the new code excluded many of the financial support strategies that had become widespread in the East and West:

Individuals subsidized by governments, educational institutions, or business concerns because of their athletic ability are not amateurs. Business and industrial concerns sometimes employ athletes for their advertising value. The athletes are given paid employment with little work to do and are free to practise and compete at all times. For national aggrandizement, governments occasionally adopt the same methods and give athletes positions in the army, on the police force, or in a government office. They also operate training camps for extended periods. Some colleges and universities offer outstanding athletes scholarships and inducements of various kinds. Recipients of these special favours, which are granted only because of athletic ability, are not eligible to compete in the Olympic Games. (cited in Killanin, 1976, p. 152)

Despite his efforts to restrict the type of athlete taking part in the Olympic Games by fiat, even the president of the IOC could not reign in the forces of modernity as they penetrated deeper and deeper into the real world of high-performance sports.

Television, Commercial Interests, and the Olympic Ideal

Although government planning and coordination would become increasingly significant in shaping the world of high-performance sports, throughout the 1960s, the market economy in the West was robust enough to support a technology that would play a major role in the transformation of sports in the period of modernity: television. While television may now seem like an antiquated technology, its impact on culture, the flow of ideas, the shaping of perceptions—to say nothing of its role in the global expansion of the commercial marketplace—is undeniable. Television thrived and expanded because the post-WWII emphasis on mass consumption created the economic context that would sustain television as an emerging technology and provided the financial incentives for its rapid refinement and development during the first two decades of the postwar period. Mass production techniques provided inexpensive products, with generous profit margins, that the growing mass market of consumers purchased. Some of those profits flowed into television as advertising revenue, and the ads continued to stimulate consumer demand. The mass production/television advertising/mass market sales cycle continued to grow, imbedding television deeper and deeper into postwar culture and society. The symbiotic relationships among television, advertising, commercial sales interests, and the growth of the market created the perfect conditions for the generous growth that occurred from the 1950s into the 1970s (Hobsbawm, 1995).

Among the beneficiaries of the rapid economic expansion were such sports interests as professional baseball, football, boxing, and wrestling in North America, soccer in most other parts of the globe, and the Olympic Games internationally as well as the emerging market for mass-produced sporting goods. Thus, for example, long before Nike took the world stage, the brothers Adolf (Adi) and Rudolf (Rudi) Dassler competed head-to-head as owners of the rival Adidas and Puma shoe companies, and a host of European ski manufacturers used the Winter Games to market their products to the world. Sporting goods producers used the Olympics to expose consumer audiences to their products through direct advertising as well as indirectly as the trademark logos on the best equipment in the world, used by world-class athletes, registered in viewers' minds. The association between technology and performance was confirmed again and again as television programs captured cutting-edge sporting equipment, producing high-performance results that consumers saw live from the comfort of their family rooms.

The television/advertising/sports/sporting goods nexus created a socioeconomic force that would dramatically alter the nature of the Olympics, the competitors taking part, and the nature of the competitions themselves.

The best athletes in the West needed money to compete against the state-supported athletes from the East bloc; television networks needed a spectacle to draw viewers and manufacturers with products to sell to that audience; the lucrative ski and shoe industries—followed by others in the 1970s—wanted to broaden their markets and increase sales; and together, they all formed complex, often under-the-table, mutually beneficial agreements.

As part of its national propaganda campaign, Nazi Germany was the first host nation to exploit the emerging technology of television. Delayed television broadcasts of the Winter Games in Garmisch-Partenkirchen marked television's inaugural use, but the live coverage of the Summer Games' opening ceremonies dramatically captured the new medium's communications potential. The Nazi Summer Games covered 175 events with 138 hours of programming. An estimated 162,000 people watching the live televised events or delayed telecasts in public venues in and around Berlin (Barney, Wenn, & Martyn, 2002).

In the first Olympiad of the postwar period, the British Broadcasting Corporation (BBC) paid about $3,000 for the exclusive rights to the 1948 London Games. At that time, only Great Britain, the United States, and the USSR had established television systems, and there were fewer than five million television sets around the world (Whannel, 2009). Even though the BBC allocated fewer hours of programming than Germany had delivered in 1936, the London Games reached an audience of a half-million people (Barney, Wenn, & Martyn, 2002). Within two decades, televised images—in "living color"—would be broadcast around the world to over 250 million homes spread throughout 130 different countries.

With each Olympiad separated by four years, the Olympic Games were not a major factor in the development of the sports/television nexus. The most important driving forces were the private commercial networks in the United States and the status, prestige, and revenue that sports coverage brought to each of them. As it became increasingly clear that sports programming attracted the key target audience of males between 18 and 40—a consumer group that responded to the "impulse needs" that television was able to project—the private networks entered bidding wars for the exclusive rights to Major League Baseball (MLB), college and professional football, and boxing and wrestling. As a result, the bids for the exclusive rights to each of these "properties" rose dramatically in the 1950s and 1960s. For example, the rights for the World Series cost only $6 million in 1951 but within five years almost tripled to $15 million. Coverage of the National Football League (NFL) cost $4.5 million per year from

1961–1964 but jumped to $7 million a year when CBS renewed its contract for an additional two years. With football quickly replacing baseball as "America's sport" in the 1960s, to avoid being completely relegated to the sidelines, NBC paid the fledgling American Football League $42 million over five years (Whannel, 2009). Bids for the rights to the Olympics rode on the coattails of the successes the American networks had experienced with domestic sports coverage and the resulting competitive scramble to secure additional high-profile sports programming.

Despite television's growing significance as a vehicle for spreading the Olympic Games' message as well as serving as a revenue source, the IOC did not begin to formulate a policy on television rights until the mid-1950s. The major impetus behind the policy was the struggle over the revenue for the 1956 Melbourne Games.

The Melbourne Olympic Organizing Committee (MOOC) recognized the potential financial windfall that television represented, but without any experience in negotiating exclusive rights, MOOC hired Fremantle Overseas and TV Incorporated to bargain with international television networks over the exclusive rights to cover the Olympic Games. In response, broadcasters from the United States, Canada, Great Britain, and several European countries argued that television covering of the Olympic Games was simply a form of journalism and that journalists should not have to pay for the right to cover an event. Fremantle refused to budge, so the broadcasters chose to boycott the Olympic Games. The resulting coverage was limited, although MOOC kept the profits that resulted from the sale of highlights packages to the networks that were not covering the Olympic Games (Gould, 1956; Wenn, 1993).

Following the networks' growing interest in sports properties and the bidding wars in the United States over sports programs, television revenue quickly became a major issue for the IOC. Some members were attracted by the potential revenue, while others were deeply concerned about the impact that television would have on the movement's ideals. Brundage tried to ensure that the IOC enjoyed the best of both worlds by shrewdly revising the *Olympic Charter* so it allowed the IOC to take advantage of the financial benefits of television while still protecting Coubertin's principles.

In 1958, the IOC modified the *Olympic Charter* regarding publicity. The change allowed the organizing committee of the Olympic Games to negotiate television rights for each Olympiad, but the IOC held final approval and had the right to determine the revenue's distribution. The *Olympic Charter* revision allowed Brundage to keep the IOC out of direct negotiations with the new commercial interests of television but allowed it to reap the financial benefits of the market forces that were creeping ever so steadily into the movement (Barney, Wenn, & Martyn, 2002). The genie in the television revenue bottle was more powerful than Brundage had anticipated as the commercial forces of television and sponsorship revenue—along with the political forces of the Cold War—would radically reshape the movement in the final decades of the twentieth century.

One gains an appreciation of how much television has meant to the Olympic Games by considering some recent data on viewers and revenue. According to Nielsen Media Research (2008), 4.4 billion people around the world watched, at one time or another, the 2008 Beijing Games—almost 70 percent of the world's population. Nielsen reported that 94 percent of the population in the Peoples Republic of China saw at least part of the Olympic Games on television, with South Korea matching that level of saturation and Mexico at 93 percent. The opening ceremonies attracted a global audience of two billion viewers. In the United States, more than 70 million Americans watched at least part of the opening ceremonies in Beijing, making them the second-most watched opening ceremonies in the National Broadcasting Company's (NBC) history—the Atlanta Games in 1996 attracted 77 million viewers. The average audience at any point in time for the Beijing opening ceremonies was 34.2 million American viewers (Atlanta averaged 39.8 million).

These data emphasize an important aspect of contemporary life, which Giddens (1990) has identified with the inelegant term "time-space distanciation"—one of the key conditions of modernity. Time-space distanciation concerns the manner in which time and space are organized so presence and absence are connected.

In premodern societies, Giddens has argued, time and space are closely bound together. Moving any distance takes time. Under conditions of modernity, movement from one place to another is far more rapid but even more importantly, and clearly illustrated by the audience data related to the Olympic Games, information from one location in the world can be distributed around the globe instantaneously. Thus, although television viewers are not in Beijing during the opening ceremonies, they feel as though they are; they are participating, as live viewers, in an event taking place far from their actual location. Time, space, and place have all been "disembedded" from the traditional experiences of time and place because they are directly experienced by humans through their regular biological capacities. Under the technological conditions of modernity, greater distances are traversed with increasing speed, so now some distances are crossed instantaneously. The time dimension of time-space distanciation has been reduced to the immediate, and the space dimension has become global.

"The advent of modernity," Giddens (1990, p. 18) wrote, "increasingly tears space away from place by fostering relations between 'absent' others, locationally distant from any given face-to-face interaction." Place, he continued, becomes "increasingly *phantasmagoric*" as a specific locale is shaped and influenced by social forces that are far removed from that specific place. Due to technology, the local is no longer shaped by what is present on the scene; it can be influenced by circumstances and events at a considerable distance. One obvious impact is the global reach of particular sports forms, but there are other profound impacts that the time-space distanciation of modernity has on sports in general and the Olympic Games in particular (the most salient are examined in the following section).

The U.S. television rights have always been the IOC's most lucrative revenue source. Looking at the Summer Games, CBS paid $394,000 for the rights to the 1960 Rome Olympics; that rose to $1.5 million, $4.5 million, and $7.5 million for Tokyo (1964), Mexico City (1968), and Munich (1972), respectively. The Montreal Games in 1976 cost the American Broadcasting Company (ABC) $25 million, and even though the United States boycotted Moscow in 1980, NBC had already paid $87 million for those rights. ABC spent $225 million for the 1984 Los Angeles Games, and the 1996 centennial Olympic Games in Atlanta cost NBC $456 million. Sydney (2000), Athens (2004), and Beijing (2008) cost $705 million, $793 million, and $894 million, respectively, with NBC and cable affiliates committing $1.181 billion dollars for the rights to the London Games in 2012 (Martzke, 2003). In Beijing, when one adds in $100 million in production expenses, the total cost still permitted more than $90 million dollars in profit after NBC had sold advertising spots (Hibberd & Landreth, 2008).

There is no doubt that television revenue has made the IOC wealthy. More importantly, television supplied a critical platform for the growth and expansion of the international marketplace. Television provided the opportunity for sporting goods manufacturers to reach consumers directly within the context of athletic events when interest would be highest. Television and the sporting spectacles it carries created market opportunities for the producers of ancillary commodities that tap into the sports market (e.g., sports drinks, nutritional supplements, diet, and fitness programs).

Finally, television created market openings for commercial interests that use athletes to market their products—everything from breakfast cereals, fast foods, various snacks, and alcohol, to investment advice, computers, and communications technology.

As the center of a global communications industry, television "challenged and then usurped the traditional authority of sports governing bodies" (Whannel, 2009, p. 214). While traditional sports-governing bodies had controlled sports without challenge, the revenues generated by television advertising and endorsement money for athletes changed the dynamics of sports considerably. Those sports-governing bodies that refused to negotiate with television found themselves losing power and influence to a variety of entrepreneurial organizations. The traditionalists lost out to the modernizers, and by the mid-1980s, all sports-governing bodies had to come to terms with sports agents, financial brokers, and television representatives. "Sport," Whannel (2009) has emphasized, "was reshaped to meet the needs of television and the advertising industry" (p. 214).

Television has reshaped sports fundamentally in another manner. Television produces a visual spectacle—one that centers on images, motion, and the apparent replication of a live experience. But as a form of technology, television had to go—and could go—beyond the mere representation of a live experience. Television reconfigured what an audience sees, hears, experiences, and expects, and this has had a profound impact on the nature of the athletic enterprise as well as the preparation of athletes for the world stage. Instant replays in slow motion from a number of different angles; zoomed images that move the viewer closer than would ever be physically possible, shown at speeds that capture what the human eye cannot at normal speed; and the accentuation of a modern, movement aesthetic have changed spectators' expectations for all major athletic events. Television has changed the aesthetics of sports.

This is partly the legacy of Riefenstahl—an avant-garde approach to the visual experience—but it is largely the impact of television as a commercial enterprise. Riefenstahl had shown how the camera could take a concrete athletic event and turn it into a universal abstraction that suggested the possibility of absolute perfection. At the same time, this modernist aesthetic tapped into deeper emotions than simply victory in a specific event. The combination of the "live" competitive experience with technologically produced, aesthetically driven reproductions of that event held out the promise of sports leading to an entirely new level of engagement between athlete and spectator. Television would deliver on that promise.

To succeed commercially, television programs must attract and hold viewers. In sports coverage, the uncertainty of the outcome is one dimension that maintains the audience's attention, but to fully enthrall viewers, television had to do more—and it did. As the technology developed and producers became more sophisticated in the presentation of sports events, television developed a wholly modernist aesthetic of sports, which then influenced how sports are performed by athletes.

The modernist aesthetic involves not only physical execution but performances that exceed all previous accomplishments. The commodity that television sells to its audiences is the high-performance spectacle, at the outer limits of human athletic potential, in slow-motion replay from a number of angles, dissected into its many components. A perfect gymnastics routine in real time or the speed of a 100-meter world championship may be dramatic, but they are no longer the extent of the sporting event. It is not until the abstracted, slow-motion, multicamera replays and expert commentary pointing to all the technical perfections on display before the viewer that the "sporting event" is properly consumed. The quest in modern sports in the contemporary era requires more than simply elite-level performances; to execute at the outer limits of human athletic potential demands the absolute perfection of anatomical, physiological, biomechanical, neural, and near intuitive, split-second decision making on the part of the athlete. The full modernist athletic aesthetic, driven by the commercial needs of television and now the multimedia cyber communications systems, requires superhuman performance capacities.

Modernity, Science, and the High-Performance Athlete

Sir Roger Bannister is widely regarded as the consummate embodiment of Coubertin's ideals—an athlete who thrived on disciplining his body and will, testing and building his character in the cauldron of competition, pursuing victory even when it could not be attained solely for intrinsic reward. The race among Great Britain's Bannister, Australia's John Landy, and the United States' Wes Santee to run the first sub-four-minute mile took those emotions and principles and expanded them outward into a drama of mythical proportions leading to what Neal Bascomb (2004) has called "the perfect mile."

Using pacers, Bannister broke the four-minute barrier (3:59.4) on May 6, 1954, at a packed Iffley Road Track at Oxford. On June 21, at a regular meet in Turku, Finland, Landy had lowered the record to 3:58, setting the stage for a Bannister/Landy showdown at the British Empire Games later that year. On August 7, 34,000 spectators at Empire Stadium in Vancouver, an estimated 100 million radio listeners, and millions more watching live televised coverage witnessed what is often regarded as the greatest race in track history. "The miracle mile," as it became known, was the epitome of the sporting ideals Coubertin cherished. But it was also the gateway to modernity and the pursuit of sports through applied science, research, and professionalized training regimes.

In his indomitable quest to shave the last two seconds off Landy's 1953 world record, Bannister believed that an athlete's capacities could be expanded through research-informed, carefully planned, systematic training. Bannister was more than just a runner; he was a medical student with an extensive background in human physiology, and he was committed to maximizing his full athletic potential. Bannister drew upon the most advanced knowledge of pure and applied physiology to configure a scientifically based training program that would produce the best results possible. Bannister's training was also tailored to the specific racing tactics that he would employ in the race. Bannister kept a fast, uniform pace throughout a race until the final finishing kick, where every last resource was expended. His steadfast commitment to breaking the four-minute barrier unintentionally undermined the *spirit* of British amateur athletics, opening the door to a wholly modernist, professionalized approach to athlete preparation and competition.

This shift in spirit was tied to and reinforced by changes in how athletes began to physically prepare for international competitions. Instead of approaching training as repetitious drill, which would allow athletes to progressively perfect and coordinate their movements to maximize output stemming from fixed performance limits, the new approach suggested that athletes' physiological capacities could be expanded through appropriate training regimes (Beamish & Ritchie, 2006). The drive to alter athletes' physiological potential had an enormous impact on the real, day-to-day practice regimes and the coaching and training strategies that soon developed. These changes to the actual, everyday training practices of amateur athletes fundamentally transformed the reality and ethos of training and competition in amateur sports. Within a decade of the miracle mile, the training regimes of high-performance athletes required an increasingly full-time commitment to scientifically based training regimes to remain competitive. Applied sports science would fundamentally change the way high-performance sports were conceptualized and carried out; it also served as the first step toward the creation of complex, state-sponsored systems of athlete development.

In writing his report following Canada's "Commission of Inquiry Into the Use of Banned Performance Enhancing Substances and Practices," Chief Justice Charles Dubin focused on one particular aspect of the testimony provided by one of Canada's premier distance runners during the 1960s. Bruce Kidd (Canada, 1989, p. 10668) had testified that in 1963, he introduced a morning run into his training program. At the Highland Games in Edinburgh that year, Kidd mentioned the addition to a fellow competitor who was one of the top 10 in the world and a veteran runner whom Kidd deeply respected. Martin Hyman surprised Kidd with the vigor of his response: "You know," Hyman responded, "you represent the thin edge of the wedge."

> If it gets to the point where people are training twice a day, then they will move on to three times a day because probably there is a marginal efficiency to be gained with a lot more training. And it will become a full time occupation and the life we lead will be impossible. And it will mean that people such as us will be forced to choose from being a full time athlete, focusing on nothing but sport, or a recreational athlete with little opportunity to travel and compete at a high level. (Canada, 1989, pp. 10668–9)

Kidd noted in his testimony that in 1989, he realized how prophetic Hyman was because by the 1980s, there was no choice; elite sports required full-time commitment (Canada, 1989, p. 10669).

In his work on modernity, Giddens has emphasized the irony of modernity's turn to science for knowledge, certainty, and assurance. With respect to natural and social scientific knowledge, Giddens (1991) argued that "the reflexivity of modernity turns out to confound the expectations of Enlightenment thought—although it is the very product of that thought."

> The original progenitors of modern science and philosophy believed themselves to be preparing the way for securely founded knowledge of the social and natural worlds: the claims of reason were due to overcome the dogmas of tradition, offering a sense of certitude in place of the arbitrary character of habit and custom. But the reflexivity of modernity actually undermines the certainty of knowledge, even in the core domains of natural science. Science depends, not on the inductive accumulation of proofs, but on the methodological principle of doubt. No matter how cherished, and apparently well established, a given scientific tenet might be, it is open to revision—or it might have to be discarded altogether—in the light of new

ideas or findings. The integral relation between modernity and radical doubt is an issue which, once exposed to view, is not only disturbing to philosophers, but is *existentially troubling* for ordinary individuals. (p. 21)

There is a lot to consider in that statement. First, Giddens' assessment of modernity includes the key feature of "reflexivity." At both the individual and at the institutional level, modernity is characterized by the constant monitoring of action—an ongoing assessment of appearance, performance, and outcomes. Freed from tradition and wedded to the notion of progress, individuals and institutions plan for a future in which more will be accomplished in less time and with better results. That orientation requires constant assessment of progress and change.

Ongoing reflexive assessment combines with and is reinforced by the fundamental principles of science. While Enlightenment thinkers and many people today associate scientific knowledge with certainty and security, Giddens has noted that the fundamental principle of radical doubt undermines the certainty of knowledge while animating an ongoing, eternal quest to test and retest all scientific claims in the name of science's fundamental principle. The perpetual testing and retesting of scientific claims has led to the continual development and refinement of knowledge, creating a further basis for adhering to the principle of radical doubt. One has to continually doubt the status of knowledge because it is changing continuously. What once seemed certain is quickly put under question and then superseded by more refined, scientifically based results.

For athletes, coaches, and a wide array of applied sports scientists, this frequently overlooked yet inescapably central conundrum of science means that the quest for improving human athletic performance is never ending. This creates a certain existential anxiety for athletes, coaches, and sports scientists themselves, but more importantly, it also establishes a constant reflexive monitoring of the institutional structures and practices that have developed that support the advancement of human athletic performance. The quest for the best is ongoing and highly competitive because the rewards have grown well beyond simply a gold medal at the Olympic Games.

It is at this juncture that time-space distanciation adds further stress and uncertainty to the system. Not only are high-performance sports a global phenomenon, as is the pursuit of podium placements, but there is heightened urgency that one nation's sports system will discover the best way to optimize athletic performance before another global competitor finds the same or an even better means. Although spread around the globe, everyone is striving for a competitive edge simultaneously within the global arena. The pressure on athletes to train intensely, for more repetitions involving less recovery time, over longer periods of precompetition preparation, and over more and more of the life course in the pursuit of smaller and smaller increments of improvement creates a world in which one's focus increasingly narrows to ends (victories) by using whatever means are necessary.

Finally, Bannister's self-administered experiments opened the door to an array of sports sciences. The professionalization of physical education—a term abandoned by many universities in favor of the more scientific-sounding and encompassing noun kinesiology—began with exercise physiology, spread to biomechanics, then sports psychology, and soon entailed a vast array of sports sciences and sports medicine professionals (Saffi 2007; Theberge 2008). The postwar expansion of the university system and its growing emphasis on pure and applied research provided the institutional basis for the growth and development of sports science. The interlinked university system across a nation allowed nation-states to draw upon and concentrate national resources in the pursuit of improved athletic performances in the national interest. As a result, a well-resourced set of institutional players—fundamentally committed to the principles of science (including the principle of ongoing, radical doubt)—continually feed into the reflexive monitoring of athletic practices to ensure that athletes can recover from training episodes as quickly as possible, reduce the risk of injury, and return to training following injury quickly so they could perform at levels that constantly push back the limits of human athletic performance.

It is the line between "recovery"—recovery from injury and recovery from training—and "enhancement" that begins to blur. Because every training episode involves some level of microtears and injury, it has become increasingly impossible to distinguish between treatments aimed at speeding athletes' recovery from training or injury and those that will enhance performance. In addition, a critical ethical question emerges: Should athletes be deprived of the best means possible for recovering from training when rapid recovery will prevent injury?

Cold War Sports: East versus West Germany

Throughout the Cold War period, most of the attention fell on the competition between the United States and the USSR. It was not until the 1976

Olympic Games in Montreal that "the miracle machine" of the GDR seemed to burst onto the high-performance sports scene (Gilbert, 1980). But rather than being a sudden, belated development in the GDR's history, the success of East Germany's high-performance sports system had its roots in WWII and the early postwar period.

At the end of WWII, Germany was a defeated nation. Physically, the nation was almost completely destroyed by the Soviets, the Western allies, and the Nazis themselves. The allied firebombing of Hamburg left a million people homeless and destroyed more than 60 percent of the city; 700,000 phosphorus bombs dropped on Dresden had produced more than 2900°F temperatures in the city center, reducing it to ashes and killing more than half a million noncombatants. The bombing of Cologne reduced the population from 730,000 to a mere 40,000 struggling for survival at the war's end in the shattered city; the allies had destroyed more than 90 percent of Düsseldorf, Frankfurt was virtually razed, and only 80,000 of its 180,000 prewar inhabitants had survived. Essen, Dortmund, Hanover, and Mannheim were also destroyed at tremendous civilian cost. As revelations of the Holocaust and other Nazi atrocities became public and German citizens internalized the shame and guilt of the nation, postwar Germany was a psychologically traumatized, hollow shell of a nation.

When Hitler launched Operation Barbarossa on June 22, 1941, his objectives were clear. The invasion of Eastern Europe and the Soviet Union would bring that vast geographical territory with its abundant natural resources and rich agricultural land under the control of Nazi Germany. More importantly, the invasion would achieve two critical objectives that Hitler had emphasized in *Mein Kampf*: the total annihilation of "Jewish Bolshevism" and the "racial purification" of the entire region (Bartov, 1991; Hitler, 1939).

German officers knew that the war in the East was one of "world historical significance"—a "war of ideologies" in which there would be no compromise. "This war," Tank Group 3 commander General Hermann Hoth wrote in a November 1941 general order, "can only end with the annihilation of one or the other; there will be no conciliation" (see Rürup, 1991, pp. 61, 63). General Field Marshal Erich von Manstein, commander of the 56th Tank Corps, was more expansive: "The German soldier is obliged to not only destroy the means of military power of this [Jewish-Bolshevik] system. He marches forth as the standard bearer of [Nazi Germany's] racially pure idea and as an avenger of all the atrocities that have been committed against him and the German people." "The soldier," Manstein ordered, "must demonstrate an understanding of the harsh atonement to be brought down upon Judaism, the spiritual bearer of the Bolshevik terror" (cited in Rürup, 1991, p. 7).

Despite the rapid German advance through Central Europe and into the Soviet Union, the vast steppes of the Soviet Union soon outstretched German supply lines, tank divisions were brought to a crawl in the mud of heavy October rain, and the early arrival of winter brought snow, bitter winds, and bone-numbing temperatures. Operation Barbarossa was reduced to a long, brutal, demoralizing war of attrition that lasted for almost four years at unprecedented human suffering (Bartov, 1991; Rürup, 1991).

When the Red Army finally repelled the German *Wehrmacht*, the Soviets were as ruthless, brutal, and merciless in their treatment of combatants and civilians as the Nazis had been in their invasion. The plunder and destruction caused by Soviet soldiers as they advanced into Germany created a vastly different relationship between German citizens and the Soviet forces of occupation than the one that existed between the Germans and the French, British, and Americans in their particular sectors. As a result, although many Germans were deeply grateful for the role and tremendous sacrifices that the Soviet Union had made in bringing an end to the Nazi nightmare, they were mixed with equally deep feelings of fear, distrust, resentment, and antipathy by many in the Eastern sector of Germany. Those sentiments remained in the GDR up to the fall of the Berlin Wall and beyond.

As a result, from the moment Stalin placed the "Ulbricht Group" in Berlin to lay the groundwork for full Soviet occupation of Berlin and Germany, there was an awkward tension between the German-born communist leader Walter Ulbricht, who became the GDR's first General Secretary, and Stalin as well as how Germans in the Soviet-occupied sector felt about their "liberators." Despite his commitment to communism, Ulbricht remained a proud German nationalist as well as an opportunist interested in advancing his own political influence within the Warsaw Pact. As a result, throughout his entire tenure as the GDR's leader, Ulbricht used East Germany's strategic geopolitical importance as leverage with the Soviet Union so he could gain greater independence from Moscow than other leaders in the Warsaw Pact were able to manage. A good deal of Ulbricht's political ambition rested on rebuilding the pride of East Germans in the nation-state they could create in the post-WWII period; nationalist pride would be more important to Ulbricht than total allegiance and submission to the Soviet Union.

Well schooled by Stalin, Ulbricht recognized how success in international sports could help rebuild the spirit of East Germany. For Ulbricht, success against athletes from the West was important, but victories over those from West Germany were the most significant. At the same time, East German victories against athletes from the Soviet Union brought a different type of national pride along with feelings of resistance as the occupied turned the tables on the occupier.

Ulbricht began to build a sports system with the formation of the Committee for German Sport (*Deutschen Sportausschusses*), but when the GDR was founded as an independent nation-state in 1949, he replaced the Committee for German Sport with the State Committee for Physical Culture and Sport (*Staatlichen Komitees für Körperkultur und Sport*—STAKO), which had a very clear mandate. STAKO was to mobilize the resources of the nation-state to develop a centralized, fully coordinated sports system.

In many respects, STAKO simply copied the Soviet sports system, including performance incentives and performance-based rankings for athletes, but they took the Soviet model a few steps further. For example, the East Germans concentrated on such individual sports as track and field, swimming, gymnastics, boxing, cycling, and wrestling where a single outstanding athlete could win gold, and in some sports (swimming, track and field, and gymnastics, for example) there was the potential for multiple medals from a single athlete in any given competition.

The most significant decision Ulbricht made was the construction of the *Deutschen Hochschule für Körperkultur* (German Academy for Physical Culture—DHfK), which opened in Leipzig in 1950 (Schumann, 2003). Not only did the DHfK serve as an elite training center for the GDR's best athletes, it housed some of the most advanced research into sports anywhere in the world.

In 1961, Manfred Ewald was appointed to head the entire sports system in the GDR (remaining there until the fall of the Berlin Wall). Throughout the 1960s, Ewald expanded the feeder system for elite athletes throughout the GDR and increased the DHfK's resources for applied sports science. By the mid-1960s, the GDR was easily surpassing the FRG in athlete development, and the contingent of athletes from East Germany on the combined German Olympic team soon eclipsed that of the more populous and prosperous FRG.

With the GDR surpassing the FRG a mere three years after the construction of the Berlin Wall, West German politicians implemented a high-performance sports plan of their own. The plan introduced funded national team coaches and the development of high-performance training centers. The training centers integrated the diffuse West German sports system to meet the increasing demands and expectations placed on world-class, high-performance athletes (Beamish & Ritchie, 2006).

The national umbrella organization for sports in the FRG—the *Deutscher Sportbund* (German Sport Federation—DSB)—introduced a sports and athlete classification system, promoted long-term planning within the different national sports organizations, and sought improvements to the instructional, medical, and psychological development of athletes. Like the East Germans, the DSB established programs of early talent identification and set up elite sports schools at strategic locations in West Germany (Bette, 1984).

Two IOC decisions changed the landscape of high-performance sports in both Germanys dramatically: awarding the 1972 Summer Games to Munich and permitting separate German teams to take part in the Olympic Games after the 1968 Olympics. Ewald immediately recognized that with each victory at the 1972 Olympic Games, the GDR's most significant political symbols—its flag and national anthem, which the FRG had never officially recognized—would be seen and heard by the world on West German soil.

Ewald quickly intensified the pursuit of Olympic gold by developing and implementing a highly classified, tightly controlled, scientifically based program that produced the best knowledge possible about the most effective performance-enhancing substances, their optimal use and dosages, and the physiological impact each substance had on an athlete. Ewald's Machiavellian plan had disastrous outcomes for many unsuspecting East German athletes, but it produced dramatic athletic success, and it was not long before aspects of the plan made their way to the West (Franke & Berendonk, 1997).

In the FRG, there was a heated philosophical debate about how the DSB should respond to the IOC decisions—should it maintain the strict code of amateurism or recognize the new reality in high-performance sports and adjust. Should it sit still and be embarrassed by the GDR on one of the world's biggest stages or should the FRG act?

The Olympic rules state that everyone should take part in Olympic competition under the same conditions. The equality of competitiveness is destroyed when sponsored athletes compete against pure amateurs whose social situation does not allow the necessary training expenditures to be covered and whose sport associations cannot supply the necessary assistance. Thus we are faced with the question: Do we want to resign ourselves in international high-performance sport to a situation that contradicts the fundamental idea of sport? Or do we want, despite the unequal starting point, to give our young athletes at least a bit more of an equal opportunity to compete? (cited in Bette and Neidhart, 1985, p. 95)

On May 26, 1967, the DSB and West Germany's NOC took the first steps toward developing a professionalized high-performance sports system. The DSB launched a state-supported high-performance athlete development system with the *Stiftung Deutsche Sporthilfe* (German Foundation for Sport Assistance—DSH). The DSH would target and fund the FRG's top athletes. The system that emerged served as the reference point for Canada, then Australia, and ultimately the American and British high-performance sports systems as they would develop from the 1970s through to the 1990s. The formation of high-performance sports systems allowed each of these countries to marshal the resources of the entire nation-state to attain specific national and international objectives through the success of athletes competing within the international spectacle of world-class, high-performance sports.

1974: Abandoning Coubertin's Dream

The 1969 and 1970 reports from the IOC/NOC joint commission documented the complete transformation of high-performance sports during the post-WWII period. For example, research showed that from 1950 to 1970, the time track athletes spent training had doubled and in some events tripled. The training regimes of the late 1960s and early 1970s significantly increased the physical demands placed on athletes. The workload grew as coaches changed the total volume of training, increased the intensity in each practice, compressed more work into shorter time frames, or increased the duration of work in each training interval. Coaches could also reduce the recovery time between intervals (Pfetsch et al., 1975). In the eight years from 1960 to 1968, the training distances for male swimmers had doubled and the percentage of each session devoted to high tempo work rose from less than 20 percent to more than half the workout. The Soviets pushed their female athletes as hard as the males, leaving little alternative for sports systems in the West (Lehnertz, 1979).

In addition to increased intensity, there was a trend toward initiating serious systematic training at earlier and earlier ages. Based on the trend toward greater specialization at younger and younger ages, Lempart (1973) argued that optimal success required the introduction of systematic training during athletes' elementary school years (see also Lehnertz, 1979). These trends in athlete development had no connection at all to the virtuous, inspirational, character-building, chivalrous contests on which Coubertin based his movement and that Brundage was then championing.

The period from 1972 to 1974 was a critical watershed point for the Olympic movement. It was becoming increasingly obvious that the real world of high-performance sports was absolutely and resolutely different than Coubertin's vision. At the 1972 Sapporo Winter Games, amid growing cries of hypocrisy and the clearest statement of eligibility in years, Brundage focused on the skiers, who, he maintained, were "more brazen than the other athletes in their subversion of Olympic rules" (cited in Barney, Wenn, & Martyn, 2002, p. 105). Brundage recommended the disqualification of more than 40 skiers for failing to comply with the eligibility code, but his recommendation was turned down. However, in the end, Austrian skiing sensation Karl Schranz served as the example Brundage wanted (Guttmann, 1984). Schranz had not simply received endorsement money—a practice common among skiers and other athletes at the time—but in a media interview, in the Olympic Village, he admitted to earning more than $50,000 annually for "testing" skis (Barney, Wenn, & Martyn, 2002). The code of silence on endorsement money was broken, shattering the myth of the amateur athlete in world-class, high-performance sports in the latter third of the twentieth century. The IOC faced a major crossroads. Steps to genuinely exclude athletes who did not meet the criteria of the eligibility code would carry heavy financial costs; pretending the code was enforced when it was not would simply discredit the movement. One interview in the Olympic Village left the central pillar of Coubertin's movement precariously unstable.

The IOC chose to adjust to the reality of world-class sports rather than defend and maintain the movement's founding principles. A new eligibility code was introduced at the 1974 meetings. "To be eligible for participation in the Olympic Games," the new Rule 26 stated:

[A] competitor must observe and abide by the Rules of the IOC and in addition the rules of his or her IF as approved by the IOC, even if the federation's rules are more strict than those of the IOC [and] not have received any financial rewards or material benefit in connection with his or her sports participation, except as permitted in the bye-laws to this Rule. (cited in Killanin, 1976, p. 143)

At first glance, Rule 26 appeared as restrictive as before, but in fact, it undermined the movement's cardinal principles in three ways. First, under the *Olympic Charter*'s bylaws, athletes could receive financial reward and material gain for their athletic prowess. Not only was the fundamental nature of the athlete taking part in the Olympic Games no longer an issue, the type of athlete taking part in the Olympic Games was the direct antithesis of what Coubertin had wanted. The fundamental reason for reviving the ancient Olympic Games was abandoned.

Second, the IOC gave effective control over eligibility to the ISFs. Because many ISFs had good reason to admit increasingly professionalized athletes to their championships, the restrictions to fully professionalized, world-class, high-performance athletes were essentially gone.

Third, the eligibility code no longer stated, reflected, or reinforced Coubertin's essential principles. The Olympic Games would no longer center on character development through chivalrous athletic competition where the joy of effort took precedence over victory. The religious experience was replaced by the secular pursuit of money and victory at almost any cost. The IOC had adapted its *Olympic Charter* so the Olympic Games would feature athletes for whom a sport was a full-time, year-round vocation and winning—the conquest of the linear record—was their solitary guiding principle. The scientifically rational, technologically assisted pursuit of the limits to human physical performance was accepted as the central ethos of the Olympic Games and open access to the finances and, by association, any other means needed in that pursuit was irrevocably recognized as legitimate. Modernity now permeated the Olympic Games fully and formally.

Olympic Principles, Performance-Enhancing Substances, and Deviant Behavior

The 1974 change to Rule 26 of the *Olympic Charter* and the actual changes to world-class, high-performance sports are directly relevant to the prohibition of performance-enhancing substances in several ways. First, Coubertin founded the modern Olympic Games as a far-reaching, innovative, educational program that would end the growing materialism of industrial capitalism and return Europe to its traditional values. Olympic competition was to be a means to a majestic end and never an end in itself. Coubertin's project was premised on the unique experience young men would gain by taking part in athletic competitions that exuded beauty and inspired reverence. The intense, competitive experience of the Olympic Games—appropriately controlled and tempered—was to build character and forge a new elite that would lead Europe back to its traditional value system.

The histories of the Olympic Games and Western Europe unfolded far differently than Coubertin had wanted. In fact, Europe followed the very path Coubertin wanted most to prevent. Commercial interests grew, narrow-minded nationalism flourished, and sports became just another part of the growing world market. It was the Olympic Games' founding principles that were becoming increasingly at variance with the reality of European life in the mid- to late twentieth century.

Recognizing that it could not control or shape the world of high-performance sports but still wanting the best athletes in the world at the Olympics, the IOC abandoned the movement's cardinal principles and adapted the Olympic Games to the social realities of contemporary world-class sports. The 1974 change to Rule 26 of the *Olympic Charter* proved that no principle or formal rule—no matter how central or sacrosanct—was immutable.

Second, the rules regulating substance use were never themselves central to the movement. They were, as Medical Commissioner Sir Arthur Porritt emphasized in 1966, intimately tied to Coubertin's original lofty principles, and indeed, the use of performance-enhancing substances was, within that context, cheating. But it was also cheating to pursue a sport on a full-time basis or to receive funding, state support, or adopting a win-at-all costs philosophy in the Olympic Games' events.

Once the Olympic Games' fundamental principles were removed, the IOC's most principled rationale for a banned list vanished. After 1974, the IOC opened the Olympic Games to world-class, high-performance athletes for whom a sport was a full-time vocation. Consistent with the realities of the competitive world in which Olympic athletes toiled for gold, that approach to sports had been taking place for years, but now it was accepted.

Reliance on state funding; the use of comprehensive, scientifically based, year-round training programs; the zeal for victory; and the personal investment in the pursuit of medals and the limits of human athletic performance were classic examples of what sociologists term *positive deviance*. By identifying so strongly with the real goals and values of high-performance sports in the late twentieth century, world-class athletes positively identified with the fundamental, modernist realities of the Olympic Games—they just followed the logic and demands of that world to the extreme. Deviants because they ignored the IOC's formal rules and regulations, high-performance athletes at the international level were conformists insofar as they did not question the all-out assault on human performance in which they took part; they merely did what was necessary to win personal fame and glorify their respective nations. The use of performance-enhancing substances is a part of that world—even though the IOC refused and continues to refuse to admit that it is the case. With the 1974 change to Rule 26, a completely new set of principles should now determine a legitimate code of conduct that would govern professionalized athletes' commitment to continually extending the limits and possibilities of human performance in sports. Decisions regarding the use or restriction of performance-enhancing substances should now be made consistent with the fundamental principles that the movement currently embraces; otherwise, the banned list will remain at odds with the modernist ethos of the Olympic Games.

There is one further point that merits commentary. After one recognizes the significant transformation of world-class, high-performance sports over the last 50 years—accelerating in speed since 1974—questions arise about the nature of world-class sports itself. Those questions extend well beyond the rules and regulations that attempt to regulate symptoms of that reality. Modern high-performance sports have become a fully professionalized and commercialized undertaking; the goal of performance maximization is pursued with single-minded determination. The means to achieving world-class results have progressively expanded to the limits of what is scientifically and physiologically possible. In addition, the pursuit of the outer limits of human performance has been actively encouraged through the complex fusion of post-WWII and late twentieth century political struggles, powerful commercial interests, and the IOC's own policies. The performance demands at the world-class level are now so extreme that ergogenic aids have become deeply embedded into the regular practices of athletes in many sports. As a result, while WADA's policy is enforced with increasing public fanfare, its legitimacy is contested on a daily basis because the use of performance-enhancing substances is woven more and more tightly into the fabric of world-class sports (Brown, 2001; Hoberman, 2001; Waddington, 1996; Yesalis & Bahrke, 2002). If breaking a rule is cheating, many of today's athletes are cheaters; if going against the dominant practices of high-performance sports makes one a deviant, then the athletes who eschew performance-enhancing substances are deviants. The question is which is the right path to follow—the outmoded yet still existing rule or the imperatives of a reality that is not yet fully recognized by the IOC leadership despite its 1974 decision to accept the premises on which the real world of high-performance sports is based?

Chapter 4

The Social Construction of Steroids in Sports

In launching the modern Olympic Games, Coubertin had one extremely ambitious, overarching objective: He wanted to create an athletic spectacle of beauty and reverence through which young men—in the chivalrous pursuit of victory with and against other brothers-in-arms—would discover, develop, and internalize the traditions and core values of Western European civilization. The unique sporting competition of the modern Olympic Games would build a new generation of elite leaders worthy of Europe's greatest cultural accomplishments and history.

From the first to the XX Olympiad, the IOC had used the notion of amateurism as the key criterion for restricting the Olympic Games to those athletes that it felt could create and take part in such a spectacle and reap the intended benefits. Amateur athletes, sports, fair play, and the philosophy of Olympism were all tightly entwined in the ensemble that constituted "the Olympic Games." While none of the terms were ever defined with precision and detail, the intent behind each was understood. The overall image the terms established became the "Olympic brand."

In view of the IOC's 1974 decision to abandon amateurism as the critical eligibility requirement, it may seem surprising that the brand was not fundamentally undermined. There were several reasons why that did not happen.

To begin with, it is important to understand how a brand and branding work. The American Marketing Association defines a brand as a "name, term, sign, symbol or design, or a combination of them intended to identify the goods and services of one seller or group of sellers and to differentiate them from those of other sellers" (cited in Kotler, 1994, p. 444). For the IOC, "the Olympic Games" is the brand. The brand is represented by several identifiable symbols—with the main symbols simply being the words "the Olympics," "the Olympic Games," "the Games," or "Games of the Olympiad" as well as the distinctive logo of five interlocking rings (IOC, 2010).

A brand is essentially a vendor's promise that the product offered will consistently deliver a specific set of goods, benefits, and/or services. The brand alleviates the need for a consumer to resort to an elaborate description of what he or she wants and consciously calculating how the product will meet those wants. Instead, a branded product provides the consumer with a very convenient, easily recalled, shorthand image of a specific product that will meet particular wants. A brand does not simply facilitate communication between a vendor and consumers—it creates a direct, reflex connection.

If one pauses to think about the "Olympic Games" as a brand and what it offers, one can readily identify what he or she expects to consume: Officially, the Olympic brand promises a live and simultaneously televised spectacle of world-class international athletes competing in selected high-performance sports contests that are conducted under the careful scrutiny of the IOC and other international bodies and officials to ensure that the competition is fair and carried out in "the true spirit of sport." But the purpose behind branding is to compress that list into its essential elements: As a brand, "the Games" promise a spectacle featuring the highest level of true sporting competition on Earth. As a form of shorthand, the compressed, holistic brand image removes the need to recall any of the details or to reflect on what the brand really represents: The branded image produces an instant association between product and want.

Many of the images and conceptions found in the current Olympic brand remain from Coubertin's original description of the athlete disciplining his muscles, nerves, and will in the pursuit of victory—whether or not it is achieved. The key concepts are still there: sport, fair play, and the vague notion of Olympism that entails—among other things—a sense of internationalism, peace, goodwill, fraternity, tradition, and the classical era. While all these were at one time strongly and easily associated with the "gentlemanly amateur"—and that was a large part of the reason the IOC used the amateur athlete as its key eligibility criterion—as the Western world continued to modernize and democratize through the twentieth century, the gentlemanly amateur became increasingly anachronistic. As a result, at the same time that the IOC was pressured by events and changing circumstances to drop the amateur restriction from the Olympic brand, it also felt certain that eliminating the amateur criterion would be broadly accepted as long as other key aspects of the brand remained—in particular, the spirit of sport and fair play.

Dropping amateurism from the brand had some important implications. For example, with amateurism removed as a key criterion for participation, the central principle of the Olympic Games became the integrity of the spirit of sport. As a result, after 1974, the Olympic brand slowly shifted to one in which the antithesis of the Olympic Games' brand was no longer the professional or even the professionalized athlete. The antithesis of the Olympic brand became the cheater. If the IOC could be tough on cheaters, it could safely abandon one of the central pillars of Coubertin's original project and still maintain the most salient aspects of its branded image. After 1974, the *Olympic Charter*'s rule on banned substances became far more important and relevant than the eligibility code. This had significant implications regarding steroids in high-performance sports.

Second, even though Coubertin had always emphasized that the most important aspect of the Olympic Games was not winning but taking part, within the context of modernity, winning always mattered, and during the postwar period, it had become virtually paramount. But the tension between the Olympic Games' ultimate ideals and the reality of win-at-all-costs sports in the Cold War era actually served the Olympic brand well. What set the Olympic Games apart from all other elite sporting competitions were the idealist aspirations of the movement and the critical notions of fair play and the spirit of sport. While all these had an association with amateurism, they could also be separated from it and pursued within the context of modernist sporting competitions themselves. As a result, the Olympic Games could continue in the post-1974 period as an inspiring movement that valued internationalism, fair play, and the spirit of sport within the context of a thoroughly modernized form of competition.

Finally, the process of branding is simply a specific instance of the broader phenomenon of social constructionism. All social actions under the social conditions of modernity are evaluated, assessed, categorized, and implicitly—if not explicitly—ranked. That is why branding is so important; when vendors succeed in branding their products properly, they gain access to people and markets that represent distinct categories of consumers. Whether it is cell phones, footwear, food, or lifestyles, having a product branded as chic, cutting edge, or even "retro" is important. But the power of definition—or branding—rests on the ability of claims-makers (frequently advertisers, but there are numerous other claims-makers—some of whom are more influential than advertising companies) to successfully achieve the three objectives discussed in the Introduction about the claims-making process: bring a particular issue to the consumer or public's attention; shape a specific conception of the product or behavior; and forge a broad consensus over their particular definition of the product, behavior, or situation.

Through branding and shifting the specifics of various claims about the value of the Olympic Games, the IOC was able to do more than simply survive its first major postwar crisis; the IOC forged a brand that was still tied to some aspects of Coubertin's original dream but fell more consistently within the social context of the increasingly predominant forces of modernity during the last quarter of the twentieth century. However, maintaining the purity of the new brand would require further, aggressive claims-making by the IOC and other organizations involved with high-performance sports.

From Caracas to Seoul: Crises and Claims-Making

If the main focus of attention under Brundage was holding firm on the principles of amateurism, during Lord Killanin's presidency, attention shifted to the use of performance-enhancing substances. Killanin had clearly defined performance-enhancing substance use as one of the Olympic movement's greatest problems; eradicating them from the Olympic Games was his foremost concern (Gafner, 1995). Thus, at the 1974 IOC meeting in Tehran, Killanin declared that the "Medical Commission of the International Olympic Committee will strive as far as it can against the creation of the artificial man or woman" (cited in Gafner, 1995, p. 257). The first step was a more aggressive stance on the use of banned substances. As a result, the *Olympic Charter* was revised to expel not only athletes who tested positive for a banned substance but also any athlete who refused to submit to a drug test.

Although the IOC had banned certain substances as early as 1968, steroids were not included because the IOC did not have a test that would detect their use. As a result, steroids were not explicitly banned until 1975, with the first tests conducted at the 1976 Olympic Games (Verroken & Mottram, 2005). In the interval between 1968 and 1976, as national sports systems began to spread around the globe and the East German sports machine went into high gear, the use of performance-enhancing substances spread. Although there is less documented evidence of steroid use by athletes from the Western bloc than there is from the Eastern bloc, it is clear that steroid use was widespread on both sides of the Cold War divide

(Berendonk, 1991; Dubin, 1990; Francis, 1990; Franke & Berendonk, 1997; Todd & Todd, 2001; Yesalis & Bahrke, 2002).

From 1952 until 1976—almost a quarter of a century—the Olympic Games were an open competition in which world-class athletes used steroids with impunity. Over that period of time, steroids and other banned performance-enhancing substances became deeply engrained in the subculture of high-performance sports.

Even though the first tests for steroids began in 1973 and the IOC conducted tests at the 1976 Olympic Games, athletes had little to fear as they were well ahead of the testers (Verroken & Mottram, 2005). But the 1983 Pan American Games in Caracas, Venezuela, were a different story—the testers had caught up to the athletes (even if only briefly).

One of the most memorable images of the 1983 Pan Am Games was the number of athletes who defaulted out of competition, performed well below expectations, or dropped out early for "personal reasons." Despite the exodus of competitors, 19 athletes, including two Canadians—weightlifters Guy Greavette, winner of two gold and one silver, and Michel Viau, who won silver—tested positive for steroids. Those who had made the podium were stripped of their medals, and all 19 were ejected from the Pan Am Games and suspended from international competition for two years (for comparative purposes, only eight athletes tested positive for steroids at the 1976 Olympics, and of the 9,292 tests at the 1980 Moscow Games, none were positive).

The Caracas debacle was particularly embarrassing for Canada's high-performance sports leadership. Once the IOC had awarded Calgary the 1988 Winter Games, the Canadian federal government began to reinvest in Canada's Olympic athletes. In June 1982, the government had launched the "Best Ever '88" Winter Olympic Team Project to ensure the nation's best performance ever at a Winter Games. The project doubled the federal government's commitment to winter sports over the previous year, but funding and support remained precarious. Canadian athletes had to fit the new Olympic Games brand if the high-performance sports system was to continue receiving public funding.

The Canadian response to the positive tests in Caracas was instructive. Some sports leaders followed the IOC's renewed commitment to fair play and the spirit of sport. For example, Barry Nye, the Canadian chef de mission for the Olympic Games, was categorical in his condemnation of the athletes. But other responses reflected a greater appreciation for the realities of high-performance sports in the 1980s. Thus, Jack Lynch, the

Canadian Olympic Association's (COA) technical director, was quick to put the positive tests within their proper context. Lynch noted that the COA tried to avoid placing undue pressure on athletes to perform beyond their abilities, but he added: "Let's face it, this is competition. You play to win. This isn't recreation" (cited in Fraser, 1983, p. 1).

While there are a number of reasons for Canadian sports leaders to officially take a strong, unequivocal position on the use of banned performance-enhancing substances and the need for public support for the sports system was only one of them, it is important to note that even before Ben Johnson's disqualification at the 1988 Seoul Games, many Canadian sports leaders presented themselves as standing at the forefront in the struggle against the use of banned substances. Canada played a far more active role in the claims-making process than one might have expected given its overall performance record in world-class sports (see, for example, Johnson, 1988b).

The surprise use of a new test at the 1983 Pan Am Games was only the first, clear statement in what would become over the next decade a concerted process by highly placed, influential claims-makers to demonize steroids and those who used them. The tests made the very public claim that the science of detection had caught up to the cheaters. The use of banned substances, the Caracas tests indicated, would be detected by increasingly refined scientific procedures, and the penalties would be harsh. Fair play and the spirit of sport would not simply be defended; they would triumph.

The Caracas testing was quickly followed by action on the part of the IOC, various NOCs, and a host of sports-governing bodies. In Canada, Sport Canada (1984a)—the body that coordinates and oversees Canada's high-performance sports system—issued a directive to the Canadian NSOs requiring them to develop a plan that would "eradicate improper drug use by Canadian athletes and support personnel." The plan was to entail 11 specific elements.

Among those elements, the plan had to include a detailed statement of the rationale behind the policy as a whole. It had to indicate that regular testing would be conducted, the penalties imposed for positive tests, and the steps for an appeal procedure that would safeguard due process and the rule of law. Each plan had to affirm all NSO personnel would not possess, use, or encourage the use of banned substances. The organizations had to detail the educational activities they would undertake to inform athletes, coaches, support personnel, and others in the organization about the dangers of drug use, and the NSOs had to indicate how they would lobby internationally for the elimination of banned performance-enhancing substances in international sports.

The IOC was also aggressive in staking out its position. The IOC's (1984) Medical Commission published a *Medical Guide* that indicated several structural changes to the commission that would make it more proactive. The *Medical Guide* claimed that the IOC, the Medical Commission, and the Biomechanics and Sports Physiology Subcommission would provide athletes with more and better information about how athletes could improve their performances "without danger and without cheating" (IOC, 1984, p. 19). Nevertheless, aside from three pages devoted to biomechanics and sports physiology, the remaining 31 pages of the *Medical Guide* dealt exclusively with drugs and drug testing.

Leading into the 1984 Los Angeles Games, Sport Canada (1984b; 1984c) launched an aggressive campaign against banned performance-enhancing substances, and the COA (1984) adopted a "Policy on Doping and Drug Usage." Both bodies emphasized that the objective was to create (or maintain) fair and equal competition among athletes and to protect their health. However, before the weightlifting competition began at the 1984 Olympic Games, two Canadian weightlifters—Terry Hadlow and Luc Chagnon—were sent home when pre-Games tests revealed traces of methyltestosterone (Christie & Fisher, 1984). Despite the pre-Olympic glitch, with the Soviet bloc boycotting the Olympic Games, Canada's 10 gold medals and total of 44 exceeded all expectations. With no other positive tests and such dramatic results, the federal government extended its "Best Ever" project to the summer sports, committing an additional $38 million to their continued development.

Canadian success in Los Angeles coupled with its aggressive stance on banned substances created a higher profile for elite sports within Canada, and the new Minister of State (Fitness and Amateur Sport), Otto Jelinek, brought the full resources of the federal government into the claims-making process. In September 1985, Sport Canada (1985) issued a revised and much stronger policy statement. Jelinek noted that since its first policy in 1983, Canada could "be regarded as a nation not only doing its duty to ensure that standards of fair play and the protection of the health of participants are upheld, but as a country endeavouring to provide significant international leadership in this important area" (Sport Canada, 1985, p. 1). He committed Canada to "initiatives in the international domain" that would ensure that "there is world-wide compliance with the rules of the international sporting bodies." The update clearly articulated Canada's position on the use of banned performance-enhancing substances:

> On the premise that the use of drugs which artificially enhance performance in training and competition is harmful to health, ethically wrong, and ultimately a threat to high performance sport as we know it today, Sport Canada has developed this policy to lay the groundwork for measures which have as their objective the eradication of the use of performance enhancing substances, not only by Canadian athletes but also by their international counterparts. (Sport Canada, 1985, p. 4)

Recognizing that "athletes from many countries are using drugs with or without supervision by medical authorities," Sport Canada would establish and maintain the highest standards possible. To emphasize the point, the new policy would result in a lifetime ban from eligibility for all federal government sports programs and benefits for any athlete "proven to have violated antidoping rules involving anabolic steroids and related compounds" (Sport Canada, 1985, p. 6). Any athlete proven to have used drugs other than anabolic steroids and related compounds would be suspended from all federal government sports programs or benefits for at least one year.

A week before the 1986 Commonwealth Games, Jelinek banned six athletes—Rob Gray (discus), Mike Spiritoso and Peter Dajia (shot put), and weightlifters Jacques Demers, Glenn Dodds, and Mario Parente (Christie, 1986). Based on the 1985 Sport Canada policy, the only appeal open to the athletes was on a technical basis—through Jelinek. Assured by the head of the Montreal testing laboratory that there was no chance of error, Jelinek was emphatic about his decision: "Their amateur careers have come to an end," Jelinek said. "There's no use pussyfooting around on this issue. . . . [T]hey didn't think I was serious," he emphasized. "[A]s difficult as it may be, they were warned. I have to stick to my guns" (cited in McAuley, 1986, p. A1).

In April 1987, the COA approved a policy that reflected Sport Canada and Jelinek's stance on banning athletes for life who tested positive for steroids. The COA (1987) would impose a lifetime ban from all COA sanctioned events for any athlete "found guilty of a doping offence within the scope of this policy" (p. 2). A hearing would be held "to determine the circumstances relating to the offence, and the sanction to be imposed," but an athlete could not challenge the results of any test conducted by an IOC-accredited laboratory.

While the leaders in Canada's high-performance sports system were stiffening their resolve against steroids and other banned substances, they were also eager to build on the momentum that Best Ever had created. The new Minister of State (Fitness and Amateur Sport), Jean Charest, established a task force to thoroughly study Canada's high-performance sports system with the view to improving Canadian performances well into the future.

The overriding, results-oriented focus of *Toward 2000: Building Canada's Sport System* was inescapable: "A commitment to excellence has been developed within the Canadian sport community," the report emphasized—"a commitment which has produced results, which has given young athletes a sense of confidence that Canada can achieve, and which has changed the attitude of Canadians to high performance sport and sport generally" (National Sports Policy Task Force, 1988, p. 28). Although the system had achieved some success, it was "still in its infancy." "There is a need to build on the accomplishments of this last quadrennial and to take advantage of the momentum which currently exists" (p. 28). The task force noted that to develop a mature high-performance sports system, Canada needed professionalized coaching, more athlete funding, better facilities, and a stronger financial commitment from the private and public sectors to the high-performance sports system. The report recommended that sports should be ranked and pointed out that Canada lacked the integrated systems of high-performance athlete development found in other countries. As a result, the task force proposed the creation of national, multisport, high-performance centers where professional administrators, coaches, sports scientists, and experts in sports medicine could serve high-performance athletes, coaches, and clubs across Canada.

The task force also emphasized that Canada's high-performance sports culture had to change. Canadian sports leaders needed to promote "the concept of sport excellence such that the achievement in high performance sport will be recognized and valued by the Canadian public" (National Sports Policy Task Force, 1988, pp. 36–7). To show it was serious about changing the culture of high-performance sports, the report outlined specific goals for the next quadrennial: Canada would rank among the top three sporting nations in the West, and with medals in six of the 10 winter sports, it would rank among the top six nations overall at the 1992 Albertville Winter Games. The report expected Canada to rank from sixth to eighth overall at the 1992 Barcelona Summer Games, with medals in 18 of the 28 summer sports. The report's unabashed commitment to medals in world-class, high-performance sports was a significant departure from earlier reports and policy documents.

The Canadian example is instructive in two specific respects. First, even though Canada was not among the most powerful high-performance sports nations in the world, from its very first 1970 *A Proposed Sports Policy for Canadians*, to the disappointments of the Montreal Games, followed by its first place finish at the 1978 Commonwealth Games in Edmonton, on to the growing momentum in the 1980s, the Canadian sports system was increasingly committed to the pursuit of victory as the defining marker of success. To achieve its goals, Canada would have to follow other nations and direct more and more of the nation-state's resources into a performance-oriented sports system. Canada's policies throughout the 1970s and 1980s showed that even the second-tier sporting nations in the world were adjusting to the full force of modernity and the thoroughly professionalized realities of high-performance sports.

Despite the shift to performance outcomes, Canada remained committed to assuming a leadership role in the struggle against steroids and other banned performance-enhancing substances. As a result, Canada became one of the leading claims-makers in the demonization of steroids while at the same time publicizing the IOC's new branded image—the quest for fair play and safeguarding the spirit of sport.

Sports Illustrated and the Claims-Making Process

Canadian sports leaders were not alone in actively supporting the IOC's position on banned substances. One of the most significant claims-makers during the early 1980s was *Sports Illustrated*. With well over five million subscribers and reaching as many as 15 million readers per issue, *Sports Illustrated* was well positioned to function as one of the most influential claims-makers in the public's perceptions of steroids.

While the IOC and various NSOs played some role in the public claims-making process, their early efforts were primarily aimed at establishing particular limits and boundaries to the practices high-performance athletes followed. It was only through their efforts to shape the culture and practices of elite athletes that the IOC and NSOs "educated" the public about steroids. *Sports Illustrated* was quite different.

On the basis of what the magazine's writers believed was occurring in sports, *Sports Illustrated* provided coverage and information about steroids—but it was more than simply the reporting of facts. The coverage showed elements of balance, but on the whole—intentionally or not—the magazine presented an antisteroid position. That agenda became an important aspect of the claims-making process that would shape how the general public thought about the use of performance-enhancing substances in sports.

The first noteworthy article was Terry Todd's (1983) "The Steroid Predicament," which noted just below the title that despite "evidence that anabolic steroids can undermine one's health, the use of these drugs is widespread among athletes, who will risk their physical well-being for the promise of stronger performance" (p. 62). Todd's informal piece set the agenda for many of the high-profile claims-makers who would follow from the late 1980s up to the present. Todd (1983) began:

> What follows are my best recollections of how I felt about anabolic steroids as an aspiring athlete, what I have learned about steroids in the past 20 years and how my feelings have changed over that time. I make no claim of objectivity, having had a front-row seat. I've watched what was at first a "secret" drug known only to a handful of elite weightlifters become a phenomenon so widespread that a majority of recent Olympic athletes, male and female, in track and field and the strength sports, are believed to have used some form of steroid; a phenomenon so widespread that pro football players have told me that as many as 50% of the active NFL linemen and linebackers have used steroids with the intent of improving their performance; a phenomenon so widespread that reports surface from time to time of teenagers being advised by their high school, or even junior high school, coaches to take steroids. (p. 62)

As a former powerlifter who had used steroids, Todd wrote from the position of an insider. Even though the article was largely anecdotal, its presence in *Sports Illustrated*—along with Todd's "credentials" as a former user—lent the story considerable credibility.

Todd's key themes were clear and straightforward: Steroid use in sports was far more widespread than most suspected; there are a number of negative side effects to steroids, and they more than outweigh the power gains that steroids provide; while widely used by elite athletes, steroids had also filtered down to high schools and "even junior high school," where people in positions of trust were recommending them to youths and children; Todd regretted taking steroids and wanted others to learn from his experiences so they would not repeat his mistakes; and, finally, steroid use had to be curtailed and preferably eliminated from sports.

Todd presented a number of disturbing images throughout the article. He noted that his wife Jan, a world record holder in powerlifting who never took steroids and was a strong critic of their use, had frequently consoled "weeping" young girls who were traumatized by the prospect of having to compete "against women who have risked virilization and God knows what else to achieve the strength advantages conferred on them by the steroids" (Todd, 1983, p. 75). Todd also described how athletes tried to avoid a positive test by using a catheter to transfer urine without any steroid metabolites from another person into their bladder. The most disturbing image was Todd's speculation that the United States might be entering an era when fathers "with large dreams for their small sons" would purchase human growth hormone (HGH) to give them an advantage over other children competing for the coveted spots in the hierarchy of the competitive feeder system for big-time sports.

William Johnson's piece in May 1985 was the first of three articles on steroids in that issue. Johnson's article touched on many of the same themes Todd had already introduced, but Johnson's role in the claims-making process was different. Johnson was writing as a highly seasoned sports journalist who was basing his story on information from several inside informants and his own research. Johnson was not an insider who might have been biased by "sour grapes"; he was a professional investigative journalist.

Johnson began with a focus on the NFL, quoting from various players (some named but others remaining anonymous), Kim Wood, who was the Cincinnati Bengals' strength coach for over a decade, and the American Medical Association's (AMA) associate general counsel, B. J. Anderson. Johnson's coverage moved into college sports, noting that in April 1985, 32 past and present Vanderbilt football players were listed as unindicted co-conspirators in a case involving the illegal sale and distribution of steroids in Nashville. Against that background, Johnson wondered how far the steroid culture had spread.

In response, Johnson (1985) presented information supplied by Richard Sandlin, a 27-year-old former powerlifter and former steroid user who was a strength consultant in Alabama. Sandlin had indicated that he had "served as a kind of consultant over the past six years to players, coaches and others interested in getting the lowdown on steroids" (p. 58). Sandlin had told Johnson that he had been approached by coaches and athletes from at least 25 universities—ranging from Alabama, Auburn, and Arizona State, to Nebraska, Oklahoma, and Texas, to Vanderbilt, Virginia and Washington State—as well as "at least 40 steroid users or would-be users on NFL and USFL [United States Football League] teams" (p. 58). Among the teams, Sandlin mentioned the Atlanta Falcons, Cleveland Browns, Detroit Lions, Green Bay Packers, Houston Gamblers, Los Angeles Raiders, Miami Dolphins, New England Patriots, New Orleans Saints, New York Giants and Jets, Portland Breakers, San Diego Chargers, and Seattle Seahawks. The conclusion that American sports were awash in steroids was inescapable.

The second important aspect to Johnson's role as a claims-maker concerns how his piece was constructed vis-à-vis the other two articles in the issue. Johnson's was the only one with a byline, giving it more authority. In addition, Johnson's discussion provided the overall context within which the next two articles would be read; certain perceptions about steroid use were introduced, which would influence how the next two articles would be viewed. Finally, using "evidence" from several sources, Johnson's piece appeared more authoritative and objective than the other articles, which were based exclusively on personal accounts.

The second article, without a byline, was entitled "Getting physical and chemical" and featured Tampa Bay Buccaneers' offensive guard Steve Courson's perspective on steroid use. Implicitly, the article presented "the other side" of the steroid story and provided some journalistic balance to the claims-making process that was taking place in that edition of *Sports Illustrated*.

Described as an "articulate, intelligent young man" who was "a military history enthusiast who loves the wars of Greece and Persia, and has a large collection of books about World War II" (p. 50), Courson was not a Neanderthal steroid junkie. The article noted that when Courson was not using Berlitz tapes to learn German, he enjoyed listening to classical music, such as Wagner, Bach, Beethoven, and Mozart. The piece also indicated that it was based on a 12-hour candid interview.

Courson noted that even though most players would not talk about steroids, he was willing because he did not want to be hypocritical: "I believe in telling the truth," he emphasized (Getting physical and chemical, 1985, p. 50). *Sports Illustrated* then framed the transition into the story: "What follows is Courson's account of—and rationalization for—his use of steroids."

In a clear, matter-of-fact manner, Courson spoke at length about his use of steroids, and while there is little doubt that the explicit content in the article provided insight into some aspects of the other side of the steroid argument, it also had several implicit themes that supported those who opposed steroid use in sports. The article concluded:

> Football is my business. I take this attitude toward drugs: They give me an edge in my business. I don't regret anything I've done so far as pharmaceutical use is concerned. It's very easy for people on the outside to criticize. But it's different when it's your livelihood, when it's your job to keep a genetic mutation from getting into your backfield. (p. 55)

There are three points about that conclusion that merit particular note. The first is that the two points I will make in a moment are the last thoughts one might have about Courson's account of steroid use.

The second point to note stems from the first four words of that concluding paragraph: "Football is my business." It is easy for outsiders to criticize, but for Courson, football is a demanding, highly competitive business—one in which others are taking steroids to gain an advantage. As a business, football is far more than sports; it is about profit and loss and people's livelihoods. Sports as a business are far removed from the ethos of the IOC's eligibility code and "amateur sport"—the term that was still widely used to identify high-performance sports and their alleged principles of fair play and the spirit of sport. As a business, one might be ready to understand and perhaps even accept the use of steroids within the context of professional sports, but one might infer from the paragraph that that is not a justification for their presence in any nonprofessional venue.

The third point of importance in the paragraph concerns the last seven words: what is required to stop a "genetic mutation" from gaining the upper hand. This point has two implicit messages. First, to the avid sports reader, the notion of a genetic mutation would have resonated with popular imagery of some of the Soviet Union's athletes—particularly some of their females—and "explained" why Western athletes had taken recourse to the same substances that the Soviets had used in Cold War sports (Ritchie, 2003). Second, is it really a genetic mutation that the athlete is facing or simply another athlete on steroids? Placing the notion of steroid use in such close proximity with the idea of an onrushing genetic mutation creates a disturbing, thought-provoking image. The reader has reason to pause, shudder, and reflect.

The second article was entitled "A business built on bulk"—the story of Charles J. Radler. Before he was arrested in July 1984, Radler, according to the article, ran "the most lucrative steroid-dealing operation in the U.S."

(A business built on bulk, 1985, p. 56). When he was dealing steroids, Radler grossed more than $20,000 a week; during the last nine months of 1983, he had deposits in four different bank accounts totaling more than $670,000. At the time of the interview, he was serving a sentence of one to two years on 18 counts of illegal sales of prescription drugs and one count of racketeering; Radler was also fined $115,000. Radler, who had become a born-again Christian a year before his arrest, had entered into a plea agreement through which he would testify against other steroid dealers in a joint investigation by the Food and Drug Administration (FDA) and the Justice Department.

Radler's involvement with steroids began after he had started weight-lifting when he purchased steroids from an outlet in Colorado. When he learned that his vendors were a legally licensed wholesale distributor and realized that if he could become licensed in Pennsylvania that he would be able to buy steroids at far better prices, Radler secured a wholesale license. To cover the costs of his own use, Radler sent out flyers to competitive bodybuilders and built up a clientele. His whole-sale business began small but mushroomed. Thinking only bodybuild-ers and powerlifters used steroids, Radler learned that "Everybody uses steroids" (p. 56):

> It's the bodybuilders, the powerlifters, it's about every sport there is. I started getting calls from college football teams. That surprised me at first. Now it would surprise me if there was a college football team out there that isn't using steroids. I'd get all kinds of calls like "I'm a boxer, what should I do?" I had this illusion I was helping people. I spent hours on the phone passing on information. (p. 56)

After turning to Christianity, Radler dropped out of the business for a while but then returned—until his arrest.

As part of the claims-making process, this story is particularly interest-ing because Radler is portrayed as such an ordinary person: The son of a Pittsburgh truck driver, he had been running a pizza shop before moving into steroids. Radler, the story noted, "is 36, a pale and bloated behemoth of a man, 6'4" and 285 pounds. He wore a bland brown prison uniform, and his body sort of sagged and flowed over a swivel chair as he told his story" (p. 56). There was absolutely nothing sophisticated about his oper-ation; most of the time, it was run out of his house until it grew so large that he had to rent warehouse space. In other words, anyone could deal in steroids, and the demand was so large that even the least sophisticated person would soon find business booming. The story left a very compelling feeling that there were "Radlers" everywhere, living and operating in everyone's own community—maybe even next door.

Taken within the context of the entire article—the entire series of articles—one of the most significant, implicit claims occurs right at the end (thus at the end of the series of articles): Even those on the inside eventually recognize that steroid use in sports must be eradicated. The final paragraph reads:

> Radler offered to turn state's evidence the same night he went to jail. "So I told them I'll tell you what I know about the steroid market in hopes it'll all collapse. I really hope that." (p. 60)

Over the next 30 years, antisteroid claims-makers would repeat—with different points of emphasis depending on the incident—the dominant themes found in these early *Sports Illustrated* articles. In addition, these themes were quickly integrated into the positions of claims-makers with far greater power and reach than a sporting magazine. The key themes included claims about how widespread steroid use in professional and high-performance sports had become; the manner in which steroids violated the principles of fair play and the spirit of sport; the extent to which steroids had trickled down into colleges, high schools, and even middle schools; the dangerous side effects associated with steroids; and the remorse that former users and dealers felt when they looked back on their reckless and careless pasts.

With just 48 strides in less than 9.8 seconds on September 24, 1988, Ben Johnson did far more than shatter a world record and crush his archrival Carl Lewis at the premier event in the Seoul Summer Games: Johnson opened one of the most high-profile chapters in the social construction of steroids. Within 72 hours of his victory, a positive test for the banned steroid stanozolol led to Johnson's disqualification and expulsion from the Olympic Games. Claims-making took on a new urgency and quickly involved some powerful claims-makers. There were three processes that are of particular note for this discussion. The first concerned *Sports Illustrated*, and the other two involved the federal government of Canada and the Senate Judiciary Committee in the United States.

There were a number of articles on steroids in *Sports Illustrated* either immediately preceding or following Johnson's disqualification; seven of them merit particular attention.

Steve Wulf's "Scorecard" continued—in a subtle yet unmistakable manner—*Sports Illustrated*'s appeal for all levels of sports to increase their vigilance and to impose meaningful punishments for athletes using steroids. Wulf contrasted the NFL's half-hearted suspension of Lawrence Taylor for steroid use with the decisive action the U.S. Olympic Committee (USOC) took when it dismissed swimmer Angel Myers from the Olympic team following a positive test for the steroid nandrolone.

Two issues later, William Johnson's "Hit for a Loss" article continued *Sports Illustrated*'s mounting critique of the NFL's steroid policy. Johnson noted that although 17 players had tested positive in 1988, none were suspended. "Indeed," Johnson (1988a) continued,

> a league handout last week announced that the 1988 testing results weren't complete yet, that they wouldn't be complete until next month and that even when they were finally finished, players wouldn't need to worry about heavy disciplinary action for using of steroids. "While suspension is possible, it is not anticipated during the '88 season," said the release. Why? Commissioner Rozelle said, "We are learning about this substance just like the medical profession is learning. . . . We are uncertain about how effective the tests are. . . . It depends on how long the drug has been in a man's system, whether it was injected or taken orally—all these things make a difference. These tests cost a lot of dough. . . . People tell players when the tests are being held. . . . We are still in a learning process." (pp. 51–2)

"Despite the wrongheadedness about steroids, the uneven disposition of justice and other flaws, there's still something to be said for the NFL's testing program," Johnson (1988a) noted optimistically at the end of the article. It forces players to think twice about their actions, and "the fact that the league is, for the first time, showing itself to be deadly serious about drug abuse can only be good in the long run" (p. 53).

The cover on the October 3, 1988, edition of *Sports Illustrated*—the first issue following Ben Johnson's positive test—showed no mercy. The headline banner "Scandal in Seoul" ran across the top. The largest text on the cover—a photo of Johnson at top speed—was explicit: "Busted!"

William Johnson and Kenny Moore's (1988) article "The Loser" was as blunt as its title. "He fled like a criminal," they wrote, "hiding his face behind a briefcase as an army of photographers and TV cameramen fought one another to take his picture." Seventy-two hours earlier, Johnson had been "a hero of truly Olympian proportions." "His fall from gold and glory," they continued, "occurred with thundering finality" (p. 22).

Johnson and Moore's article dramatically pieced together a sequence of events that extended from Ben Johnson's withdrawal from pre-Olympic competitions following two August losses to Lewis in Zurich and Cologne; his clandestine training/rehabilitation program on the island of St. Kitts with his physician and steroid supplier, Dr. Jamie Astaphan; and the events in Seoul before, during, and after the 100-meter final. The article did more than report the facts; it was written to evoke some specific reactions within readers.

Readers learn in the first paragraph that information contained in the article came from sources who had claimed they were present when Johnson and Astaphan had talked about the different steroids Johnson was taking and how he could fool the drug tests in Seoul (Johnson & Moore, 1988, p. 22). The two sources claimed that Astaphan had told them that the Americans and Soviets did not know how to use banned substances without being detected but that the Bulgarians did. The cloak and dagger secrecy added an important underworld flavor to Ben Johnson's story, but the article was written to make a more important set of claims.

Johnson and Moore (1988) wrote: "The source told SI that, under the Bulgarian-Astaphan regimen, [Ben] Johnson was receiving 'incredible quantities of this stuff.' However, he said, Johnson's advisers did not even do blood profiles on Johnson to see if his liver and his kidneys were capable of handling the steroids. 'It was like he was a racehorse. A commodity,' said the source" (p. 23). Given the regime of steroids Johnson was taking, the source later commented: "I fear for his liver now"—a view that was reinforced by an American trainer who claimed that Johnson's eyes "were so yellow with his liver working overtime processing steroids that I said he's either crazy or he's protected with an insurance policy" (p. 24).

Johnson and Moore (1988) concluded with two starkly contrasting images—one of hope and optimism and the other of shame and despair. They noted that Johnson's positive test might signal a tougher stance on steroids, quoting Mary Slaney: "I think it's wonderful. Not because of Ben, but because I want a clean sport. The fact that a thing this big can't be swept under the rug is a sign of hope." In contrast, there was no hope for Johnson. He had been "transformed from a man with one of the brightest, richest futures in all of sport to a man with nothing to look forward to but days of shame" (p. 27).

It is worth noting that Slater would face her own controversy when a routine test at the 1996 U.S. Olympic trials revealed a testosterone-to-epitestosterone ratio that exceeded the 6:1 parameter allowed by the IAAF

Chaikin also wrote about the potential psychologically addictive aspects to steroid use. He noted that there is a "vicious cycle" involved with them; the muscle growth, increased aggression, and other psychological changes fuel an athlete, making him or her want to get even bigger by taking more steroids. But there are also deep emotional troughs coming off a cycle. Steroids, he noted, create a continuous cycle of extreme highs and depressing lows.

Almost six months after quitting steroids, Chaikin still had vision problems and could not deal with stress the way he had before. He could not exercise aggressively without getting headaches and could not work full time because he tired easily. One might have to be a bit crazy to play football, Chaikin argued, but one should not take steroids. When he met a former teammate in the spring of 1988 who was still using steroids, Chaikin told the player that he would end up just like Chaikin had. The teammate dismissed the comment, saying steroids affect some more than others. "Maybe that's true, maybe not," Chaikin concluded. "God help those who find out" (p. 102).

The full claims-making significance of the Chaikin and Telander article is twofold: what was written and how it was framed—what was emphasized and what was glossed over or omitted.

Concerning the content, the article is a moving and powerful warning to anyone considering taking steroids. The pain and suffering Chaikin experienced and detailed for others to see was real and probably far deeper than most readers could really appreciate. The account should not be ignored, trivialized, or dismissed out of hand.

However, at the same time, as a contribution to the claims-making process—intentionally or not—the article was constructed and framed to demonize steroids while deflecting attention away from other important issues and concerns. For example, Telander (1988) wrote a short piece that put the larger article into a particular context. "A Peril for Athletes" focuses the reader's attention on two key points: This is the story of an individual who has chosen, with great difficulty and ambivalence, to "purge himself before someone who was empathetic" while hating to have to "recite his own failings" (Telander, 1988, p. 114). "When I gave him the manuscript of his story to review, he almost broke down as he labored through it," Telander noted. "Sweat poured from him as though he were running grass drills in the South Carolina heat." But does that frame the story correctly?

While Chaikin himself probably saw his abuse of steroids as a personal failing, his account shows how deeply integrated Chaikin was within the powerful football culture of NCAA Division I football. There is little question, on the basis of Chaikin's article, that the NCAA Division I football culture celebrates hypermasculinity, violent competitive combat, unrestrained aggression, and physical excess. Thus, Chaikin's failings were not simply his own; they were clearly related to his intimate connection to a much broader set of social forces and his desire to "chase the American dream" (Chaikin & Telander, 1988, p. 85). At the same time, while steroids in Chaikin's case may well have been a problem, the story is framed by Telander as though they were the cause of Chaikin's path to near suicide—but were they? Or are steroids a critical and dangerous symptom of much more deeply rooted problems?

Chaikin's account of his experiences makes it clear that every decision that he made—from his senior year in high school pursuing a football scholarship, to making the University of South Carolina Gamecocks team but not dressing in his first year, to dressing, and then starting and wanting to star—was heavily shaped by an extremely powerful sports culture that is held in high esteem throughout the United States. Moreover, each of Chaikin's decisions drew him deeper and deeper into that culture until he and the culture had become one. Had he not made that culture such an integral part of his self-identity, Chaikin might have remained a member of the scout team for a couple of years and would have been dropped by the wayside sooner or later as another young stud took his place.

Telander is not solely responsible for making steroids and Chaikin's individual decisions the focus of the story. It is clear that when Chaikin reflected on his experiences, he did the same thing. In Chaikin's case, that may have been due to the extent he had internalized the overwhelmingly individualist ethos of elite sports, where the individual is constantly held responsible for his or her successes and failures. Through long-term dedication and personal self-sacrifice, every athlete learns as he or she moves up through the ranks that the individual controls his or her own future. "I often sit and wonder how it all happened," Chaikin noted, "how I let anabolic steroids lead me into this mess." "I feel there's something in me— a flaw maybe, a personality trait—that brought me down" (Chaikin & Telander, 1988, p. 85). Chaikin took full responsibility for his actions, noting that he was headstrong: "I can't blame others for my mistakes, certainly not for making me take dangerous drugs." However, at the same time, Chaikin also felt that part of the problem was due to the pressures of college football, overzealous coaches, and "our just-take-a-pill-to-cure-anything society."

Reading Chaikin's piece now, with so much attention currently focused on the impact of repeated concussions in contact sports, it is clear that many of the symptoms that Chaikin experienced and expressed may very well have been related to repeated head trauma. Six months after he left football, Chaikin was still unable to exercise without experiencing severe headaches, could not work full time because he tired easily, could not deal with stress, and his vision was still problematic. None of those conditions are among the normal side effects of steroid use, but along with Chaikin's severe depression, they all fit the profile of an athlete who has experienced repeated incidents of head trauma.

Telander's article in that issue frames steroid use in two particular respects. First, Telander linked Chaikin's account with an April 1988 *American Journal of Psychiatry* article on the psychotic symptoms associated with anabolic steroid use. Telander noted that Harrison Pope and David Katz had written that "[m]ajor psychiatric symptoms [manic behavior, depression, paranoia, visual and auditory hallucinations, grandiose delusions] may be a common adverse effect of these drugs" (p. 114, Telander's insertions). Pope and Katz, Telander (1988) continued,

> recounted horror stories of athletes who became deranged from steroid use, but then added that psychological damage "cannot easily be studied in the laboratory or clinic. Only by observing the effects of these drugs in natural settings, in the doses and combinations actually used by athletes, are we likely to better understand them." (p. 114)

"Tommy [Chaikin] offers us just such an opportunity," Telander concluded.

The citation and quotations seem to lend the authority of scientific research to Telander's claims and construct a direct link between Pope and Katz's work and Chaikin's experiences. However, there are some problems with that construction.

First, the quotations Telander used are taken from the summary abstract to Pope and Katz's (1988) paper. When one reads the full article and then the abstract, it is clear that in writing that "[m]ajor psychiatric symptoms may be a common adverse effect of these drugs [i.e., steroids]," Pope and Katz (1988) have deliberately qualified their claim with the use of "may" (p. 487). The study is based on interviews with 41 bodybuilders and football players. Pope and Katz noted in the abstract that according to the criteria found in the 1987 *Diagnostic and Statistical Manual of Mental Disorders* (DSM-III-R), "nine subjects (22%) displayed a full affective syndrome, and five (12%) displayed psychotic symptoms in association with steroid use" (p. 487). Within the discussion, Pope and Katz indicated that none "of the 41 subjects recalled an adverse medical effect of steroids requiring medical consultation" (p. 489). While 18 had experienced acne, five indicated testicular atrophy, three had gynecomastia, two experienced difficulty urinating, three reported hair loss, and both females in the study had deeper voices, all were in sound physical health.

With respect to psychological problems, five subjects had "met DSM-III-R criteria for psychotic symptoms during periods of steroid exposure," Pope and Katz (1988) indicated, but "no subject had psychotic symptoms during periods of no steroid exposure" (p. 489). All the subjects reported a "remission of symptoms within a few weeks after stopping steroids." None of the subjects had any psychotic symptoms when they were off steroids, suggesting that steroids were the cause of the psychotic events and that the events were temporary.

Five subjects "met DSM-III-R criteria for a manic episode" and eight others "only narrowly missed a diagnosis of manic episode." "Many others," Pope and Katz (1988) continued, "described pronounced euphoria and grandiosity, believing that nothing in the world could hurt them" (p. 487). No subject described that behavior when off steroids.

Pope and Katz recognized that their findings were far from definitive; on the contrary, they were highly exploratory: "Our findings must be considered descriptive rather than quantitative, since it is unclear whether our observations were representative of the experiences of steroid users as a whole." While it certainly seems, from reading the article, that Pope and Katz may have felt that their results were conservative in reflecting the incidence of affective or psychotic symptoms, they also recognized that they were only getting a glimpse of a large underground subculture. It was in this context that they noted that the impact of steroids on one's mental state could not be easily studied in a clinic or laboratory. "Only by observing the effects of these drugs in natural settings, in the doses and combinations actually used by athletes, are we likely to better understand them" (p. 489).

Pope and Katz (1988) suggested the need for research outside a clinical setting because the doses athletes tended to use were "frequently 10–100 times as high as those used in medical studies of these agents." Second, the practice of "stacking" (including several drugs in a single injection) as many as five or six drugs, "including oral preparations, parenteral preparations [a preparation introduced under or through one or more layers of skin directly into the body fluid system], veterinary preparations, and other hormones (such as chorionic gonadotropin) may be responsible for psychiatric effects (as well as muscle gains) far beyond those witnessed in research settings." In other words, while this exploratory study was suggestive and one might want to draw preliminary hypotheses from it, there was still significant scientific research to be done before one could begin to make statements anywhere close to definitive.

In addition to implying far more conclusive statements to Pope and Katz's research than the authors had indicated in their article, Telander also used some very evocative terms that were not in the article. Telander (1988) wrote that Pope and Katz had "recounted horror stories of athletes who became deranged from steroid use, but then added that psychological damage 'cannot easily be studied in the laboratory or clinic.'" While the construction of the sentence makes it clear that the terms "horror stories," "deranged," and "psychological damage" all come from Telander, the construction could also imply to the casual reader that those emotive terms were used by the researchers—and Telander had certainly connected them to steroids.

In stating their claim, claims-makers often provide a clear, unambiguous picture or position that does not fully reflect the complexity of reality; it is a distortion of the real situation. While Pope and Katz exercised caution and circumspection due to the limited and provisional nature of the data they had examined, by not retaining that caution, Telander's presentation creates a very different context for the Chaikin story than Pope and Katz's article suggests. Working with Chaikin while he was so emotionally distraught, Telander may not have realized that he had overstepped Pope and Katz's circumspection, but the fact remains that the association constructed between Chaikin's confessional and the work of Pope and Katz created some significant distortions.

In addition to using Pope and Katz to contextualize Chaikin's story, Telander identified another authority in a manner that suggested he was an impartial, objective source regarding steroids. On the basis of *Death in the Locker Room*, Bob Goldman (1984) has left little doubt about his past experiences with steroid use. Nevertheless, identifying Goldman, "the director of the High Technology Fitness Research Institute of the Chicago College of Osteopathic Medicine," as "perhaps this country's foremost authority on steroid abuse" was as misleading as if Telander had identified Dan Duchaine (1981), the author of *The Underground Steroid Handbook*, with the same words. Duchaine also had extensive experience with and knowledge of steroids, their use, and their impact on individuals, but he was as active an advocate for steroids as Goldman was an opponent. Neither could ever claim much objectivity to their particular interpretations of steroid use; they both had strong, vested interests in the statements they made about steroids. Goldman, like Duchaine, was a useful source for information, but he was not a disinterested expert. As a result, when Telander cited Goldman's claim that there were more than a million steroid users in the United States in 1988—"one in every 250 people"—he was presenting the exaggerated claim of a high-profile steroid opponent as a simple point of fact and inaccurately contextualizing Chaikin's story.

The final article of note was Telander's (1989) "The Death of an Athlete." The main subject of the piece is Benji Ramirez, a member of the Ashtabula (Ohio) High football team who collapsed at practice on October 31, 1988, and died in the hospital from an apparent heart attack. The autopsy was conducted in Cleveland, and although the county coroner does not normally test for steroids, following rumors that Ramirez had used them, Dr. Robert Malinowski took that into consideration when performing various tests during autopsy. Telander (1989) related two of the coroner's findings. The first indicated that although the coroner could not identify any specific steroid in Ramirez's blood, through his "field investigation and some changes seen in the body at autopsy," he concluded that Ramirez had used steroids. Second, Telander wrote that it was the coroner's firm opinion that steroids had, in some way, contributed to Ramirez's death (p. 71).

While Malinowski had been careful to state that it was his opinion that Ramirez had used steroids, that they had been a contributing factor to his death, and that it was possible he was wrong, he then added: "But I doubt it" (p. 71). "If Malinowski is right," Telander wrote, "Ramirez is the first U.S. athlete whose death has been linked officially to the use of steroids, a practice that, by all accounts, is spreading across the country faster than experts can track it" (p. 71).

This article is particularly noteworthy for three reasons. First, it contributes to the previous claims in *Sports Illustrated* concerning the dangers associated with steroid use—in this instance, leading to the ultimate tragedy of a youth's unnecessary death.

Second, the article introduces a new dimension to the problems associated with steroids—youths taking steroids not to enhance their athletic performance but to improve their appearance. Many of Ramirez's friends cited in the article state that he took steroids simply to get bigger to impress girls. Despite the active discouragement of Danny Wells, a body-builder and former steroid user, Ramirez and some of his friends persisted in taking steroids to "get big." In Telander's (1989) words: "To be big means to be in control, macho, bad. It means you have bypassed adolescence and jumped straight to manhood" (p. 74).

This is an extremely important dimension to the use of steroids, but it receives little attention in the popular media. To indicate that Ramirez and his friends were not unique, Telander cited the work of Charles Yesalis, a researcher with particular expertise in the sociocultural aspects of steroid use and the extent of such use in the United States. Although he did not identify the study precisely, Telander appeared to be referring to Buckley, Yesalis, Karl Friedl et al.'s (1988) lead article in the December 16, 1988, issue of the *Journal of the American Medical Association*, which estimated the prevalence of steroid use among male high school seniors.

The study was the first nationwide survey of the general American adolescent male population regarding steroid use. The authors noted that 6.6 percent of male high school seniors use or had used anabolic steroids. While the survey revealed that most of the users were involved in sports—with football and wrestling predominating—the data also showed that about a third (35.2 percent) of the users had no sports involvement at all. The authors compiled a profile of adolescent steroid users: Steroids were used by youths at all grade levels in high school as well as junior high school; self-identified users had gone through from one to five cycles of six to 12 weeks duration; only 18.2 percent reported a single cycle, and almost 40 percent reported five or more; of those starting at age 15 or younger, less than 10 percent had used steroids for only one cycle; 12 percent reported cycles of steroid use lasting 13 weeks or longer; about 44 percent had stacked their steroids, and more than 38 percent had used oral and injectable steroids; the largest single reason for using steroids (47.1 percent) was "to improve athletic performance," with "appearance" indicated as the main reason by 26.7 percent of respondents; the most common source for steroids (60.5 percent) was "other athletes, coaches, gyms, etc.," but 20 percent reported a health care professional (physician, pharmacist, or veterinarian) as their source (p. 3443).

The final aspect to Telander's piece concerns the impact that this article would have in the overall claims-making process. On the one hand, the article drew attention to five extremely important and, to that point in time, neglected aspects of steroid use among adolescents—the age at which use began, the extent to which steroids were used by adolescents, the duration of steroid use among many youths, and the fact that while most took steroids to improve athletic performance, there was a significant percentage of users who, like Ramirez, were simply interested in improving their appearance. However, because it was such an early study, the categories of users were not broken down on the basis of specific background variables (such as socioeconomic status or other risk behaviors). Later work would begin to identify important background variables that differentiated the sports-oriented users from the appearance-based users (see DuRant, Escobedo & Heath, 1995; Faigenbaum et al., 1998; Hoffman et al., 2008; Kanayama et al., 2006, 2007; Kindlundh, Isacson, Berglund, & Nyberg, 1999; Labre, 2002; Miller, Barnes, Sabo et al., 2002; Pope & Brower, 2008; Pope, Olivardia, & Gruber, 1999; Parkinson & Evans, 2006; Pedersen, Wichstrøm, & Blekesaune, 2001; Scott, Wagner, & Barlow, 1996). As a result, the perception created was that all youths were susceptible to the temptations of steroid use, and that would become a predominant image in further claims-making.

The change in the Olympic brand, coverage of positive tests for steroids tests, the policies of national sports systems regarding substance use, and various media representations of "the growing problem" with steroids established the foundation on which later, more powerful claims-makers would stake their claims with respect to steroid use in sports. The social construction of steroids as demonized substances was well under way by 1988, but far bigger players would soon become involved.

Chapter 5

Interests of the Nation-State, Sports, and Steroids

The "war on drugs" in the United States began as early as July 14, 1969, when President Richard Nixon, in a special message to Congress, called drug abuse a serious threat to the nation. On the basis of increasing juvenile arrests and street crime related to drugs, Nixon called on state and federal governments to implement a national antidrug program. In June 1971, Nixon identified drug abuse as "public enemy number one" and officially declared a "war on drugs" (National Public Radio, 2007). Two years later, Nixon created the Drug Enforcement Agency (DEA) to coordinate the activities of the various agencies fighting to eliminate drugs from the United States.

The rhetoric on drugs cooled somewhat under President Jimmy Carter. Carter had campaigned on a platform that included decriminalizing marijuana and eliminating the federal criminal penalties for possession of an ounce or less of cannabis. But the Reagan Administration returned to a hard-line antidrug position.

Following criticisms over her extravagance as the First Lady and an inability to relate to the average American, in the second year of Ronald Reagan's presidency, Nancy Reagan launched the "Just Say No" campaign.

"Just Say No" had its origins in work pioneered in the 1970s by the University of Houston social psychologist Richard Evans as part of a substance abuse prevention research program funded by the National Institutes of Health. Evans believed that students needed to be "inoculated" with skills that would help them resist various social pressures that encouraged unhealthy behaviors. "Just Say No" was one of the resistance skills that children could use to lower peer pressure (Evans, 2002). Whatever its merits, "Just Say No" was successful in bringing national attention to the Reagan Administration's commitment to winning the war on drugs.

By October 1986, Reagan had signed the Anti-Drug Abuse Act of 1986, directing $1.7 billion to drug enforcement agencies (Library of Congress, 1986; National Public Radio, 2007).

Within that overall "war on drugs" context, the early articles in *Sports Illustrated* reinforced the general claims-making process and focused attention on drug abuse in sports. Ben Johnson's disqualification at Seoul created an ideal opportunity for antisteroid claims-makers to go on the offensive.

Prior to 1988, steroids in the United States were regulated as prescription drugs under the Food, Drug, and Cosmetic Act. The unauthorized sale of steroids was considered an instance of "misbranding," which was a misdemeanor (U.S. Sentencing Commission, 2006). The most significant steps taken to criminalize steroid use took place within the Anti-Drug Abuse Act of 1988—an act that went well beyond its 1986 predecessor. Certainly, the most ambitious objective of the new act was the goal of a "drug-free America" by 1995.

The comprehensive nature of the new act sought, first of all, to create a strong "law and order" context for the elimination of drug use in the United States. The act would also establish the institutional structures and resources needed to reach its ultimate objective. Finally, the act created the opportunity for those who wanted to target steroid use in sports to support legislation that would specifically address steroids and establish harsher penalties for their possession and distribution.

The Anti-Drug Abuse Act of 1988 contained three sections dealing specifically with steroids. With the approval of Congress, the act became the extremely far reaching and, as a result, controversial Public Law 100-690 of 1988—a law that many felt seriously infringed on individuals' constitutional rights and civil liberties.

Public Law 100-690 is long and extremely encompassing. The law is more than 360 pages in length, containing 10 major chapters, which each have numerous subtitles or chapters (Library of Congress, 1988a). The various titled sections provide an indication of how comprehensive the law is with respect to combating drug abuse: Coordination of National Drug Policy, Treatment and Prevention Programs, Drug Education Programs, International Narcotics Control, User Accountability, Anti-Drug Abuse Amendments Act of 1988, Death Penalty and Other Criminal and Law Enforcement Matters, Federal Alcohol Administration, and Miscellaneous and Supplemental Appropriations. The law was introduced on August 11, 1988, to the House of Representatives as H.R. 5210, the

Omnibus Drug Initiative Act of 1988, and it passed, with amendments, on October 22, 1988 (Library of Congress, 1988a).

The first title of the act—"Coordination of National Drug Policy" (and under "Subtitle A: National Drug Control Program")—established the Office of National Drug Control Policy within the Executive Office of the President. The office is run by a director who is assisted by deputy directors for "demand reduction" and "supply reduction." Each position is filled by the president, with the advice and consent of the Senate. The status and location of these positions indicate the importance that the Reagan Administration was placing on the war on drugs.

Title V of the act—"User Accountability" (and under "Subtitle A: Opposition to Legalization and Public Awareness")—deplored an earlier position taken by Congress on the legalization of illegal drugs, terming it a surrender in the war on drugs. The 1988 act required the director of National Drug Control Policy to develop a program that would inform Americans of the government's renewed efforts to eliminate drug abuse from the United States, indicate the nature of the new provisions of the act, and the penalties for the possession or use of illegal drugs. This section called for the establishment of a National Commission on Drug-Free Schools, the implementation of the Public Housing Drug Elimination Act of 1988, and the Drug-Free Workplace Act of 1988. It was within "Subtitle F: Drug-Free America Policy" that Congress made its dramatic commitment to make the United States drug-free by 1995 (Library of Congress, 1988a).

Following different committee readings and amendments, in the final text of the act, steroids were dealt with under "Title II: Treatment and Prevention Programs—Subtitle A: Provisions Relating to Public Health Service Act," "Chapter 4: Miscellaneous," and "Subtitle E: Provisions Relating to Certain Drugs." In many ways, this relocation of the sections dealing with steroids represented the success that various senators and representatives had in raising the profile of the steroid problem. But there had been more to the committee reading and amendment process than simply moving steroids up in the act. A few key changes were also introduced as the act moved to its final passage.

The original proposal only mentioned steroids once. The reference occurred within "Title X: Committee on Energy and Commerce—Comprehensive Alcohol Abuse, Drug Abuse, and Mental Health Amendments Act of 1988." In the first draft, this section of the act declared that any criminal conviction under the Federal Food, Drug, and Cosmetic Act involving steroids or HGH that was subject to criminal forfeiture under the Controlled Substances Act would be treated as a violation and conviction under the Controlled Substances Act (see the "Introduced" summary at Library of Congress, 1988b).

On September 22, citing "disturbing evidence" of steroid use among high school students, New Jersey Democratic Representative William Hughes proposed Amendment 909, which would make the distribution of steroids without a prescription a felony punishable by fines and up to three years in prison (Library of Congress, 1988a). "Echoing Rep. Hughes' concerns," the *2006 Steroids Report* indicated, "Representatives [Richard] Baker and [Daniel] Lungren denounced the use of steroids in high school and college athletics, and noted that the amendment signaled the beginning of greater congressional involvement in the regulation of steroids" (U.S. Sentencing Commission, 2006, p. 4). This amendment resulted in the House adding a second clause on steroids. The amended act made it a criminal offence—in instances other than those in which a physician had ordered them for the treatment of a medical condition—for an individual to distribute or possess with the intent to distribute steroids (see the "Passed House Amended" summary at Library of Congress, 1988b).

In the Senate, Joe Biden, citing many of the same concerns as Hughes, proposed an amendment that would double the penalty in the Hughes proposal for the distribution of steroids to a minor. The Senate amendment was accepted in a slightly altered form. As a result, when the legislation passed the House of Representatives on October 22, 1988, steroids were dealt with in three specific sections of the act. The act declared any criminal conviction under the Federal Food, Drug, and Cosmetic Act involving anabolic steroids or HGH punishable by more than a year of imprisonment and subject to criminal forfeiture under the Controlled Substances Act to be a violation of the Controlled Substances Act. The legislation directed the Comptroller General to study and report to Congress by June 1, 1989, on the extent to which steroids and HGH were being used by high school and college students and other adults. Finally, the act would amend the Federal Food, Drug, and Cosmetic Act to "make it a criminal offense to distribute or to possess with the intent to distribute any anabolic steroid other than in accordance with a physician's order for the purpose of treating disease" (Library of Congress, 1988a). In instances where the distribution or intent to distribute was directed at an individual under the age of 18, the act authorized a longer prison term.

H.R. 5210, the Omnibus Drug Initiative Act of 1988, was refined further and became Public Law 100-690 on November 18, 1988. It was the "first major steroid legislation" in the United States (U.S. Sentencing Commission, 2006, p. 3).

Under section 2403 of the new public law, the terms of imprisonment were not more than three years, or a fine, or both for anyone distributing or possessing with intent to distribute anabolic steroids for purposes other than the treatment of disease pursuant to the order of a physician. Consistent with Biden's amendment, the term of imprisonment increased to up to six years for anyone distributing or possessing with the intent to distribute to individuals under the age of 18 (see Dubin, 1990, p. 615). As the act became law, Biden indicated that it was only the first step in controlling steroid abuse (U.S. Sentencing Commission, 2006).

Despite this early success, Biden and other claims-makers ran into some difficulties as they sought to toughen the laws around steroids. One of Biden's chief objectives was to place steroids directly under the Controlled Substances Act as a highly restricted Schedule I substance. To that end, even before the Comptroller General had reported back to Congress about the extent of illegal steroid use in the United States, on February 9, 1989, Fortney Stark and 141 cosponsors proposed H.R. 995, Anabolic Steroid Restriction Act of 1989 (Library of Congress, 1989c). Biden introduced a companion bill, S.466, Anabolic Steroid Restriction Act of 1989, to the Senate on the last day of February. H.R. 995, Anabolic Steroid Restriction Act of 1989, proposed amendments to the federal criminal code such that anyone who knowingly used the mail system to distribute or receive anabolic steroids or other controlled substances for purposes other than the medically authorized treatment or used any communication facility to cause or commit a violation of the act would be subject to criminal prosecution. The bill was referred that same day to the House Judiciary Committee and on March 21 to the House Judiciary Committee's Subcommittee on Crime. The subcommittee began hearings the next day.

A diverse but select group of individuals, including a postal inspector, high school principal, professor of medicine, and Carl Lewis—the ultimate winner of the 100-meter dash in Seoul following Johnson's disqualification—testified before the subcommittee. Despite the early action, neither H.R. 995 nor S. 466 moved beyond the committee stage (U.S. Sentencing Commission, 2006).

On October 5, 1989, Democrat Mel Levine introduced H.R. 3421, To Provide for the Control of Anabolic Steroids Under the Controlled Substances Act, and for Other Purposes, into the House of Representatives (Library of Congress, 1989a). This proposal also sought to classify steroids as a controlled substance (H.R.3421.IH, 1989). The act was immediately referred to the House Committee on Energy and Commerce and on October 20 referred to the Subcommittee on Health and the Environment. Like the Stark and Biden initiatives, Levine's bill fell dormant until it was ultimately incorporated into H.R. 5269, Comprehensive Crime Control Act of 1990 (Library of Congress, 1989a).

The goal of classifying steroids as a controlled substance was proving to be difficult. There were two hurdles in the way: One was major, and the other was inconvenient. The major hurdle concerned the criteria for classification as a controlled substance. To become a controlled substance, there had to be medical evidence confirming that it was addictive and psychoactive. For steroids, that was not as easy as one might think.

In 1989, there was very little research on steroids concerning their psychoactive character or any addictive properties. The work by Pope and Katz (1988) had suggested that psychotic symptoms "may be a common adverse affect of these substances [steroids]," but the data were not conclusive (see also Katz & Pope, 1990). Almost a decade later, such researchers as Bahrke, Yesalis, and Wright (1996) continued to caution that even though there appeared to be "an association between anabolic-androgenic steroid use and affective and psychotic syndromes and psychological dependence" at the high levels used by many athletes and bodybuilders, "the psychological and behavioral effects of anabolic-androgenic steroids are complicated by a variety of methodological limitations" (p. 367). Of the estimated million past or current steroid users in the United States, Bahrke, Yesalis, and Wright (1996) noted that "an extremely small percentage of individuals using anabolic-androgenic steroids appear to experience mental disturbances severe enough to result in clinical treatment and medical case reports." Moreover, among those affected, "the roles of previous psychiatric history, genetic susceptibility to addictions or mental disorders, environmental and peer influences" make the connection between steroids and addictive and psychoactive conditions difficult to establish (see also Bahrke, Yesalis, & Wright, 1990; Yesalis, Vicary, Buckley et al., 1990).

Writing almost a decade after the first wave of intensive scientific interest in the impact that steroids have on athletes and nonathletes alike,

Yesalis and Cowart's (1998) comprehensive discussion of steroid use in sports was careful in addressing the psychoactive aspects of steroids. They noted that the negative effects of steroids on behavior had been a subject of controversy, with "roid rage" receiving considerable attention. Their conclusions about the relationship between steroids and psychological problems were cautious and carefully worded:

> Where the absolute risk may be open to debate, most experts do agree that some individuals will have psychological problems as a result of taking steroids. It stands to reason that those who are better adjusted psychologically will have fewer consequences than those who are farther out on the behavior continuum, but nobody really knows who is at risk. (Yesalis & Coward, 1998, p. 3)

Thus, despite their opposition to steroid use in sports or any other nonmedically prescribed and supervised situation, Yesalis and Coward did not want to overstate what the scientific community had established: "[S]ome individuals will have psychological problems," "but nobody really knows who is at risk" (p. 3). Whether steroids were addictive and psychoactive had not really been demonstrated after a decade's worth of investigation.

The second hurdle was the AMA. Although the AMA was usually very supportive of antidrug legislation, in this instance, it opposed the inclusion of steroids as a Schedule I controlled substance (the highest level of legislated control) (American Medical Association, 1991).

To build his case, as the chair of the Senate Judiciary Committee, Biden initiated and then presided over two days of hearings on "Steroids in Amateur and Professional Sports: The Medical and Social Costs of Steroid Abuse." The committee heard testimony from almost 20 individuals. The first session, taking place on April 3, 1989, in Newark, New Jersey, featured high-performance athletes Evelyn Ashford, Diane Williams, and Pat Connolly—who was a former Olympian and then Ashford's coach—two researchers—Yesalis and Katz—AMA spokesperson Edward Langston as well as Pat Croce, the conditioning coach for the Philadelphia 76ers of the National Basketball Association (NBA) and the Philadelphia Flyers of the National Hockey League (NHL); Mike Quick, an all-pro receiver for the NFL's Philadelphia Eagles; Otho Davis, the Eagles' head trainer and executive director of the National Athletic Trainers Association; and Dorothy Baker, chair of the United States Olympic Committee (Senate Judiciary Committee, 2002).

It was the AMA position that created the greatest difficulty for Biden's proposal. In its submission to the committee, the AMA (1991) was clear on why it opposed the scheduling of anabolic-androgenic steroids:

> Anabolic steroids do not meet the statutory criteria for scheduling under Schedule I of the CSA [Controlled Substances Act]. First, anabolic steroids have an accepted medical use in medical practice. Moreover, anabolic steroids can be used safely under medical supervision. Second, abuse of steroids does not lead to physical or psychological dependence as also is required for scheduling under the other schedules of the CSA. (p. 121)

Furthermore, the AMA (1991) noted that the existing regulation of steroids through the CSA "has proven to be a highly satisfactory means of reviewing and evaluating drugs for almost twenty years."

In his testimony before the committee, Langston (1991) emphasized each of the AMA's main points while specifically focusing on the criteria required to schedule a substance:

> We believe that anabolic steroids do not meet the statutory criteria for scheduling under the CSA. The CSA provides that in order to be placed in Schedule I, a drug must have a high potential for abuse *and have no currently accepted medical use in treatment in the United States.* In addition, there must be a *lack of accepted safety for use of the drug under medical supervision.* In order to be controlled under one of the other schedules of the CSA, a drug must have some *potential for abuse that could lead to physical or psychological dependence.*

The medical facts do not support scheduling anabolic steroids under the CSA. (p. 127, all emphases in the original)

Langston then reviewed the medical facts, emphasizing again that "anabolic steroids should not be scheduled under *any* other schedule of the CSA since abuse of the drugs does *not* lead to physical or psychological dependence as is required by scheduling under the Act" (p. 127).

The second session was held on May 9, 1989, in Washington, D.C., and focused on football. The committee heard testimony from Bill Fralic, a three-time all-pro lineman with the NFL's Atlanta Falcons and their NFL Players Association representative; Chuck Noll and Marty Schottenheimer, head coaches of the NFL's Pittsburgh Steelers and Kansas City Chiefs, respectively; Joe Paterno, Bo Schembechler, Joe Purzycki, and Harold Raymond, the head football coaches at Penn State University, the University of Michigan, Madison University, and the University of

Delaware, respectively; Jay Moyer, an NFL executive vice president; and Pete Rozelle, the outgoing commissioner of the NFL (Senate Committee of the Judiciary, 2002).

Biden played a particularly active role in framing the discussion. "The NFL's words and actions, together with those of successful college and pro athletes and coaches around the country," Biden told the committee, "can demonstrate that taking steroids is dangerous [and] wrong" (cited in Assael, 2007, p. 51). He emphasized that tens of millions of Americans look to the "stars on the athletic field as the role models in our schools, in our colleges, and in our lives." If athletes were allowed to use steroids without any penalties, Biden argued, it would send a message that "is over-whelmingly clear to the rest of America that drug abuse in any form is not that big a deal" (p. 52). Throughout the proceedings, Biden skillfully emphasized four simple themes: steroids are dangerous, their use is wrong, allowing star athletes to use them will corrupt young people, and ignoring steroid use is the same as allowing heroin junkies to use drugs without any legal consequences. The same themes were also emphasized in two House of Representatives' inquires into steroids and sports: ste-roids pose serious potential health risks, they run against the rules and spirit of sport, and allowing athletes to use steroids sends a dangerous message to American youth (see House of Representatives, 1989, 1990; Assael, 2007).

By the end of the Senate Judiciary Committee hearing, Biden indicated that he felt it was appropriate to introduce legislation that would make steroids, like heroin, crack, and cocaine, a controlled substance. As a con-trolled substance, simple possession would be a criminal offense.

Despite the absence of full support from the AMA and the challenge Biden faced in convincing legislators that steroids were addictive and psychoactive, the material in the records of the hearings before the Senate Judiciary Committee, the manner in which that material would be incor-porated into the presentation of the act to the Senate—along with the gen-eral claims-making environment around steroids—were sufficient for Biden to pursue the legislative initiative. On November 1, 1989, Biden introduced S. 1829, The Steroid Trafficking Act of 1989.

The purpose of the act was simple: It would "amend the Controlled Substances Act to further restrict the use of steroids. By designating ana-bolic steroids as a Schedule II controlled substance, the bill would crack down on illegal steroid use" (Senate Judiciary Committee, 2002, p. 282). The act indicated four ways in which it would "crack down on illegal steroid use." First, the act would increase steroid trafficking penalties to match those related to cocaine, heroin, and other dangerous drugs; second, it would impose "tight record-keeping and production control regulations to prevent the diversion of legally produced steroids into the illicit market; third, it would transfer the investigatory and regulatory powers from the Food and Drug Administration (FDA) to the DEA; and, finally, it would require "U.S. demand reduction agencies to incorporate steroids in all federally supported drug abuse prevention, education, and treatment programs" (Senate Judiciary Committee, 2002, p. 283).

By November 19, the proposed act had been referred to the House Judiciary Committee and on to the House Judiciary Subcommittee on Crime as well as the House Energy and Commerce Committee and on to its Subcommittee on Health and Environment and the Senate Judiciary Committee, which Biden chaired. The Senate Judiciary Committee revised the text in minor ways and returned it to the Senate on March 8, 1990, giving the bill its full support.

The Senate Judiciary Committee reported that it supported the Schedule II designation of steroids and provided arguments for its position based on the three criteria required to schedule a substance under the Controlled Substances Act. Concerning the potential for abuse, the committee was unequivocal: "Steroid abuse has become a major drug abuse problem in America" (Senate Judiciary Committee, 2002, p. 284). The report noted that as many as a million Americans "have used or are currently using steroids for nonmedical purposes, primarily to increase athletic performance and improve physical appearance" (Senate Judiciary Committee, 2002, pp. 284–5). "More disturbing," the committee noted, was the "widespread abuse among high school students and other young people." Citing a study that showed that the number of students who had used steroids in the previous 30 days was about 75 percent of the level of individuals who had used crack, the report emphasized that: "Steroid abuse by male high school seniors is nearly as widespread as the use of 'crack' cocaine." The committee claimed that "up to 500,000 male high school students use or have used steroids" apparently selecting the maximum number noted in range of 250,000 to 500,000 indicated in the report's source: Buckley, Yesalis, Friedl et al. (1988) (Senate Judiciary Committee, 2002, p. 285). Irrespective of the real number of users, with Buckley, Yesalis, Friedl et al., reporting that about 6 percent of high school seniors in their survey had used steroids, the committee felt that the potential for abuse was clearly established.

The second criterion for inclusion under the Controlled Substances Act was straightforward. The substance must be used in the treatment of a medical condition, and steroids certainly met that test.

Addiction was the most challenging criterion. Although the conclusions drawn in the various studies that the committee cited were qualified and sometimes tentative, the committee presented its findings with clear certainty:

> The leading study of the addictive nature of steroid dependence cites the following four symptoms: (1) loss of control; (2) continued use despite adverse consequences; (3) tolerance; and (4) withdrawal [(see Brower, 1989)]. Almost every leading expert in the field agrees: steroids are addictive. (Senate Judiciary Committee, 2002, p. 287)

While the committee felt it was on solid grounds in making that claim, the sources cited were far more circumspect in their language and terminology.

Moore (1988) is one source cited. His piece is actually an editorial in the same issue of the *Journal of the American Medical Association* as the Buckley, Yesalis, Friedl et al. (1988) study—the first "nationwide survey of AS [anabolic steroids] use among the general adolescent male population" (p. 3443)—that estimated the prevalence of steroid use among high school seniors. The editorial was designed to call attention to the Buckley, Yesalis, Friedl et al. piece, and within his editorial comments, Moore engaged in some speculative extrapolations from the data in the actual article. Thus, Moore (1988) wrote: "Since many of the users among high school seniors might be described as habitual, the data may also be important in describing AS misuse in the adult population, the prevalence of which is not known and may be virtually impossible to ascertain" (p. 3484). The term "habitual" is Moore's and not that of Buckley, Yesalis, Friedl et al.; moreover, Moore then noted that because the primary reason identified in Buckley, Yesalis, Friedl et al. for taking steroids was to increase strength among high school football players, the prevalence of use "may decrease after high school, when participation in football declines" (p. 3484). In other words, "habitual" was not synonymous with "dependence" or "addiction."

Following a review of the various clinical uses for steroids, Moore (1988) did examine the "psychological effects of AS" (p. 3486). In that section, he noted: "As with other aspects of AS abuse, the psychological reaction to AS has not been documented" (p. 3486). In that section, he did not mention the terms "habitual," "dependence," or "addiction."

A paper forthcoming at the time of the report by Brower (1989) was the one referred to as "the leading study," but there are reasons to argue that the report overstated the paper's claims and exaggerated its status. The Brower paper was based on an earlier publication by Brower, Blow, Beresford, and Fuelling (1989). That earlier paper was centered on one specific case of a patient "whose dependence on a combination of anabolic and androgenic steroids meets the *DSM-III-R* criteria for psychoactive substance dependence" (p. 31). The discussion in Brower (1989) outlined what one would look for with respect to steroid dependence and how to treat it, but it did not document any cases of such dependence.

Writing about the potential for psychological dependence through steroids, with a decade's more research completed, Brower (2000) indicated that although anabolic steroids had not been included in the *DSM-III-R* (APA, 1987), they had been included in the 1994 *DSM-IV* (APA, 1994). This, he wrote, indicated that steroids have been associated with "mental or behavioral changes that could come to the attention of practicing psychiatrists and other health professionals" (Brower, 2000, p. 281). However, he continued to note that "the *DSM-IV* does not specifically state that anabolic steroids can cause dependence (as it does for drugs such as alcohol and cocaine)," although, he also wrote, the inclusion "does allow for this possibility in its diagnostic code and classification, *304.90—Other Substance Dependence*" (pp. 281–2). At the same time, Brower noted that the 1993 "*ICD-10* [the World Health Organization's *International Classification of Diseases*] defines all steroids under the category of 'non-dependence-producing substances'" (p. 282).

The two criteria—addictive and psychoactive—are complex designations. That is why researchers, physicians, psychiatrists, and psychologists are so careful before they use either term. Legislators may not feel the same constraints of precision and might rely on more commonsense interpretations of what each term should mean in making their case for or against the classification of steroids as a Schedule II controlled substance. Clearly, the members of the Senate Judiciary Committee felt that the testimony they had heard and the research that they had reviewed met the third test necessary for the Schedule II classification of steroids, and while some hearing the same testimony and reading the same research might concur, others would reach a very different conclusion.

Confident that the report of the Senate Judiciary Committee was enough to convince legislators that steroids should be classified as Schedule II substances, Biden addressed the Senate on October 24, 1990. Rather than belabor the technical aspects to the act, Biden focused on some key pragmatic issues. He emphasized that the Steroid Trafficking Act of 1989 was important because it would remove steroids from the jurisdiction of the FDA and place them under the DEA. Making four specific arguments, Biden maintained that the FDA did not have the ability or resources to regulate steroids. A third of the illegal steroids in the United States were diverted to the black market by drug manufacturers; the FDA did not have the resources to police a $300 to $400 million illicit market; the FDA personnel did not have the authority and were not properly trained to effectively combat illicit drug trafficking; and the FDA did not have a system that was reliable enough to track the production of steroids and determine what percentage made their way to the black market. Biden also emphasized that in addition to moving regulation to the DEA, the act made the penalties for trafficking in steroids the same as those for heroin, crack, and cocaine. Finally, the act made steroids a component of all general drug prevention and treatment programs (U.S. Sentencing Commission, 2006).

During the lengthy time period between the November 1, 1989, introduction of S. 1829, The Steroid Trafficking Act, and its movement through the Senate committee and then back to the floor, Jack Brooks—one of the most senior Democrats in the House of Representatives—introduced H.R. 5269, An Act to Control Crime, on July 13, 1990. The bill was similar to Biden's, proposing that steroids be added to the Controlled Substances Act as a Schedule II substance (H.R.5269.EAS, 1990). The reception in the House was more critical, and although the bill passed on October 5, 1990, as H.R. 5269, The Comprehensive Crime Control Act of 1990, Section 301 classified steroids as a Schedule III rather than as a more restrictive Schedule II substance. Accepting the fact that steroids had at least been classified as a restricted substance, Biden brought the Senate legislation into line with the House decision by introducing on October 27, 1990, S. 3266, A Bill to Control Crime, which also classified steroids as a Schedule III substance (see S.3266.ES, 1990). The bill was approved by the Senate and the House of Representatives on November 29 and became Public Law 101-647 (see S.3266.ENR, 1990; Library of Congress, 1990b).

Dubin Commission

From the tremendous heights of instant exhilaration, exuberant national pride, and the bursting sense of accomplishment that Ben Johnson's victory in Seoul brought to Canadians, his disqualification left them plummeting into the deepest depths of disbelief, loss, and even feelings of betrayal. But as path breaking and dramatic as the IOC's decision was to disqualify the gold medal winner in the Summer Games' premier event, the most significant and enduring outcome of the events in Seoul began with the Canadian parliament's October 5, 1988, Order in Council PC 1988-2361, which established the Commission of Inquiry into the Use of Drugs and Banned Practices.

Better known as the Dubin Commission, the inquiry lasted almost a year (beginning on November 15, 1988, and ending on October 3, 1989). During that time, the Honorable Charles Dubin heard sworn testimony from 119 witnesses (creating 14,817 pages of transcripts), viewed and considered 295 exhibits, and received 26 briefs from the public. In terms of the resources expended, the status of those providing testimony under oath, and the scope of the material presented, with the release of his final report on June 26, 1990, Dubin brought to a close the most thorough examination of the nature of contemporary high-performance sports ever undertaken by an independent investigator. This is the foremost reason that the inquiry is so important for understanding the current situation regarding the prohibition of steroid use in high-performance sports. At the same time, the inquiry is significant because its recommendations shaped several key legal regulations and policies in Canada regarding steroids and other performance-enhancing substances. In turn, those decisions have influenced policies and laws in other nations and jurisdictions. In addition, the inquiry concentrated a wealth of information into one highly respected report. The report of the commission became one of the leading references in all discussions of steroid use in sports after 1990.

Finally, because Dubin's investigations were conducted under the legal format of a national commission of inquiry, there is the strong perception that it represents a completely objective, dispassionate assessment of high-performance sports and the use of banned substances and practices. In actuality, the inquiry and its representation in the 1990 report are fascinating social constructions of what the IOC, NSOs, national sports administrators, politicians, and the media have portrayed as the most pressing problem in world class, high-performance sports—the use of banned substances. For this reason, the report merits some close and careful scrutiny as a key element in the claims-making process around steroids.

The social construction process began with the original Order in Council PC 1988-2361. The order's opening statement—"Whereas there is a clear public concern with respect to the use of drugs and banned practices intended to increase athletic performance"—was not as much one of fact as it was one that created a particular departure point for the inquiry (Canada, 1989, p. 3). After claiming there was a public concern, the order continued: "And whereas recent events warrant the establishment of an inquiry with the capacity to examine the issues and determine the facts with respect to the use of drugs and banned practices," implicitly justifying the enormous expenditure of resources over the simple forfeiture of an Olympic medal for disobeying an IOC regulation. The order then set out the task and mandate for the inquiry:

> Therefore, the Committee of the Privy Council, on the recommendation of its Prime Minister, advises that a Commission do issue under Part I of the Inquiries Act and under the Great Seal of Canada, appointing the Honourable Charles Leonard Dubin, the Associate Chief Justice of Ontario, to be a Commissioner to inquire into and report on the facts and circumstances surrounding the use of such drugs and banned practices by Canadian athletes, including the recent cases involving athletes who were to, or did, compete in the Olympic Games in Seoul, South Korea, and to inquire into and to make recommendations regarding the issues related to the use of such drugs and banned practices in sport. (Canada, 1989, pp. 3–4)

Although the remaining paragraphs are less dramatic in their construction, they were fundamental in the actual conduct of the inquiry, providing Dubin with the freedom to socially construct the inquiry and report in line with his own particular assessment of the use of banned substances and practices in high-performance sports. The order indicated that it was up to the commissioner to determine the appropriate methods and procedures for the inquiry; to establish, as necessary, advisory panels comprised of "sports, medical or legal experts"; and authorized consultations with "groups, bodies or individuals having responsibility for, or authority or expertise in dealing with, on a national or international basis, the use of such drugs and practices" insofar as the commissioner felt they could assist the inquiry (Canada, 1989, pp. 4–11).

What is often overlooked in reading the report of the inquiry is the fact that although it appeared to be the product of an impersonal parliamentary Order in Council, which initiated a process that was governed by government statutes and the Canadian legal system, the commissioner of the inquiry had tremendous discretion in determining exactly how the inquiry would be conducted, the testimony he would hear, and the manner in which the final report would be written. None of this is to question

Dubin's integrity; it is simply to indicate how socially constructed this apparently impersonal, statute-driven process actually was. The full importance of the social construction of the Dubin report is the central theme in the discussion that follows. However, before examining the report in detail, there are four particular points that one must recognize.

First, one of the major focal points of the Dubin inquiry was the Canadian high-performance sports system per se. It only considered other national systems of high-performance athlete development tangentially. Nevertheless, the analysis of the Canadian system did not reveal anything that dramatically set it apart from other athlete development systems around the world. No matter where one looks now or looked at that time, the national sports systems in the industrially advanced, Western, liberal democracies were and remain very similar in their most essential features. All the national high-performance athlete development systems in the advanced nations of the West involve a mix of considerable government and private sector funding to support the ongoing operations and further development of increasingly sophisticated, scientifically based systems of athlete development (see Beamish and Ritchie, 2006). The primary objective for that investment is to increase medal counts in major international competitions (Allinger & Allinger, 2004; Own the podium, 2010; UK Sport, 2007a, 2007b, 2007c, 2010; USOC "Podium 2002" Programme, 1999). This is a reality that is easily overlooked, but it is critical to understanding the context of the highly competitive world of international athletic competition that is heavily subsidized and directed by individual nation-states.

Second, Dubin grounded much of his analysis of high-performance sports within what he understood as the principles of the Olympic movement. The principles that he identified were primarily those of Coubertin, with particular reference to "the spirit of sport," the importance of "fair play," and sports' potential for building character. At the same time, Dubin's investigation of Canada's high-performance sports system in particular and high-performance sports in general identified the central tensions and contradictions that existed (and continue to exist) between the Olympic movement's founding principles and the reality of contemporary world-class sports.

Third, Dubin identified a significant divergence between the principles and pronouncements upon which the federal government of Canada had become involved in the funding, organizational support, and promotion of sports, physical activity, and healthy lifestyles and the principles and practices that informed and animated Canada's athlete development system in particular and the larger not-for-profit sports system in general. Dubin noted that although government policies and statements often emphasized fitness and health promotion through broader participation in sports, the democratization of opportunity, and the removal of barriers created by gender, race, ethnicity, regional disparity, and/or disability, government action and funding fell disproportionately to the elite levels of high-performance sports, and various resources were increasingly being tied to athletic success determined by specific indicators set by the system. Dubin did not investigate the extent to which the same processes occurred in other democracies, but the Canadian situation was and is not unique.

Finally, while it is unlikely that Dubin had any particular agenda as he opened the inquiry, by its end, he had settled on some very specific philosophical principles that provided the context and framework for his recommendations. These philosophical principles stemmed from his understanding of the main tenets of the Olympic movement and the fundamental principles of the modern welfare state. This combination constituted the most important elements in the socially constructed recommendations on steroids found in the inquiry's final report.

The Report of the Commission of Inquiry

At first glance, the *Commission of Inquiry Into the Use of Drugs and Banned Practices* seems to conform precisely to the mandate established by the Order in Council. The report is comprised of six parts: Part one is an overview of government involvement in sports; part two focuses on performance-enhancing substances; part three examines the events in Seoul and the athletes in the two sports—the Canadian sprint team and the weightlifters—most involved; part four deals with the use and control of various banned substances; part five considers various rights and ethical issues; and the final part contains the commissioner's conclusions and recommendations (Dubin, 1990). The center of the report—parts three and four—focuses on the events in Seoul and an examination of the use and control of banned substances.

Looked at more closely, the report's total length is 638 pages (581 pages if the appendices and notes are excluded). Taking the entire report into consideration, the midpoint is page 319, which occurs at the end of the discussion of the disqualifications in Seoul. Looking at the report's chapters alone (excluding the notes and references), the midpoint is between pages 290 and 291, which occurs within the section covering Johnson's positive test. In short, the report appears to center on the "clear public concern with respect to the use of drugs and banned practices intended to increase athletic performance" as mandated by the Order in Council (Canada, 1989, p. 4).

However, this appearance is deceiving. The heart of the report is located between two "bookends" that do more than introduce and summarize the report. The first and fifth parts establish the critical context for the discussion found in the middle parts of the report and set out the specific ethics and morality that are more than proposed guidelines for the future direction for Canada's high-performance sports system; parts one and five thoroughly inform the form and substance of the report as a whole, including its conclusions and recommendations.

Concerning the bookend at the front of the report, Dubin had begun the hearings with the testimony of the Assistant Deputy Minister for Fitness and Amateur Sport at the time: Lyle Makosky. Makosky provided a detailed account of the overall structure of Canada's sports system as well as the high-performance components within it. Makosky was followed by the Director General of Sport Canada, Abby Hoffman, who provided additional insight and detail, rounding out Makosky's presentation. It was not until five days before the end of the hearings that Donald Mackintosh, coauthor of *Sport and Politics in Canada: Government Involvement Since 1961*, appeared before Dubin. In the final report, Mackintosh's testimony would play a far more significant role than his position in the hearing's schedule might indicate.

While drafting his report, Dubin chose to put the discussion of the structure and nature of Canada's high-performance sports system within a particular historical and philosophical context. As a result, Dubin opened the report with a selection of statements and arguments that placed the Canadian federal government's involvement with sports within its broader mandate to govern and meet the needs of the nation as a whole. One of the report's main premises, which Dubin cited in his report, stemmed directly from Mackintosh, Tom Bedecki, and Ned Franks' (1986) key arguments in *Sport and Politics in Canada* concerning the legitimacy of government involvement in sports. "Government has a legitimate and essential role to play in sport," they wrote.

> Promoting sport and physical activity for all Canadians is one such role. Providing equality of opportunity to high-performance sport is another.

Sport also has an important role to play in any government efforts to promote unity and a unique Canadian identity. Government support of sport for these purposes is justified to the same extent as these functions are widely accepted in other areas of cultural practice. (Mackintosh, Bedecki, & Franks, 1986, p. 186)

Dubin (1990) then drew upon the latest federal government publication—the 1988 task force report *Toward 2000: Building Canada's Sport Systems*—and excerpted some specific quotations from the then Minister of State for Fitness and Amateur Sport Jean Charest's lengthy introduction. Among the points that Dubin extracted from the report and emphasized were the following: sports reflect the nature of Canada—"diverse, proud, and competitive"; the sporting activities Canadians choose to pursue and the meaning they draw from them say a good deal about who Canadians are; sports are a part of Canadian culture, they are vital to the economy, and they serve as vehicles for presenting Canada proudly to the world; the federal government invests in the sports system, Charest had emphasized, "simply for what it is—a part of human nature; a social movement made accessible and equitable through the national sport system"; sports allow individual Canadians to pursue excellence to the highest level possible and provide "opportunities for Canadians in general to observe and share in their pursuit and their celebration and to draw important meanings from their performances"; and, finally, Charest had written and Dubin cited this: "I believe the financing of sport is a worthy and important social responsibility of government" (National Sports Policy Task Force, 1988, pp. 16–7; see also Dubin, 1990, p. 4).

Throughout the inquiry, several high-profile members of the Canadian sporting community with impeccable sports, civic, and professional credentials had made similar points and observations. For example, former Olympian, sport historian, community leader, and professor in the School of Physical Education and Health at the University of Toronto, Bruce Kidd, had indicated that increasing the surveillance of athletes was not the way one would eliminate the use of banned substances. Kidd (Canada, 1989, p. 10710) testified that one needed to recreate "sport as an important international cultural practice where people are valued, regardless of their position, for outstanding performances." He suggested that "we need to recreate the moral basis of sport. You know it is almost as if the exchange-value of sport is the only value."

To document the philosophy that led to the federal government's involvement in creating a publically supported not-for-profit system in Canada—a philosophy that, in Dubin's estimation, remained the foundation for the system—Dubin (1990) cited from the pivotal 1969 *Task Force Report on Sports for Canadians*. Even though there was an overall sports- and performance-oriented emphasis to that foundational report, the authors recognized that Canadians wanted their federal government to do more than simply govern them; they wanted governments to help Canadians establish their country and then to continually recreate it in the face of every new challenge posed to subsequent generations.

The 1969 task force report led to the 1970 government white paper *A Proposed Sports Policy for Canadians*, which formally announced the establishment of Sport Canada and Recreation Canada. The federal government's Minister for Health and Welfare, John Munro (1970), announced: "Our policy is about people—the greatest number of Canadians possible—increasing their participation in sports and recreational activities, and improving the benefits they can enjoy from such participation" (p. 1). "If, along the way," he continued,

> it also serves to upgrade the caliber of Canadian participation in the world sports arena—which we are completely confident it will—then we will be able to really take pride in ourselves for having achieved something that very few other nations have been able to develop—a successful yet well balanced total national sports program. (Munro, 1970, p. 1)

Dubin (1990) cited liberally from the *Proposed Sports Policy* to emphasize its overall tenor and the specific commitments it made. The points Dubin selected also established parts of the philosophical foundation that he would develop with respect to sports and his recommendations at the end of the report.

The *Proposed Sports Policy*, Dubin (1990, p. 14) noted, specified four specific reasons for government involvement in sports. Sports helped overcome the economic dehumanization of a society that tended to overly focus on material gain; sports provided opportunities for improving mental and physical health; involvement in sports increased social interaction, thereby improving the quality of life; and, finally, life in an industrial society is improved through recreational activities in the workplace (see Munro, 1970, p. 15). According to the *Proposed Sports Policy*, Dubin indicated, sports help "restore a human soul and sense of human fraternity to what otherwise might remain just another agent of depersonalization" (Munro, 1970, p. 15).

With regard to sports, Dubin (1990, p. 14) also emphasized that Munro had identified three ways in which sports were being robbed of their potential for recreation. Drawing from Munro's white paper, Dubin noted that sports were robbed of their potential when the work ethic of industrial society was carried over into sporting activities, when there was a total devotion to elite-level competitive sports, and when there was too close an identification of sports with economic and commercial ends (see Munro, 1970, p. 16). Dubin continued to build his case by drawing further from the *Proposed Sports Policy*. Citing directly from the white paper, Dubin emphasized Munro's fundamental claim that a Canadian sports system should emphasize participation over a win-at-all costs philosophy. "Competition is healthy and victory is pleasant," Munro (1970, p. 19) had noted,

> but so is plain participation in a recreational manner or in a loose, pick-up competitive fashion. If sports is to be an alternative to destructive social forces and not a mirror, it should cease to ape excess of technology in the elaboration and regimentation of its competitive system—especially when the labyrinthian structure is exclusively devoted to the small handful of top national and international athletes.

It should also not enshrine victory as a sole worthy objective of sports participation.

Dubin also noted that the *Proposed Sports Policy* had promised a new focus for the administration of Canadian sports. The white paper had indicated that the pursuit of success in international sports was to be seen as a consequence of mass participation—not as the main goal. The value of sports, Dubin emphasized as he cited from the *Proposed Sports Policy*, was not the "glitter of gold" but the inspiration it provided for Canadians of all ages and classes to become more involved in sports. "This is the fundamental reason," Munro (1970, pp. 23–4) had emphasized,

> why we feel that the time has come for the pendulum to take a healthy swing in the opposite direction from the way it has been going on in Canada's sports scene. We firmly feel—and we strongly hope—that it will also work to the advantage of excellence. But even if its success in meeting that objective is not better than the current status quo, we—all of us—will at least have assisted in achieving something very tangible and meaningful—the

most important component in the strength of our nation—a greater opportunity for all of our people to enjoy themselves and rehabilitate their environment, in their leisure time.

Despite all the noble claims for inclusion, building a broad base of participation, and reorienting the objectives of the sports structure—which
Dubin had documented from the *Proposed Sports Policy*—the specific program proposals in the white paper, Dubin (1990, p. 16) emphasized, were
consistent with the specific recommendations of the 1969 task force
report, which was aimed at building a high-performance sports system.

Dubin continued to work his way through all the major white papers
and policy documents that had shaped Canada's sports system from
1970 up to 1989. Dubin cited from the 1979 *Partners in Pursuit of
Excellence* (Campagnolo, 1979), the 1981 *A Challenge to the Nation: Fitness
and Amateur Sport in the '80s* (Reagan, 1981) and the 1988 task force
report *Toward 2000: Building Canada's Sport Systems* (National Sports
Policy Task Force, 1988).

In structuring and writing his final report, Dubin had decided to go
well beyond the structural diagrams of the sports system that Makosky
had provided. Dubin carefully reviewed the federal government's own
documents and found policy statements and commitments that he felt
were appropriate to a government's involvement in sports as well as
those that he felt created tensions and problems. The choice of the title
for part one—"Overview of Government and Sport in Canada"—was
far more telling than many have recognized. It was not just an overview
of the government and sports in Canada; it was fundamentally concerned
with the principles of good government and good governance and how
the process of government should become engaged with sports, sports
policy, and sports governance.

Dubin indicated the extent to which the federal government had essentially removed itself from maintaining the original principles on which the
system was initiated. Thus, Dubin acknowledged, even though Makosky
was correct that, in principle, the federal government's role in high-
performance sports was restricted to financing the system, in practice,
Dubin asserted, that meant that the entire system depended on the
government and, as a result, its real role was much larger. Because the
federal government made such a substantial investment in high-
performance sports, Dubin (1990, p. 27) argued, it should have taken a
greater interest in how its funds were being dispersed. The government

had the authority to withdraw funding if the various national sports organizations were not meeting the government's primary objectives. In that sense, the government did have a regulatory authority, but it chose to let the system emphasize the pursuit of gold medals.

Drawing extensively from *Toward 2000*, Dubin (1990) documented the degree to which Sport Canada and the federal government fully supported a performance-oriented system in the 1980s. In that report, Dubin (1990, p. 52) emphasized, the orientation to sports was clear: Winning medals in major international competitions was the foremost goal and would be one of the main criteria for the allocation of future funding.

In his discussion contained in the section on sports as policy instruments, Dubin returned to the nation building and welfare state themes of the 1970 *Proposed Sports Policy*. Over the course of the hearings and writing the report, Dubin saw sports as policy instruments that could help achieve some of the particular goals one would expect under good government. Based on all he had learned, Dubin considered sports as means of improving Canadians' health and fitness, promoting and facilitating gender equality, and increasing opportunities for those with disabilities or those from low socioeconomic status backgrounds. He saw sports as means for forging and promoting a healthy national identity. "In sum," Dubin (1990) concluded his discussion of sports as policy instruments,

> the federal government, in its role as guide, motivator, mentor, and source of funds for sport, is perhaps the only entity capable of exercising sufficient moral and economic suasion to ensure equality of access by all Canadians— regardless of gender, physical disability, socio-economic or cultural background, or language—to sport, to sport facilities, and to programs it supports. (pp. 61–2)

In his summary to part one, Dubin (1990) emphasized that since the beginning of the federal government's involvement in sports in 1969, as the level of involvement and funding had increased, there had been a shift in the focus and nature of that involvement. Despite the appropriate references to the benefits of broad-based participation, Dubin noted that from the mid-1970s onward, government funding and the actions of Sport Canada had been increasingly directed toward the specific goals of winning medals in international competitions. "Notwithstanding protestations to the contrary," Dubin (1990) emphasized, "the primary objective has become the gold medal."

This changed emphasis from broad-based support of sport for the general community of ordinary Canadians to high-level competitive sport demands a re-examination of the role and mandate of government sport agencies.

In light of the evidence and disclosures made before this Commission, I think the time has come for the Government of Canada to consider whether those premises upon which government involvement in and funding of sport have been founded are still valid and whether, if they are indeed still valid, the legitimate objectives of such involvement are being pursued and achieved. (pp. 64–5)

Dubin's position was becoming clear already: Did the funding of Canada's sports system in the 1980s produce outcomes that were the *legitimate* objectives of government involvement in sports?

Sports, Ethics, and Morality

The first of the two bookends had three objectives. First, it provided an overview of government policies and actions in the establishment, development, and ongoing operations of the federally supported and sponsored Canadian sports system, including the high-performance elements within that system. Second, in reviewing that history and structure, Dubin drew out the philosophy of governance that legitimated government involvement in that sports system. Finally, having determined the basic principles behind government involvement in sports, Dubin contrasted those principles with the actual practices found within the sports system, and he discovered a number of tensions and contradictions. Thus, although the section contained considerable factual material, it was the underlying principles that Dubin drew out that constituted the most significant elements in part one of the report. A very specific tenor and set of principles were established to shape the way one would read the remaining sections of the report.

The second bookend was much more overt in its focus on issues of ethics and moral conduct. The discussion followed parts two, three, and four. Part two presented an overview of the policies and definitions related to performance-enhancing substances within the IOC and Canada, the identification of various banned substances and practices and their impact upon athletes, and the various procedures testing for those substances. Part three dealt primarily with the Canadian weightlifting team, field athletes involved in the throwing events, the individuals involved with Canada's sprint team in 1988, the disqualification at Seoul, and the involvement of several other athletes with Jamie Astaphan and Charlie Francis. Finally, part four reviewed material on the extent of banned substance use, their supply and distribution, the legal regulation of different banned substances, drug testing policies, and various initiatives to control the use of performance-enhancing substances in high-performance sports. It was against this background that Dubin developed his discussion in part five on athletes' rights and ethical considerations related to the use of performance-enhancing substances.

In the first section of part five, Dubin began with testimony from three of Canada's long-standing, prominent, highly regarded former athletes and pillars of Canada's sporting community: Bill Crothers, one of world's premier middle-distance runners when he was competing; Bruce Kidd, Crothers' former East York Track Club and University of Toronto teammate; and Andy Higgins, a former athlete who had become a track and field coach and instructor at the School of Physical Education and Health at the University of Toronto. Higgins was an important figure because he was a strong opponent to the use of steroids throughout the 1980s and was critical of what he regarded as Sport Canada's lack of attention to numerous claims that certain athletes on the Canadian national track and field team were using steroids.

Drawing from his testimony during the hearing, Dubin (1990, p. 474) noted that Crothers had always kept his track commitments in perspective. Despite his highly successful international career, track had remained an avocation—never taking precedence over his university studies. Dubin used a lengthy excerpt from Crothers' testimony to reinforce the notion that once sports become more than an avocation—once they are professionalized—then the nature of the activities is fundamentally altered. Crothers, Dubin emphasized, thought that money was the root of the problems currently manifesting themselves in world-class sports.

Crothers' point had really been somewhat different than the emphasis Dubin put on it, although his position did not contradict Dubin's interpretation. Crothers was really emphasizing the extent to which the large, complex system—driven by the specific goals and interests that constituted the high-performance sports system internationally in the late 1980s—dictated the entire ethos of sports. More specifically, as long as there were the resources to support that system, athletes would continue to use banned substances. "As long as there is sufficient money in sport

to produce the kind of rewards that the athletes can receive for their performances," Crothers (Canada, 1989, p. 11620) had testified,

> and, more importantly, that there is enough money to support all the sup-
> port personnel, the trainers, the physicians, the agents, the promoters, that
> is far more important. As long as there is sufficient money in sport to make
> it possible for them to benefit by the performances of individual athletes,
> there will always be the problem. Because they achieve their benefits, not
> by virtue of the enjoyment they get out of the sport, but they achieve their
> benefits by virtue of the success that the individual athlete receives.
>
> And as long as they can receive material, significant material benefits
> from that, there will always be some people who are looking for an edge
> and an angle.

Crothers and Dubin agreed: Once sports moved from avocation to vocation, their fundamental ethos changed. But Crothers' point was more profound: Within a complex, modernist sports system, constituted by an
elaborate division of labor in which numerous individuals, with a variety of
professionalized credentials, all working toward the enhancement of athletes'
performances, there would be continual pressure to gain an advantage—
especially as the margins of victory became slimmer and slimmer and the
level of performance reached the outer limits of human potential.

From Kidd's testimony at the inquiry, as noted in Chapter 3, Dubin
focused on the impact that the addition of one more training session per
day had on other competitors and the implications it held for high-
performance athletes just a decade later. By the 1980s, high-performance
sports had become a full-time occupation for most world-class athletes.

Dubin was using the testimony of Crothers and Kidd to establish two
points that had significant implications for his discussion about the ethical
and moral dimensions of sports. Dubin wanted to demonstrate how much
sports had changed over the period of time in which the federal
government had introduced and then supported Canada's sports system.
Second, Dubin wanted to emphasize how much that change had fundamentally altered the nature of what stood as high-performance sports.

The testimony cited from Higgins was critical in putting forth the position that Dubin had reached regarding the values of sports and the reasons
that governments should become involved in supporting sports and
broadening the opportunities for citizens to engage in sporting activities.
Dubin (1990, p. 478) drew upon Higgins' discussion of why it mattered
how far a person could project a 16-pound metal ball in the shot put.

"[W]e have machinery today that can make it go much further, so just projecting metal through the air some distance is an absolutely useless activity," Higgins (Canada, 1989, p. 12573) had testified. "What was the point?" he had asked. Higgins continued: "I think that's a discussion that has to be generated from the very beginning." It was something he believed should have been taking place throughout the Canadian sports system— from the highest levels down to the grassroots.

> We should understand why we are doing sport, and the only value, it seems to me, is what happens to the individual in the process of trying to make that piece of metal go as far as he [or she] is capable of making it go. Because once one commits to that kind of endeavour, then all kinds of possibilities begin to arise. We are going to meet all the challenges that many of these athletes [who had testified before the inquiry] spoke about, and they will come in minor ways and in major ways, and at every challenge we are faced with options.
>
> It seems to me the value of sport to the individual and to the country is to help young people to make the choice that will make them stronger when you meet the challenge, and not go the easy route, not to take what I refer to as the "fear choice."

Dubin continued the section by citing material and ideas from a number of Canadian athletes in the prime of their competitive careers. Based on material cited from their testimony and contained in the report, Dubin (1990, p. 488) concluded that each of those athletes recognized that there was more to sports than simply winning medals; they realized that if sports are to survive, more attention must be paid to the moral and ethical aspects that are critical constituents of sports.

In the final section of the bookend, Dubin addressed the ethical and moral aspects of sports. It is in this section that Dubin presented the view he had arrived at concerning the importance of sports to human life. Perhaps not surprisingly, he returned to some of the fundamental principles that Coubertin had advocated when he launched the modern Olympic Games.

People look to sports, Dubin (1990, p. 499) emphasized, to build character and instill the virtues of dedication, self-discipline, and perseverance. He noted that one may learn as much from defeat as victory. Most importantly, Dubin emphasized, people look to sports to impart moral and social values into individuals and foster the healthy integration of people into society.

Dubin (1990, p. 501) used this final section to bring together the two key issues he wanted to feature in each of the bookends and use to hold the entire report together: the principles behind government involvement in sports as well as sports as character-building undertakings. If winning a gold medal at all costs—including risking one's health and cheating—is the only goal of high-performance sports, then, he unequivocally affirmed, there was no justification for the continued financial assistance of sports through public funds.

Dubin (1990, p. 501) used Jean-Marie Brohm's *Sport: A Prison of Measured Time* to distinguish the true sports experience—as he had, by the end of the inquiry, come to understand and value it—from its commercialized form. "It is impossible to deny," René Maheu wrote in text cited by Brohm (1978, p. 8), "that the development of spectator sport has turned attention away from the moral value of sport for the individual towards its entertainment potential."

> For the mass of people, sport has become a form of entertainment of which they are mere spectators; radio and television spare them even the trouble of getting to the sportsground. The success of spectator sport and the importance it has come to assume in everyday life are unfortunately too often exploited for purposes alien or even opposed to sport—commercialism, chauvinism and politics—which corrupt and deform it. *If we want to save sports' soul, the time has come to react and react quickly.*

Dubin (1990, p. 502) returned to Coubertin to formally frame the position on sports that he wanted to advocate following the inquiry. In 1892, addressing the members of the *Union des Sports Athlétiques* assembled at the Sorbonne, Coubertin had noted that, above all else, the characteristics of nobility and chivalry, which had distinguished sports in the past, had to be preserved. It is only in this way that sports could continue to play the same educative roles that they had fulfilled so admirably in classical Greece. For Dubin (1990, p. 511), the significance and value of sports was clear, as were the forces that corrupted the sporting experience: placing too much emphasis on winning and ignoring the moral and ethical dimension of the sports experience. Sweeping ethics and morality aside in the pursuit of victory had significant implications for the athletes who made that tradeoff because, Dubin maintained, personal integrity cannot be compartmentalized into specific areas of their lives. Living in a competitive society, any athlete who cheats in sport might carry that attitude into other competitive situations in his or her everyday life.

Dubin (1990) drew his discussion to a close with the following final remarks:

> We must examine to what extent our expectations of our athletes have contributed to the current unacceptable situation in sports in Canada. We must

examine, too, whether the programs supported by the federal government have contributed to the problem, and indeed whether the funds provided by the government are being utilized in a manner consistent with the fostering of those values and ethics which are so important to us as Canadians. (p. 511)

Thus, although the Dubin commission began as an inquiry into the use of banned substances and practices and Dubin gathered a vast amount of information that ranged over the structure of Canada's high-performance sports system, the resources invested in it, the government policy documents, the use of banned substances and practices, the policies that banned their use and the various impacts they had on athletes, and detailed testimony by athletes, coaches, and sports administrators, his final report ultimately centered on key questions of governance and the nature of sports. Dubin chose to support and promote a very specific, transhistorical, essentialist notion of sports, and it was only this form of sports that he felt merited federal government support. By viewing the essence of sports in those terms, Dubin believed there was no place for performance-enhancing substances. As a result, in the preface to the report, Dubin (1990) could state quite categorically: "The use of banned performance-enhancing drugs is cheating, which is the antithesis of sport."

> The widespread use of such drugs has threatened the essential integrity of sport and is destructive of its very objectives. It also erodes the ethical and moral values of athletes who use them, endangering their mental and physical welfare while demoralizing the entire sport community.
>
> I have endeavoured to define the true values of sport and restore its integrity so that it can continue to be an important part of our culture, unifying and giving pleasure to Canadians while promoting their health and vitality. (p. xxii)

The "true values of sport," "its integrity," and sports' place in Canadian culture as a unifying, pleasurable activity became the central issues in the report of *Commission of Inquiry Into the Use of Drugs and Banned Practices*, and they informed Dubin's most important recommendations.

The Commission of Inquiry's Conclusions and Main Recommendation

During the inquiry's first public session, Dubin (Canada, 1989, p. 17) had asked: "Have we, as Canadians, lost track of what athletic competition is all about? Is there too much emphasis by the public and by the media on

the winning of a gold medal in Olympic competition as the only achievement worthy of recognition?" As he concluded his report, Dubin (1990,
p. 515) noted that the answers to those questions would determine the
future of Canadian high-performance sports.

After all the testimony and study of policies and documents, Dubin
(1990, p. 516) chose to locate his own response and recommendations
within the Olympic movement's fundamental principles as they stand in
the *Olympic Charter*: promoting and developing the physical and moral
qualities that are the basis of sports; educating young people through sports
to create better understanding and friendship and thereby help build a
more wholesome and peaceful world; spreading the principles of Olympism and creating international goodwill; and bringing the athletes of the
world together in the sports festival of the Olympic Games. Dubin then
underscored the claim that the Olympic Games "*unite Olympic competitors
of all countries in fair and equal competition*" (p. 516, Dubin's emphasis).
Unfortunately, he candidly continued, the *Olympic Charter*'s lofty sentiments and ideals no longer prevail in international high-performance
sports. The extent to which they have been lost was not widely recognized,
but the conspiracy of silence had been broken and the truth revealed—and
it was a very unpleasant truth.

Dubin's (1990, pp. 517–24) preamble to his first recommendation
sketched out some of that difficult truth—documented in detail throughout the report. He emphasized in several ways the manner and extent to
which he believed that the use of banned performance-enhancing substances undermined the integrity of sports; Dubin noted how widespread the
use of banned substances had become while also indicating the various
social pressures that encouraged or supported their use; he was extremely
critical of athletes, officials, sports-governing bodies, and Olympic officials
for not doing more to eradicate their use in sports. "We cannot allow
sport," he continued, "which we expect to build character, to become a
means of destroying it, encouraging hypocrisy and cynicism in athletes
and other young people" (Dubin, 1990, p. 523). Although some, he continued, would see his position as idealistic and out of touch with the times,
if that were indeed the case—and he did not believe it was and that most
Canadians did not hold that view—then there was no justification for
the government funding of sports. With his position made very clear,
Dubin proceeded to make 70 different recommendations.

Recommendations 13 to 15, 18, 20 to 23, and 42 to 44 were specifically
aimed at steroid use, testing, or education. Recommendations 20 to 23

were similar to the legislative actions taken in the United States regarding the classification of steroids as controlled substances, an increased range of penalties for offences involving minors, and urging government officials to recognize, when classifying steroids and other similar substances, their potential abuse by young people in sports as well as in the pursuit of particular body images. However, it was in his first recommendation that Dubin put forward the context within which the other recommendations fell.

The essence of sports, Dubin began, is fairness; in athletic competition, there must be an equal opportunity for every participant—based on his or her own natural ability—to strive for victory in accordance with sports' fundamental principles of morality and ethics. "That is what sport is all about" (Dubin, 1990, p. 525). International competition should develop and promote sports' physical and moral qualities while also bringing athletes together from around the world within a context that is conducive to building genuine friendship and better understanding. These objectives, Dubin emphasized, are the valid and legitimate basis for government funding in sports. However, Dubin continued, as the Canadian government has increased its involvement in sports, gold medals have become the overriding focus. The change in emphasis from broad-based participation among all Canadians to elite-level competitive sports needed to be carefully re-examined.

> The pursuit of excellence is worthwhile and should be encouraged. But all Canadians, not just our high-performance athletes, should have the opportunity to pursue personal excellence through sport while broadening their experience and abilities with a view to their future contribution to society. Success in national and international competition should be viewed as a consequence and not as a goal of mass participation in sport. Its main value is not the glitter of gold but the inspiration it gives for even greater popular involvement in sport from all ages and interests. (Dubin, 1990, p. 526)

Dubin hoped to take sports out of their sociohistorical contexts and all the social pressures that had shaped them in the postwar period. He wanted to start afresh with Coubertin's fundamental premises and reasons for launching the modern Olympic Games. Dubin's position as a claims-maker regarding steroids in sports came directly from Coubertin at the end of the nineteenth century.

Chapter 6

Steroids in Sports: The Social Construction of a New Moral Panic

"Hegel remarks somewhere that all great, world-historical facts and personages occur, as it were, twice," Karl Marx (n.d., p. 13) once noted. "He has forgotten to add, the first time as tragedy, the second as farce." Marx could not have anticipated that in the twenty-first century, many great world-historical issues and people would appear more than twice—often falling from the poignant precipice of epic tragedy to the humiliating depths of media-created disgrace.

Today, very little escapes the attention of the vast media complex that captures, records, plays, and replays events great and small from around the world. Those events that are deemed "newsworthy" may begin with live network television coverage—consumed around the globe with an unmistakable feel of immediacy and reality. The viewer has the sense that he or she is directly participating in the events and emotions as they swirl and unfold. Those same events are picked up and relayed from person to person as tweets, text messages, and on social network pages before they appear on nightly newscasts and then as headlines and front page stories in print media. People and events soon find themselves on numerous roundtable analyses and panel discussions before they are turned into a wide variety of conflicting partisan editorials and commentaries. The seemingly endless repetition of sound bites on radio and TV are eventually reduced to talk shows, and ultimately, as the next event takes hold, the earlier world-historical facts and personages end up in an eternal, ignominious existence on YouTube.

Throughout the journey from "live action" to yesterday's news, the lives of real men and women may be broken irrevocably. That was certainly the fate of athletes as diverse as Marion Jones, Tim Montgomery, Kelli White, and Tammy Thomas; it was partially true of Jose Canseco, Mark McGwire, and Rafael Palmeiro; and although Rob Garibaldi, Taylor Hooton, and

Efrain Marrero were spared the impact of the media coverage that followed their suicides, their stories have been heavily shaped and framed by media representations. The lives of Greg Anderson, Brian McNamee, and Kirk Radomski have also been dramatically recast through media coverage of their involvement with steroids.

In *Life: The Movie—How Entertainment Conquered Reality*, Neal Gabler (2000) argued that the media and entertainment have become the "new cosmos" within which people live and ultimately understand and interpret the major issues and events of their time. Although it is not hard to understand why this has happened, the implications of "entertainment as reality" merits some reflection—particularly with respect to steroids, their use, and what people think they known about them.

Gabler noted that in 1960, American novelist Philip Roth posed one of the most troubling questions that contemporary writers would have to face: How could fiction possibly compete with reality? "Life had become so strange, its convolutions so mind-boggling" that, Roth noted, a writer "has his hands full in trying to understand, and then describe, and then make *credible* much of American reality" (cited in Gabler, 2000, p. 3). Roth noted that a writer's creative capacities seem almost feeble as reality continually goes beyond artists' imaginations and "the culture tosses up figures almost daily that are the envy of every novelist." In his book *The Image: A Guide to Pseudo-Events*, Daniel Boorstin described how "everywhere the fabricated, the inauthentic and the theatrical were driving out the natural, the genuine and the spontaneous from life until reality itself had been converted into stagecraft" (cited in Gabler, 2000, p. 4).

Following decades of media hype, countless public relations stunts, and a steady diet of theatrics, Gabler (2000) emphasized that life "has *become* art" (p, 4). The application of drama and theater techniques to politics, religion, commerce, education, diet programs—virtually everything—has turned them into offshoots of show business, where the central objective is to capture, entertain, and satisfy an audience. Life in the contemporary world is one of constant distraction and amusement.

While an entertainment-driven, celebrity-oriented society does not necessarily destroys all moral values, Gabler (2000) argued, it does produce a culture where value is determined by what holds public attention. Serious literature, reasoned political arguments, and complex and challenging ideas are all marginalized because they do not conform to the entertainment format. Celebrities become the examples people follow because they know how to capture center stage and exploit the media. Gabler maintained that in the contemporary period, people value the skills that permit them, like actors, to perform whatever role a situation demands; people "perform" their lives rather than living them. *Homo sapiens* has been replaced by *Homo scaenicus* (man the entertainer).

The critical point is that unless an event is presented through the medium of entertainment, it fails to register with the public at large. But any event as entertainment is filtered and constructed in a particular manner—one that allows a consumer to digest it quickly, easily, and without reflection. The cosmos of entertainment determines what information reaches us and the depth of our knowledge about it. Nowhere is this truer than in the social construction of steroids. What do we really know and how do we know it are the questions one must ask.

Beginning with the events that followed Ben Johnson's positive test in Seoul, to Steve Wilstein's (1998a, 1998b) first revelations of McGwire's use of the steroid precursor androstenedione, to Canseco's, McGwire's, and Palmeiro's 2005 testimonies before the House Committee on Government Reform (hereafter CoGR), followed by the Mitchell report, Brian McNamee's statements before the House Committee on Oversight and Government Reform (hereafter CoO&GR) regarding Roger Clemens' alleged use of steroids and HGH and Clemens' responses, North Americans' understanding of steroids and their use has been constructed far more by and for "man the entertainer" than "man the knower." This chapter traces out the manner in which steroid use became "infotainment" and the impact that has had on one's ability to truly understand the real issues involved in steroid use in contemporary high-performance and professional sports.

The passage of H.R. 5269, The Comprehensive Crime Control Act of 1990, and S. 3266, A Bill to Control Crime, in October 1990, followed by the enactment of Public Law 101-647 in November of that year, did not—despite the efforts of a number of civil libertarians who were concerned with the infringements on personal freedom contained in the new law—receive much public attention. Little in the bill captured the media's interest, and it was difficult to present any aspect of the law as riveting entertainment.

The death of colorful and controversial former Los Angeles Raider defensive lineman Lyle Alzado in 1992 was a different story. The cover of the July 8, 1991, issue of *Sports Illustrated* featured a gaunt Alzado staring out grimly, with a scarf concealing his hair loss from chemotherapy treatments. The accompanying text read: "'I LIED' Former NFL star Lyle Alzado now admits to massive use of steroids and human growth hormone—and believes they caused his inoperable brain cancer" (Alzado, 1991). The article began:

> I lied. I lied to you. I lied to my family. I lied to a lot of people for a lot of years when I said I didn't use steroids. I started taking anabolic steroids in 1969, and I never stopped. Not when I retired from the NFL in 1985. Not ever. I couldn't, and then I made things worse by using human growth hormone, too. I had my mind set, and I did what I wanted to do. So many people tried to talk me out of what I was doing, and I wouldn't listen. And now I'm sick. I've got cancer—a brain lymphoma—and I'm in the fight of my life. (Alzado, 1991 p. 21)

"Everyone knows me as a tough, tough guy," he continued. "And I've never been afraid of anything. Not any human, not anything," but his cancer diagnosis, Alzado (1991) wrote, was different. "Cancer. I couldn't understand it. All I knew was that I was just so weak. I went through all those wars on the football field. I was so muscular. I was a giant. Now I'm sick. And I'm scared" (p. 21).

Alzado (1991) indicated that although there is no documented proof linking steroids and HGH to cancer, it was something to consider—and if there was a link, then a lot of athletes were in danger. Concerned only with success, athletes will use steroids to get ahead, no matter what the risk, Alzado maintained.

Within the article, Shelly Smith (1991) interviewed Robert Huizinga, a former Raiders team doctor, about the possible connection between steroids, HGH, and cancer. While there were so many factors involved in Alzado's life that could have influenced his health negatively, in response to the question "Could Lyle's cancer have been caused by what he took?" he replied: "I think there's no question. We know anabolic steroids have cancer-forming ability. We know that growth hormones have cancer-growing ability" (p. 22).

Following Alzado's death, media coverage of the steroid issue fell quiet. Because it did not meet the entertainment requirements of the media, the significance of the transfer of responsibility for steroid investigations from the FDA to the DEA never made it to the news despite the real magnitude of the outcome. The reassignment of steroids to the DEA completely eliminated the expertise of the most informed federal agent regarding steroid production, distribution, and use: Dennis Degan (Assael, 2007). Degan had waged a number of successful prosecutions—including the imprisonment of Duchaine in 1988—and accumulated massive Stasi-like paper and computer files on steroid production sites, distribution networks, and the key players in the steroid trade within the United States and internationally. By 1993, Degan's FDA supervisor informed him that his office was to be shut down, he would be reassigned, and he had to turn his files over to the newly created Office of Criminal Investigations. The DEA put Degan's massive files into storage, and virtually unused, they were ultimately destroyed.

In addition, whereas steroids mattered to the FDA agents, DEA investigators and federal prosecutors were far more interested in the limelight associated with heroin, cocaine, and other Schedule II controlled substances. Catching athletes, bodybuilders, wrestlers, and recreational gym users with a few vials of Schedule III steroids had no glamour or status; there was little incentive for time-consuming investigations and enforcement related to steroids (see Thompson et al., 2009).

The main sports media focus in 1994 was the labor negotiations between MLB owners and the Major League Baseball Players Association (MLBPA), which resulted in the 1994 strike that ultimately cancelled the World Series. In the end, the owners were able to hold firm and enforce a league-wide salary cap, which effectively regulated players' salaries. Despite their success in holding out for the salary cap, the strike was a disaster for owners, as attendance in 1995 fell well below previous levels.

It was the majestic home runs hit by some of baseball's premier hitters that rekindled fan interest (CoGR, 2005). In 1995, Albert Belle became the first player since 1990 to hit 50 home runs in a season. The next season, Brady Anderson duplicated Belle's performance, and McGwire hit 52 in only 130 games. In 1997, McGwire went head-to-head with Ken Griffey Jr. in pursuit of Roger Maris' 1961 record of 61 home runs in a single season. Both fell just short—Griffey with 56 and McGwire with 58.

In 1998, McGwire, Griffey, and Sosa began what appeared to be a new era in baseball, and their home run totals during the season suggested that any one of them—and perhaps all three—would surpass Maris' mark. When Griffey fell off the pace, Sosa and McGwire kept baseball in the forefront of the sports pages as they entered the final three games of the season tied at 65. Sosa hit one more against the Houston Astros, but McGwire smashed five off five different Montreal Expo pitchers.

In the year before Lance Armstrong began his string of seven consecutive Tour de France victories, few North Americans were aware of the drama that was taking place in Reims, France. However, those events would have a significant impact on McGwire, Sosa, Barry Bonds—who would soon eclipse McGwire, Sosa and Griffey as the premier home run hitter in MLB—as well as Roger Clemens and other baseball celebrities. The events in France would ultimately involve President George W. Bush.

"[A]nything that doesn't Adversely Affect the Health of the Athlete . . . isn't Doping"

Although steroids were not involved in the 1998 Tour de France drug seizure, that event became the catalyst for several far-reaching decisions concerning the use of performance-enhancing substances in sports. The events began with an unprecedented seizure of 24 vials of HGH and testosterone, 234 doses of erythropoietin (EPO), and 60 capsules of the blood thinner Asaflow from the Festina cycling team's van by customs officials at Reims. Two weeks later, TVM team director Cees Priem and team doctor Andrei Mikhailov were arrested for transporting poisonous substances and the possession of dangerous merchandise.

Those events took on a much higher profile when in an interview published by the Spanish daily newspaper *El Mundo*, IOC president Juan Antonio Samaranch stated that if a performance-enhancing substance could damage an athlete's health, then that was a problem, but if it simply improved performance, he did not think it was doping (Beamish and Ritchie, 2006).

Samaranch's remarks virtually forced the IOC to support a proposal it had long resisted—the creation of an independent body to oversee the testing of all Olympic and world-class athletes. Created in 1999, the World Anti-Doping Association (WADA) quickly became the most aggressive claims-maker in the war on drugs in sports. Barrie Houlihan (2004) has emphasized the power and influence that WADA would exert. Prior to the formation of WADA, the movement opposing the use of banned performance-enhancing substances was "characterized by fragmentation of effort, mutual suspicion among key actors, a general lack of momentum and a severe lack of resources." "While there was much activity," he continued, "there was little effective action" (p. 19).

WADA was the outcome of the first World Conference on Doping held in Lausanne, Switzerland, in February 1999. At that time, the conference, which involved participants from governments, intergovernmental and nongovernmental organizations, the IOC, ISFs, and NOCs, passed the "Lausanne Declaration on Doping in Sport" (1999). Clause four stated:

> An independent International Anti-Doping Agency shall be established so as to be fully operational for the XXVII Olympiad in Sidney in 2000. This

institution will have as its mandate, notably, to coordinate the various programs necessary to realize the objectives that shall be defined jointly by all the parties concerned. Among these programs, consideration should be given in particular to expanding out-of-competition testing, coordinating research, promoting preventive and educational actions and harmonizing scientific and technical standards and procedures for analyses and equipment. A working group representing the Olympic Movement, including athletes, as well as the governments and inter-governmental organizations concerned, will meet, on the initiative of the IOC, within three months, to define the structure, mission and financing of the Agency. The Olympic Movement commits to allocate a capital of US $25 million to the Agency. (Lausanne Declaration, 1999, pp. 17–8)

When it was constituted in Switzerland, WADA had an explicit mandate. Its first objective was "to promote and co-ordinate at the international level the fight against doping in sport in all its forms" (Agence mondiale antidopage, 1999, p. 1). "[T]o this end," the mandate continued:

the Foundation will cooperate with intergovernmental organizations, governments, public authorities and other public and private bodies fighting against doping in sport, inter alia the International Olympic Committee (IOC), International Sports Federations (IF), National Olympic Committees (NOC) and the athletes; it will seek and obtain from all of the above the moral and political commitment to follow its recommendations.

WADA's first order of business was the creation of a set of universally applicable regulations concerning the use and detection of banned substances. Over its first 18 months in existence, the World Anti-Doping Code team consulted with a number of relevant groups, organizations, and individuals. The list included several national antidoping organizations, several ISFs, internationally recognized experts in drug testing and detection, athlete groups, various national governments, the Council of Europe, and the International Intergovernmental Consultative Group on Anti-Doping in Sport.

By April 2002, a draft code had been completed and was then vetted by many of the same individuals, groups, and organizations consulted originally. On the basis of their feedback, a second draft was prepared by October, followed by further consultations. The third draft was completed in February 2003 and presented at the second World Conference on Doping in Sport held in Copenhagen, May 3–5, 2003. The conference was attended by members of the IOC, representatives from 80 governments,

60 NOCs, 70 ISFs, 30 national antidoping organizations, and some athletes. At the end of the conference, the delegates agreed to the "Copenhagen Declaration on Anti-Doping in Sport" (Copenhagen Declaration, 2003). The declaration positioned WADA as the primary international actor in the antidoping movement and established the WADA Code as the basis for establishing the list of banned performance-enhancing substances and the procedures by which they would be controlled. The purpose of the declaration was "to articulate a political and moral understanding among Participants" to four key points:

1.1 Recognise the role of, and support, the World-Anti-Doping Agency (WADA);

1.2 Support the World Anti-Doping Code (the "Code") adopted by the WADA Foundation Board at the World Conference on Doping in Sport (Copenhagen, 3–5 March 2003);

1.3 Sustain international intergovernmental cooperation in advancing harmonisation in anti-doping policies and practices in sport; and

1.4 Support a timely process leading to a convention or other obligation on points 3–8 below, to be implemented through instruments appropriate to the constitutional and administrative contexts of each government on or before the first day of the Turin Winter Olympic Games. This process should draw upon the expertise of representatives of governments from all the regions of the world and international organisations. (Copenhagen Declaration, 2003, p. 3)

Because WADA was constituted as a private organization, it could not force any jurisdiction to formally comply with its code. As a result, WADA sought to bind governments—as much as possible—to the Copenhagen Declaration through a UNESCO Convention.

At the Third International Conference of Ministers and Senior Officials Responsible for Physical Education and Sport held in Uruguay in December 1999, ministers had "expressed concern over unethical behaviour, in particular doping in sport," and urged the international community to take action (UNESCO, 2010). While finalizing its code, WADA also worked with UNESCO to gain its support and involvement. In January 2003, during the 32nd session of the UNESCO General Conference, UNESCO (2010) agreed "to tackle the question of doping in sport through an international convention." The convention provided the legal framework that would permit governments to act on undertakings that are outside the domain of various sports organizations. The convention was drafted, revised, and finally adopted in October 2005, at which time it was ratified by almost 100 countries (see UNESCO, 2005a, 2005b).

With the Copenhagen Declaration approved and work under way on the UNESCO Convention, WADA chairman Richard Pound openly expressed his outrage over Washington's disingenuous stance about performance-enhancing drug use. Pound alleged that the U.S. Track and Field Association (USTFA) had covered up positive tests, and he condemned MLB and the NFL for trivializing drug use in sports (Assael, 2007). To some, it seemed like odd timing because many Americans were consumed with the March 20 invasion of Iraq. At the same time, Americans reading the sports pages had almost daily reports on news that linked the previously unknown Bay Area Laboratory Co-Operative (BALCO) with drug scandals involving the world's fastest man and fastest woman: Montgomery and Jones. The BALCO news soon appeared to also link Bonds, whose 73 home runs in 2001 had easily eclipsed McGwire's single-season record, to BALCO and steroids.

BALCO, the World's Fastest Man Project, and Bonds

Long before 2003, Victor Conte had laid the groundwork for what would ultimately become one of the defining investigations into steroid use by high-performance and professional athletes. In polite terms, Conte was a salesman, although he would be more accurately labeled a huckster. Conte was an expert at manipulating perceptions and exploiting people's inner dreams for his own particular ends. Conte began his career as a "sports nutritionist" when he and his wife established the Millbrae Holistic Health Center in 1983. Within a year, Conte closed the center and opened BALCO (see Fainaru-Wada & Williams, 2006).

Conte's first scheme developed with the purchase of a device called the "inductively coupled plasma" (ICP) spectrometer. The spectrometer's legitimate commercial use was the analysis of welds on castings, examining jet engines for defects, and assessing the chemical composition of soil samples. Conte's Balcolab.com website indicated that the ICP spectrometer would provide a "high tech nutritional assessment for Olympic athletes, weekend warriors and even business executives" (cited in Novitzky, 2003, p. 6). The website information claimed that the spectrometer could identify toxic metals in a person's system as well as mineral deficiencies and then determine the supplements that would overcome the deficiencies and increase athletic performance.

Conte's enterprise was small until 1988, when he was able to include American shot-putters Greg Tafralis and Jim Doehring among his 25 "BALCO Olympians" (Fainaru-Wada & Williams, 2006). Based on their testimonials, Conte initiated the Scientific Nutrition for Advanced Conditioning—or SNAC—System Inc., which involved a variety of different supplements that, Conte claimed, provided athletes with the ideal nutritional foundation to their workouts. SNAC is still active, listing a variety of products that allegedly enhance physiological response, speed recovery from workouts, promote REM sleep, overcome nutritional deficits, fight fatigue and build energy, provide essential minerals, and suppress appetite to lose weight quickly and effectively (see Novitzky, 2003, p. 5; SNAC Products, 2010).

Despite Conte's financial setbacks, divorce, and fraud allegations in the 1990s, his connection with NFL linebacker Bill Romanowski created an opportunity to aggressively market his newly developed zinc-magnesium supplement ZMA to NFL players to gain celebrity endorsements for the product (Fainaru-Wada & Williams, 2006). Shortly thereafter, Conte became involved with bodybuilder Milos Sarcev—a two-time Mr. Yugoslavia and 1989 Mr. Universe—who helped him promote ZMA.

In the June 2003 issue of *Muscle & Fitness*, Jim Schmaltz (2003) ran a story on Bonds that claimed that Bonds' tremendous success as a hitter began in 2000 when he became involved with trainer Greg Anderson and began to use Conte's line of BALCO supplements. Schmaltz quoted Bonds' claim that he went to BALCO every six months to have his mineral levels checked. The article included a detailed listing of Bonds' nutritional regimen that was allegedly based on the measurements taken by BALCO. The regimen included a long list of BALCO supplements, including ZMA. Conte featured—and continues to feature—the article on his website (Bonds, 2010). But ZMA, Mark Fainaru-Wada and Lance Williams (2006) have indicated, was simply the front for Conte's growing involvement with the steroid underground.

With an eye for publicity and an apparent need for attention, Conte began a project that succeed in "producing" the world's fastest man. That project also became one of the key dominos that, when it fell, would ultimately put baseball under the microscope—McGwire and baseball commissioner Bud Selig before the CoGR and Selig, Mitchell, McNamee, and Clemens before the CoO&GR. Most importantly, the events that began in 2000 with Project World Record and their coverage by the media would construct the dominant perception and understanding of steroids and steroid use in sports among North Americans. Like a classical Greek tragedy, the dominos began to fall when the participants in Conte's scheme, who were sworn to secrecy, had a petulant falling out (Fainaru-Wada & Williams, 2006).

Six months after the close of the 2000 Sydney Games, Conte brought disgraced Canadian sprint coach Francis, bodybuilder Sarcev, and sprinter Montgomery and his coach Trevor Graham together in California. With Francis' nuanced knowledge of sprint training and technique, Sarcev's bodybuilding and steroid background, Graham's protégé, and various cocktails of performance-enhancing substances supplied by Conte, including Patrick Arnold's newly manufactured and undetectable tetrahydrogestrinone (THG)—a drug that was not classified by the Justice Department as a steroid until January 2005 (Littman, 2009a)—Montgomery had moved, within a year, from barely ranking among American sprinters to number two in the world with the third-fastest 100-meter time ever.

Although Montgomery's training and performances continued to go as planned, he began to drift away from Conte. Part of the reason was the romantic relationship he had developed with Jones, another beneficiary of BALCO's performance-enhancement programs, but it also concerned money and Conte's constant need for public recognition (Fainaru-Wada & Williams, 2006). By the end of 2001, Conte had abandoned Montgomery and started over with British sprinter Dwain Chambers.

In a scenario fit for Hollywood, Chambers and Montgomery met in a showdown at the Grand Prix Finals in Paris on September 14, 2002. The BALCO-backed Chambers clocked the fastest time in his career—9.87 seconds—but Montgomery blew him away with a 9.78 (the first time Ben Johnson's 1988 time of 9.79 was bettered).

However, it was during the postrace celebrations that the first domino fell. Rather than praising Graham for his success, Montgomery credited Francis with his accomplishments. The Montgomery/Graham rift took place alongside a larger one between Conte and Graham—and each of them planned something dramatic.

On June 5, Conte drafted a letter to the IAAF and the U.S. Anti-Doping Association (USADA), claiming that Graham was giving his athletes "oral testosterone undeconate from Mexico" (Fainaru-Wada & Williams, 2006, pp. 140–1). Conte never sent the letter.

On that same day, via overnight FedEx, Graham sent the USADA a syringe containing a "mystery steroid" that, he claimed, high-ranking American athletes were using (Fainaru-Wada & Williams, 2006, pp. 141, 167–9).

Novitzky, BALCO, and Baseball

Jeff Novitzky is a former track athlete on scholarship at the University of Arizona who, at six feet seven inches in height, became a moderately successful scholarship basketball player at San Jose State University. Upon graduation in 1992, Novitzky joined the Internal Revenue Service's Criminal Investigations division (Littman, 2004; Fainaru-Wada & Williams, 2006). Although the full story behind Novitzky's steroid investigation is not known—accounts vary in their detail—it appears that his primary focus was Bonds and not BALCO. Furthermore, it was only Bonds' connection to his high school friend and personal trainer Anderson and the latter's association with BALCO that led Novitzky to Conte's operation (Assael, 2007, pp. 220–1; Fainaru-Wada & Williams, 2006, pp. 165–7; Littman, 2004).

While Novitzky's motivation is not of major consequence, in September 2002, he began sifting through BALCO's garbage for any information on Anderson or Bonds. However, what Novitzky found—along with syringes, empty boxes of HGH and testosterone, and underground steroid publications—were "various small envelopes and letters from an elite track and field athlete, who is currently the Unites States champion in his event," and two "personal notes from an elite track and field athlete and world record holder" (Novitzky, 2003, pp. 9–10). The information changed everything—instantly.

Normally, there is little incentive or reward for arresting the distributors of Schedule III substances, but with high-profile athletes involved, there was considerable prestige and intrinsic reward for building a case that would lead to arrest and conviction. As Novitzky proceeded to gather more information, the search for guilty offenders became the reverse of typical drug investigations. Normally, users are pressured to identify the street suppliers and general distributors higher up the chain of command; in this case, the distributors and suppliers would be pressured to give up the names of the direct users.

On September 3, 2003, Novitzky filed an affidavit with Howard R. Lloyd, a U.S. magistrate judge with the Northern District of California, to search five locations "under the authority and control of Victor Conte" (Novitzky, 2003, p. 1). The request was based on facts establishing probable cause concerning allegations that Conte and others were involved in a scheme distributing performance-enhancing substances, including anabolic steroids, to professional athletes across the nation. Novitzky presented the facts in support of probable cause, indicating that the case had begun in August 2002, that there was reason to believe Conte was selling steroids—a controlled substance—as well as masking agents, such as epitestosterone, to perpetrate fraud on sports governing agencies, and "laundering the proceeds of his illegal activities" (Novitzky, 2003, p. 3).

Granted the warrant to search Conte's premises, Novitzky and other federal agents raided BALCO that same day (see Novitzky, 2003; see also Thompson et al., 2009, pp. 63–5). Conte was there as agents entered through the unlocked front door; faced with the reality of armed federal agents and a search warrant, Conte agreed to cooperate. Within a few hours, according to Fainaru-Wada and Williams (2006), Conte had implicated 15 track and field athletes, including Jones, seven NFL and four MLB players as well as Bonds. The agents seized Conte's ledger listing athletes, their drug regimens, and blood and urine test results. Anderson, who was secured on a separate warrant, admitted to supplying BALCO substances to "the little guys" on his list of MLB clients but denied supplying steroids to Bonds (Fainaru-Wada & Williams, 2006).

By the end of September, a federal grand jury was convened to investigate BALCO. Three dozen MLB and NFL players, Olympic track and field athletes, swimmers, cyclists, boxers, and bodybuilders were subpoenaed to give sealed testimony. With few exceptions, they admitted to steroid use (Fainaru-Wada & Williams, 2006). However, at his December 4 appearance, Bonds never admitted to knowingly taking steroids (see Fainaru-Wada & Williams, 2006, pp. 199–206).

The sealed grand jury testimony provided critical leverage for Novitzky and other federal agents. First, although the list of athletes testifying was supposed to be secret, media personnel swarmed the Phillip A. Burton Federal Building, where the proceedings were taking place. The sports pages across the nation reported the names of athletes subpoenaed to appear. More importantly, even though the list of names published was incomplete, word spread through the athlete underground as to who had been called before the grand jury.

The second point of leverage concerned Section 1001 of Title 18 of the *United States Code* (2006), which makes it a criminal offense—punishable by fine and imprisonment up to five years—for anyone who, in interacting with a federal agent, "knowingly and willfully falsifies, conceals, or covers up by any trick, scheme, or device a material fact; makes any materially false, fictitious, or fraudulent statement or representation; or makes or uses any false writing or document knowing the same to contain any materially false, fictitious, or fraudulent statement or entry to a federal agent." Due to the seals on the grand jury testimony, none of the people

Novitzky subsequently investigated knew exactly what information he already had. As a result, any misrepresentation that he could substantiate with information gathered prior to the statement could mean a federal prison sentence. That was a decisive lever in all the ensuing investigations.

From the State of the Union Address to Naming Names

On January 21, 2004, President Bush spent the bulk of his State of the Union address focusing on the war on terrorism, reforms in education and Medicare, a defense of the Patriot Act, ongoing U.S. military involvement in Afghanistan, and the war in Iraq. Toward the end of the speech, Bush (Associated Press, 2004) reminded Americans that the "fundamental institutions, such as families, and schools, and religious congregations" were "the unseen pillars of civilization" and they "must remain strong in America, and we will defend them." Families helped "children make right choices," and with that opening, he addressed the war on drugs:

> One of the worst decisions our children can make is to gamble their lives and futures on drugs. Our government is helping parents confront this problem, with aggressive education, treatment and law enforcement. Drug use in high school has declined by 11 percent over the past two years. Four hundred thousand fewer young people are using illegal drugs than in the year 2001. In my budget, I have proposed new funding to continue our aggressive, community-based strategy to reduce demand for illegal drugs. Drug testing in our schools has proven to be an effective part of this effort. So tonight I propose an additional $23 million for schools that want to use drug testing as a tool to save children's lives. The aim here is not to punish children, but to send them this message: We love you, and we don't want to lose you.

With his next comments, Bush brought the claims-making process regarding steroids to the highest office in the nation. The single-most powerful individual in the world paved the way to a series of investigations, hearings, and depositions that would powerfully shape public perceptions about steroid use in sports and involve an investigative process that fully embroiled the U.S. Congress in the steroid issue:

> To help children make right choices, they need good examples. Athletics play such an important role in our society, but, unfortunately, some in professional sports are not setting much of an example. The use of

performance-enhancing drugs like steroids in baseball, football and other sports is dangerous, and it sends the wrong message—that there are short cuts to accomplishment, and that performance is more important than character. So tonight I call on team owners, union representatives, coaches and players to take the lead, to send the right signal, to get tough and to get rid of steroids now. (Associated Press, 2004)

The *San Francisco Chronicle* had already been publishing some significant investigative pieces on the grand jury hearings involving athletes and BALCO. Following the State of the Union address, the *Chronicle* continued its coverage of Anderson, Conte, BALCO, and alleged links to Bonds and the mystery steroid THG. As the ongoing war in Iraq became the central focus of more and more Americans' attention and the coverage on steroids faded, Novitzky continued to work behind the scenes to gather more evidence and build his case against BALCO, Bonds, and other MLB players suspected of steroid use.

With the same raw, explosive power that Jose Canseco exhibited in many of his 462 career home runs, *Juiced* drove the entertainment value of steroids in baseball into the upper deck. Michael O'Keeffe (2005), under the headline "Canseco Confessions: Tell-All Outs Steroid Users," leaked news of the book early, so HarperCollins had to rush the book's publication, releasing it on February 6 (O'Keeffe and Quinn, 2005). Canseco's (2005) exposé was more than just a pumped-up tale of *Wild Times, Rampant 'Roids, Smash Hits, and How Baseball Got Big* (the book's subtitle); it was the right book appearing at the right time to capitalize on the growing public interest in steroids in professional sports. More importantly, the book stimulated that interest even further. At any other time, *Juiced* would have been little more than a self-indulgent rant where Canseco took cheap shots at Cal Ripken Jr., Alex Rodriguez, McGwire, and others whom he disliked.

As an insider naming names, Canseco caused a furor. MLB instantly denied any knowledge of steroid use in baseball, but the strategy backfired. Biden in the Senate and Henry Waxman of the CoGR wasted no time in becoming involved.

Although Waxman may not have known very much about steroids and the law, as he revealed in an interview with Chris Bell (2008; 2008b)—the producer of *Bigger, Stronger, Faster*—Waxman is a tenacious investigator with 33 years of experience as the representative for California's 30th Congressional District. Waxman is also a long-standing opponent of steroids, and he had a reputation for taking on big issues. For example,

Waxman had overseen the 1994 hearing where tobacco executives claimed, under oath, that nicotine was not addictive (Thompson et al., 2009). In addition to his interest in addressing the steroid issue with zeal, Waxman must have also recognized that it provided a very high-profile opportunity to demonstrate his importance and effectiveness as a legislator to the voters in California.

Waxman successfully lobbied Republican Tom Davis, the chairman of the CoGR, to investigate steroids in baseball through the committee. As one watched the proceedings and read through the transcripts, the hearings were clearly becoming much more than an investigation. The hearings on steroids in baseball became political theater in which members of the CoGR took full advantage of the opportunity to posture and speak directly, at no cost, to voters in their constituencies through a nationally televised broadcast about an "apple pie issue"—cleaning up baseball. To underscore the public and media interest in the hearings, unlike Biden's 1989 Senate Judiciary Committee investigations into steroid use in sports, which garnered almost no media attention, the publicity surrounding *Juiced*, the names of McGwire, Jason Giambi, Rodriguez, and Palmeiro, and the media coverage of MLB's and players' denials meant the session drew "more media requests than President Clinton's impeachment hearings" (Thompson et al., 2009, p. 89).

Despite the entertainment value of the proceedings and the theatrics different members of the committee employed when they were in the spotlight asking questions, the CoGR hearings were a serious undertaking. Critical to the hearings were the committee's power to issue subpoenas and to hear sworn testimony. No witness could refuse to appear before the committee, and any deviation from the truth could have serious consequences.

The Committee on Government Reform Hearings on Steroids in MLB

On March 17, 2005, the CoGR convened televised hearings with a carefully scripted agenda. Hall of Fame pitcher and Kentucky senator Jim Bunning led off in the first panel. Bunning, with his long-standing reputation as a conservative Republican, represented baseball as it was and should be. Bunning was the embodiment of the "old school" values that had made the game great.

Two sets of parents and four medical doctors, including the medical advisor to MLB, were in panel two. The families would establish the deeply emotional costs of steroid use by youth in the United States, and the doctors would present some of the lurid factual details about steroids and MLB's negligence.

Panel three was the centerpiece of the session, with Canseco, McGwire, Palmeiro, and Sosa selected to represent the "dirty" ballplayers (CoGR, 2005, pp. 208–28). Curt Schilling and Frank Thomas (CoGR, 2005, pp. 229–37) expressed the interests of all those who were clean.

Panel four included Selig and MLBPA executive director Don Fehr. They would receive the sharpest questions and comments as the committee flexed its muscle for the voters at home. Their situation was made even more uncomfortable when committee members learned of a hastily revised proposal for drug testing in baseball—one that fell far short of the committee's expectations (see Democratic Staff, 2005).

Bunning set the tone for the committee and put forward the key theme of the entire proceedings: integrity. "As a member of the Hall of Fame, as someone who helped found the Players Association, and as a lifelong fan," Bunning (CoGR, 2005) began, "protecting the integrity of our national pastime is a matter that is near and dear to my heart" (p. 55). To emphasize the point, Bunning re-emphasized the theme: The committee must protect "the integrity of the greatest game ever invented."

Denise Garibaldi's (CoGR, 2005) stark claim that "[t]here is no doubt in our minds that steroids killed our son" (p. 115) and Don Hooton's (CoGR, 2005) summary statement—"On behalf of Taylor Hooton, Rob Garibaldi, Efrain Marrero and other kids around the country who have lost their lives to steroids, let me implore you to clean this mess up" (p. 120)—provided the riveting sound bites the committee wanted to frame the next two panels. Committee members would frequently recall those impassioned words in subsequent televised hearings.

Canseco's hulking physical presence—a pariah shunned by his former MLB brothers—said as much as, if not more than, his prepared statement. Because Conseco was denied immunity for any testimony that might be used against him in any subsequent hearing over parole violations, the testimony he gave added little to the proceedings other than setting the stage for McGwire.

McGwire became the central figure in the hearings. His opening dismissal of Canseco's book and its allegations was expected. However, when McGwire indicated to committee members that, following his lawyers' advice, he would not "answer questions about who took steroids in front of television cameras" because it would jeopardize his friends, family, and himself, rather than avoiding scrutiny, McGwire turned himself into the media's focal point. McGwire's (CoGR, 2005) evasive "I'm not here to talk about the past" under questioning left a lasting negative impression on viewers (p. 242). McGwire's testimony ensured that the hearings were widely covered in the print and electronic media, spurring detailed analyses and discussions across the United States.

Palmeiro, in contrast, was as believable as he was adamant (and possibly deceitful). "Let me start by telling you this," he began as he wagged his finger at the chairman and television cameras: "*I have never used steroids. Period. I don't know how to say it any more clearly than that. Never*" (CoGR, 2005, p. 227, underlining in original). But Palmeiro was, at least at the moment, a bit player clearly overshadowed by Canseco and McGwire.

Selig and Fehr were questioned aggressively by members of the committee. Selig wisely exploited the questioning to unilaterally launch MLB's own investigation into steroid use in baseball. The decision was brilliant because it showed that the commissioner took the issue of steroid use seriously but allowed him to control who would investigate the issue further and the conditions under which the investigation would be conducted. What he could not foresee were some behind-the-scenes activities that would make the resulting report far more explosive than Selig might have anticipated. In the end, through some of its more sensational discoveries and the sense that it left more questions unanswered than it resolved, the report heightened the steroid drama rather than dissipating it.

The investigation that would lead to the "Report to the Commissioner of Baseball of an Independent Investigation Into the Illegal Use of Steroids and Other Performance Enhancing Substances by Players in Major League Baseball" was launched on March 30, 2006. Despite the impressive title, Kirk Radomski (2009) was not impressed: "Baseball," he stated flatly, "had set up Senator George Mitchell to fail" (p. 173).

While chastened by the CoGR, Selig was far from defeated. Taking the initiative and launching an inquiry into steroid use in baseball, Selig appointed former Senate majority leader George Mitchell to lead the investigation. Selig (2006) lauded Mitchell's extensive investigative experience as an attorney and judge, his work as the head of the inquiry into the Salt Lake City Olympic Games scandal, service as the chair of a fact-finding investigation into violence in the Middle East, and his conduct as Senate majority leader. Mitchell had, to echo the CoGR's dominant theme, an impeccable reputation for integrity (see also Mitchell, 2007, pp. A1–A2).

Despite his credentials, Mitchell's investigative power was limited. The inquiry was not a government investigation, so Mitchell had no power to subpoena potential witnesses, and they were not sworn in for testimony. Furthermore, MLB and the MLBPA were far from cooperative, although Mitchell would emphasize the MLBPA's obstruction rather than MLB.

Mitchell (2007) reported that he had pored over 115,000 pages of documents from the commissioner's office and 30 MLB clubs and 20,000 electronic documents and had conducted more than 700 interviews with witnesses, more than 550 of whom were current or former MLB officials, managers, coaches, team physicians, trainers, or resident security agents. He noted that the task force attempted to interview almost 500 former players, but only 68 agreed to interviews. The MLBPA, Mitchell (2007) noted, "was largely uncooperative," rejecting all requests for relevant documents, permitting only one interview with Fehr, and sending a memorandum to players "that effectively discouraged players from cooperating" (p. SR7; see also Mitchell, 2007, pp. B7–B10).

Radomski's observation about the Mitchell report came from a unique insider position. Radomski was a trainer for the New York Mets when, at 6:00 a.m. on December 15, 2005, Novitzky and a team of federal agents, tipped off by an FBI informant, arrived with a warrant to search Radomski's premises (Radomski, 2009). Although he knew nothing about Section 1001 of Title 18 of the U.S. Code, the search warrant was apparently enough to convince Radomski to cooperate even as Novitzky disarmingly said: "We're not here to arrest you. We just need to talk to you" (Radomski, 2009, p. 7). When asked on his doorstep if he had any steroids or HGH in the house, Radomski could have been trapped; instead, he said yes, swung the door open, and let the investigators enter his home.

That day, federal prosecutor Matt Parrella told Radomski that he faced charges of possession, distribution, and money laundering—the last alone could result in 25 years in a federal penitentiary. Radomski's lawyer, John Reilly, told him it would cost at least a couple of million dollars to fight the charges (Radomski, 2009). Lacking adequate financial resources, Radomski agreed to plead guilty and cooperate with investigators in exchange for little more than hope.

Under U.S. federal law, agents can only promise to support a recommendation for leniency to a federal court judge; they cannot promise a reduced sentence. That circumstance creates a significant hidden incentive to be as cooperative as possible so one receives as much support as possible in the official's recommendation for leniency (see Radomski, 2009, p. 165). The conditions of Radomski's plea bargain were particularly intriguing because in addition to cooperating with federal investigators,

Novitzky also stipulated that Radomski had to cooperate with the Mitchell investigation (see Mitchell, 2007, pp. 138–9, SR19–SR20; Radomski, 2009, pp. 174–5). The same condition would apply to McNamee—whom Radomski had identified to Novitzky (see Mitchell, 2007, pp. 167–8, SR20–SR21; Thompson et al., 2009, pp. 137–9, 142–3).

While one can only speculate about the motivation behind those conditions, the outcome is clear: Without those unusual plea agreements, the Mitchell report would have had little substance. The report would have been the whitewash that many had anticipated and, one imagines, would have met Selig's objectives. Consider the following: Of the 89 players Mitchell identified, only six came from sources other than Radomski and McNamee (Mitchell, 2007, p. SR20); a major section of the report relies on IRS affidavits and memoranda related to the BALCO raid (Mitchell, 2007, pp. 112–7). The other major source of information in the Mitchell report was Fainaru-Wada and Williams' articles in the *San Francisco Chronicle*, which drew upon illegally leaked testimony from the grand jury hearings—a much less solid source than the Novitzky-related information (see Mitchell, 2007, pp. 117–20).

In his final report, Mitchell indicated that although the investigation was prompted by revelations of player involvement with BALCO, it uncovered evidence substantiating that steroid use was not a problem isolated to a few players or a few teams (see Mitchell, 2007, pp. SR1, SR5, SR17; see also 1–2, 112–37; CoO&GR, 2008a, pp. 20–8). Mitchell placed the burden of the blame for what he perceived as an inadequate testing program on the shoulders of the MLBPA—a point he reiterated for emphasis in his appearance before the CoO&GR following the completion of his report (see Mitchell, 2007, pp. SR11–SR14, 24–59; 2008, p. 4; see also CoO&GR, 2008a, pp. 27, 30–1, 32–6, 62, 68–70, 85).

One of the key concerns Mitchell (2007) expressed about steroid use in MLB was the example it set for young Americans—although he did not draw the causal relationship Bush and others had before him (pp. SR8–SR9, 4, 15–7). A second concern was the issue of fairness among MLB players—"the illegal use in baseball of steroids and other performance enhancing substances victimizes the majority of players who do not use those substances," although the first sentence in Mitchell's report suggested that few players were victimized in that manner (Mitchell, 2007, p. SR9). "For more than a decade," the opening "summary and recommendations" section of the report began, "there has been the widespread use of anabolic steroids and other performance enhancing substances by players in Major League Baseball" (Mitchell, 2007, p. SR1; see also 14–5, SR35, 310).

With those concerns expressed, Mitchell (2007, pp. SR14–SR17, 60–111) outlined what he identified as "The Steroids Era"—a discussion almost fully indebted to Radomski's materials and meetings, in the company of federal agents, with Mitchell (see also Mitchell, 2007, pp. SR17–SR21, 138–67; Radomski, 2009). The material Novitzky seized from Radomski's home and Mitchell used in his report included names, signed checks or money orders from players, mailing and shipping receipts to and from players, and an address book with players' names and/or telephone numbers. (Mitchell also had access to Radomski's telephone records.) Mitchell (2007) noted that Radomski's testimony and evidence had helped identify dozens of current or former players who had possessed or used performance-enhancing substances (pp. SR18–SR19). On the basis of the Radomski material, Mitchell (2007) discussed in some detail 50 players ranging in stature from such high-profile all-stars and MVPs as Lenny Dykstra, David Justice, Mo Vaughn, Miguel Tejada, and Eric Gagné, to such journeymen as Larry Bigbie, Jack Cust, Gregg Zaun, and Ryan Franklin, to such career minor leaguers as Phil Hiatt, Cody McKay, Stephen Randolph, Adam Riggs, and Bart Miadich (pp. 149–229; see also pp. D1–D32).

Mitchell (2007) also identified McNamee as an inside source who had indicated that he was a direct participant in the alleged illegal use of steroids by Clemens, Andy Pettitte, and Chuck Knoblauch while he was working as a personal trainer (pp. SR20, 147–8; see also pp. 167–77).

In his conclusions, Mitchell (2007) noted that there had been considerable speculation about the report, much of it focused on players names—who was involved and how many. After careful consideration, Mitchell decided to include names in the report, although he hoped that the media would look beyond the names and focus on the report's central conclusions and recommendations.

It was, of course, names that fans and voyeurs wanted, so journalists provided them with the entire list the same day Mitchell issued the report (see Associated Press, 2007). Of the 89 identified players, one stood out from the rest: Roger Clemens.

Naming Names: The Mitchell Report and Roger Clemens

Under the long, ominous shadow of McCarthyism and the tactics of the House Committee on Un-American Activities (HUAC) during the 1940s that ignored First and Fifth Amendment rights and the rule of law, "naming names" has become fraught with difficulty in the United States (for example, see Bentley, 1971; Navasky, 1980; Schrecker, 2002).

No matter how one judges the questions and commentary of Republican Representative Dan Burton during the committee's televised hearings on February 13, 2008, he was absolutely correct to note that the principle that a person is innocent until proven guilty is seriously undermined in any trial by media (CoO&GR, 2008b, p. 103). Furthermore, whether one believes Clemens' denials about steroid or HGH use, the Mitchell report and the CoO&GR hearings left Clemens, like the "unfriendly witnesses" who faced HUAC interrogation 60 years ago, in a position where his name may never be restored. "I have been accused of something I'm not guilty of," Clemens contended under oath before the committee—"How do you prove the negative" (CoO&GR, 2008b, p. 21)?

Like the HUAC hearings at mid-century, there is far more involved in the investigations into steroid use in MLB than the statements, questions, and answers that one may read in the transcripts of the House Committee's 2008 hearings or find in the Mitchell report. The Mitchell report and Clemens' challenge are only the visible elements in a complex process where particular individuals wanted "justice" no matter how it was achieved. Ultimately, the standards of American jurisprudence were bypassed because a victory in the court of public opinion seemed preferable and ironically appropriate.

The release of the Mitchell report resulted in two outcomes. First, the members of the CoO&GR (2008a) reconvened to question Mitchell about the report and then address questions and concerns to Selig and Fehr. The new committee chair, Henry Waxman (CoO&GR, 2008a), began the CoO&GR hearing on January 15, 2008, by informally setting a rather wide-open agenda—one that included aspects of steroid use that he felt the media had overlooked and Mitchell had underplayed. He set the main context of his agenda with a calculated opening statement:

> When our committee held its first hearing 3 years ago on Major League Baseball's steroid scandal, I talked about how the culture of Major League clubhouses trickled down to become the culture of the high school gym.
>
> Later that same day, Dan Hooten and Denise and Raymond Garibaldi proved that connection with their powerful testimony about the deadly impact that steroids had on their sons. (p. 3)

To address the growing scandal in MLB, Waxman argued, one had to begin with the facts, and the Mitchell report had taken a "hard look at baseball's steroid era" (CoO&GR, 2008a, p. 4). Although the report did not cover everything, what it did discover was damning.

Waxman argued that the report demonstrated that everyone in baseball was responsible for the use of performance-enhancing drugs. "Despite that shared responsibility," he (CoO&GR, 2008a) continued, "most of the media attention over the past month has focused on the players. They are the face of the game, and they are the ones our kids emulate" (pp. 4–5). But, Waxman (CoO&GR, 2008a) emphasized, the steroid scandal was about more than the players, and not enough attention had been paid to those who run baseball. After citing two specific examples, Waxman (CoO&GR, 2008a) noted: "It is a dismal record and it needs to be put front and center; not hidden" (p. 8).

Following a review of some of the changes to drug testing that MLB had instituted since the report's release, Waxman returned to his opening theme: Steroid use in MLB filters down to the youth of the United States. Entering a statement from Efrain Marrero's parents into the committee record, Waxman (CoO&GR, 2008a) concluded by reading from their statement: "[S]imple, honest accountability is all we're asking for. . . . [N]o family should have to endure the anguish we've suffered, but tens of thousands of youngsters are at risk. For them we ask you to dig deep, find the unvarnished truth and report if fairly." Waxman concluded, "To Mr. and Mrs. Marrero, and Mr. Hooton, and to all the concerned parents around our nation, I want you to know we're trying to do just that" (pp. 9–10).

Former committee chairman Davis' opening statement contrasted with Waxman's. He saw the Committee's task in very precise terms. "Let's be clear about our purpose," he (CoO&GR, 2008a) began.

> We're not self-appointed prosecutors trying the claims of the Mitchell report. This is not a court of law. And the guilt or innocence of the players accused in the report of steroid abuse is not our major concern. Our focus is on Senator Mitchell's recommendations more than his findings. We're here to save lives, not ruin careers. We want steroids and other dangerous drugs out of sports, period. (p. 11)

After emphasizing the same theme about the impact of steroids on adolescents, Davis returned to directing the committee: "[A]s a panelist in our last baseball hearing famously said, We're not here to talk about the past."

The committee should address only one question: What should baseball's leadership do to implement the Mitchell report's recommendations?

For his part, Mitchell (2008) mirrored Davis' assessment of the task at hand by emphasizing that it was time to look to the future and tackle the difficult tasks that lie ahead. He urged everyone in baseball to bring an end to the use of steroids and HGH in baseball through a coordinated, systematic plan of action.

In the statements and questions that followed, committee members expressed their admiration for Mitchell, his integrity and dedication, and the quality of the report. The questions posed to Mitchell focused, for the most part, on the logistics of the investigation, the lack of support from the MLBPA, and the dangers steroids posed to American youth (for example, see CoO&GR, 2008a, pp. 30–6, 37–40, 68–70; 85–6). However, there were three substantive issues that Mitchell had to address.

The first centered on whether players named in the report had the opportunity to view the evidence that Mitchell had deemed sufficient to identify them in the report (CoO&GR, 2008, pp. 32–7). Mitchell stated that players had every opportunity to do so on the condition that they agreed to an interview with Mitchell and his investigators.

The second concerned the limitations Mitchell faced in collecting information. Jessica Lynch asked how fruitful it would have been if the investigation had the ability to subpoena witnesses and could enter into plea bargains. Whether it was by design or not, Mitchell essentially avoided the question by addressing the context within which the question was first asked. Not satisfied, Lynch made her point clearer by noting that his investigation related directly to the Controlled Substances Act but that it took place without the power of subpoena (see CoO&GR, 2008a, pp. 60–2).

The third issue foreshadowed the Mitchell report's most controversial outcome—Clemens versus McNamee—and the partisan split that would ensue in the Committee's February 13th meeting. Eleanor Norton (CoO&GR, 2008a) began:

> I would like to give you an opportunity to respond to the criticism, however, to the naming of players; and some have alleged that you had too little corroboration. In doing so, could you tell us what standard of evidence you used in deciding when to name players and when not to name players? (p. 71)

After Mitchell explained the standard of evidence he used, Norton then noted that Clemens had strongly denied the allegations in a highly public manner—Clemens had used his own website, YouTube, an interview with

Mike Wallace on *60 Minutes*, and the print media to adamantly deny Mitchell's statements about his use of steroids and HGH (see Clemens, 2007; *60 Minutes*, 2008a; 2008b). Why, Norton asked, did Clemens refuse Mitchell's invitation to talk to him before the report was released (see CoO&GR, 2008a, pp. 72–3)?

"I do not know why," Mitchell replied, and as he began to explain the legal process that he had followed, Norton cut in: "Obviously, he hasn't told you and he hasn't told us. That's why I wondered" (CoO&GR, 2008a, p. 73).

Norton followed with questions about why McNamee's testimony was credible, and Mitchell provided a lengthy reply. When he had finished, to underscore the point, Waxman asked: "Senator Mitchell, in other words, despite the public presentation by Clemens that the testimony was not accurate, you continue to feel comfortable with Mr. McNamee's credibility?" Mitchell responded: "We believe that the statements provided to us were truthful" (CoO&GR, 2008a, pp. 73–6).

The two Democrats had used Mitchell's integrity and credibility to undermine Clemens; they made the circumstances under which McNamee had given his information fully transparent and thus the reasons why one could be confident his statements were truthful. The committee would move on to question Selig and Fehr at length, but the stage was already being set for the strongest test the Mitchell report would face: the Clemens/McNamee confrontation (on Selig and Fehr, see Bodlander 2008; CoO&GR, 2008a, pp. 86–169).

Clemens adamantly denied the Mitchell report's allegations that he had used steroids. In an almost two-minute video posted on his own website and YouTube on December 22, Clemens (2007) was emphatic:

> And let me be clear the answer is no! I did not use steroids, human growth hormone and I have never done so. I did not provide Brian McNamee any drugs to inject into my body. Brian McNamee did not inject steroids or human growth hormone into my body when I played in Toronto for the Blue Jays or the New York Yankees. This report is simply not true.

Clemens indicated he would talk with Mike Wallace on *60 Minutes* after Christmas, where he was equally categorical.

> I'm angry that, that what I've done for the game of baseball and as a person, in my private life what I've done, umm that I don't get the benefit of the doubt. The stuff that's being said, it's ridiculous; it's hogwash for people to

even assume this. Twenty-four, twenty-five years Mike, you'd think I'd get an inch of respect. An inch. How can you prove your innocence? (60 *Minutes*, 2008a; see also 60 *Minutes*, 2008b)

When Wallace asked Clemens about McNamee's specific and detailed statements to Mitchell regarding his injecting Clemens with steroids, quoting directly from the report, Clemens replied: "It never happened. Never happened. And if I have these needles and these steroids and all these drugs, where did I get 'em? Where is the person out there gave 'em to me? Please, please come forward." After Clemens denied further allegations, Wallace read from the Mitchell report:

"The next season, 2001, from the Mitchell Report, quote, 'According to McNamee, Clemens advised him in August of 2001 that he was again ready to use steroids and shortly thereafter, McNamee injected Clemens with a steroid on four to five occasions at Clemens' apartment.'" "Yeah," [Clemens replied], "never happened."

"In two of the three years that McNamee claims that he injected you—'98 and 2001—you won 20 games and the Cy Young Award as the American League's best pitcher" [Wallace noted].

"I won in 1997, I won the Cy Young Award. 2004 when he supposedly, I wasn't doing it. . . ." "Yeah [Wallace interjected], but these are the years in which McNamee claims that he injected you."

"It didn't happen. It didn't happen. It just didn't happen." (60 *Minutes*, 2008a; see also 60 *Minutes*, 2008b)

McNamee stayed away from the controversy and declined a *60 Minutes* interview. He had fulfilled the conditions of his plea agreement with Novitzky and wanted to disappear, but Clemens would not let the issue die. Clemens' challenge was about more than simply clearing his name; symbolically, it challenged the very truth of the Mitchell report, and some members of the CoO&GR did not want that to happen. For others, it was purely a question of political allegiance. The Dixie Chicks had been black-balled from country music south of the Mason-Dixon Line for speaking out against a Texan; no Southern politician wanted to risk his or her reputation by questioning the claims of a man that Bush had identified as a close friend and fellow Texan.

The transcript of the February 13 hearing documents the end of the bipartisan attack on steroids in baseball.

Between the release of the Mitchell report and Clemens' instant attack on the allegations that he had used steroids or HGH, members of the

CoO&GR used their power of subpoena to secure depositions from Clemens, McNamee, Pettitte, and Knoblauch. This was the type of sworn testimony that Mitchell could not gather.

In his opening statement to the committee as it was about to hear statements from Clemens and McNamee, Waxman (CoO&GR, 2008b) emphasized that it was a highly unusual hearing. He noted that "given the committee's past work and our interest in an accurate record of baseball's steroid era, we [Waxman and Davis] have investigated the evidence in Senator Mitchell's report that relates to Mr. McNamee and the players he identified" (p. 2). The committee chairs felt this was necessary because "if the Mitchell Report is to be the last word on baseball's past, we believe we have a responsibility to investigate a serious claim of inaccuracy" (CoO&GR, 2008b, pp. 2–3). Waxman then overviewed the evidence.

Davis' (CoO&GR, 2008b) opening statement reflected the same tenor as Waxman's—this hearing was a test of the Mitchell report.

> It gives me no joy to have joined you in calling this hearing. We were faced with an unenviable choice: Allow a strenuous challenge to the Mitchell Report to stand without review, or open ourselves up to criticisms that we were grandstanding, that we are acting like self-appointed prosecutors trying the claims of that report.
>
> In the end, we decided we had a duty to probe the challenge, that we needed to help determine whether the Mitchell Report, with its 409-page sordid picture of back-room drug deals and players injecting each other with illegal substances right in their locker rooms, whether that report could or should still stand as proof positive that baseball's efforts to combat illegal drug use needs a fresh look. (p. 15)

Davis' view of how the outcome would be determined differed from that of Waxman: "Today, we will let the American people judge who is to be believed in this unfortunate battle of wills, memories and reputations."

The agenda was clear—the status of the Mitchell report "as the last word on baseball's past," and it was equally clear that the American people would decide. The major difference between this hearing and the previous one was that no one could draw upon Mitchell's credibility and integrity; they would have to frame their truth claims on the backs of either McNamee or Clemens.

After being formally sworn in to testify before the committee, Clemens, who appended photos of himself pitching and a 49-page analysis of his career to his statement, and McNamee read abbreviated versions of their prepared statements which probably hurt Clemens (see CoO&GR, 2008b, pp. 19–77, 78–85). The prepared statement distributed to the committee began: "I appreciate the opportunity to tell this Committee and the public—under oath—what I have been saying all along: I have never used steroids, human growth hormone, or any other type of illegal performance enhancing drug" (CoO&GR, 2008b, p. 22). Clemens' statement then drew upon his history as one of baseball's most dominant hard-throwing pitchers in a manner that was carefully crafted so he could speak directly to the American people: "I have tried to model my baseball career, and indeed my entire life, on the premise that 'your body is your temple.'" His prepared statement then noted that any suggestion that Clemens had used steroids was incompatible with who he was and what he stood for (CoO&GR, 2008b, p. 23). Clemens' statement touched on how he had come from a poor family, the values his mother instilled, his work ethic, and his struggles growing up. Clemens then spoke about his own family and his charity work. It was a carefully drawn portrait.

However, in the statement he read, Clemens (CoO&GR, 2008b) adopted a very informal approach: "Thank you for allowing me to tell you a little bit about myself and how I have conducted my career for the past 25 years" (p. 20). He noted: "I have always believed that hard work and determination were the only ways to be successful and to reach goals. Shortcuts were not an option. This was instilled in me since I was a young boy by my mother and by my grandmother."

The conclusion to Clemens' prepared statement also differed from his oral statement. "At the end of the day," the conclusion to the prepared statement began:

> I have been accused of doing something that I did not do. I have been asked to prove that I did not do it. How in the world can I prove a negative? No matter what we discuss here today, I am never going to have my name restored. I know that a lot of people want me to say that I have taken steroids and be done with it. But I cannot in good conscience admit to doing something that I did not do; even if it would be easier to do so. That's not the type of person I am. Instead, I will try to set the record straight, and I will do so directly to Congress and under oath. I have been told that by doing this, I am subjecting myself to possible criminal prosecution. I know that some people will still think I am lying no matter what I say or do. And I know that because I've said that I didn't take steroids, it will look like an attack on Senator Mitchell's report. I am not saying Senator Mitchell's report is entirely wrong and I am not trying to convince those who have

already made up their minds based only on an allegation. For those with an open mind, however, I am saying that Brian McNamee's statements about me are wrong. Once again, I never took steroids or human growth hormone. (CoO&GR, 2008b, p. 26)

The oral statement made some of the same points but with less impact:

No matter what we discuss here today, I am never going to have my name restored, but I have to try and set the record straight. However, by doing so, I am putting myself out there to all of you, knowing that because I said that I didn't take steroids that this is looked on as an attack on Senator Mitchell's report. Where am I to go with that?

I'm not saying Senator Mitchell's report is entirely wrong. I am saying Brian McNamee's statements about me are wrong.

Let me be clear. I have never taken steroids or HGH. Thank you. (CoO&GR, 2008b, p. 21)

McNamee (CoO&GR, 2008b) had to establish his credibility. After noting that the Mitchell report documented widespread use of steroids in MLB, admitting he was part of the problem and apologizing for his conduct, McNamee indicated that by testifying that he could contribute to the solution (p. 81). McNamee (CoO&GR, 2008b) confessed that he was not proud of what he had done nor did he find any satisfaction in testifying against "a man I once admired" (p. 81). McNamee made all the points he needed concerning his specific actions while dispelling any doubts about his motivation for telling the truth.

"**Make no mistake:**" McNamee began in the most critical section of his statement:

When I told Senator Mitchell that I injected Andy Pettitte with performance enhancing drugs, I told the truth. Andy Pettitte—who I know to be honest and decent—has since confirmed this.

Make no mistake: when I told Senator Mitchell that I injected Chuck Knoblauch with performance enhancing drugs, I told the truth. Chuck Knoblauch, I believe, will confirm this as well. [Knoblauch had already testified to this under oath in a deposition to the committee.]

And make no mistake: when I told Senator Mitchell that I injected Roger Clemens with performance enhancing drugs, I told the truth. I told the truth about steroids and human growth hormone. . . . Unfortunately Roger has denied this and has led a full court attack on my credibility. . . .

I have no reason to lie, and **every reason not to.** If I do lie, I will be prosecuted. I was never promised any special treatment or consideration for fingering star players. I was never coerced to provide information against anyone. All that I was ever told, was to tell the truth to the best of my ability, and that is what I have done. (CoO&GR, 2008b, pp. 82–3, all emphases in the original)

In the questions that followed, the Democrats forcefully and critically cross-examined Clemens, and the Republicans were even more aggressive in their questioning of McNamee (e.g., CoO&GR, 2008b, pp. 129–30, 147, 156–57). Each side directed their questions at the areas where they felt Clemens or McNamee were the weakest. Republicans also jumped to the defense of Clemens when he faltered with Democrats doing the same with McNamee.

Democrat Elijah Cummings spoke first, establishing Pettitte's credibility by quoting Clemens' lawyers and referring to Pettitte's religiosity. Reminding Clemens he was under oath, Cummings asked Clemens if he thought Pettitte was lying when he told the committee that Clemens had used HGH. Clemens responded: "I believe Andy has misheard" and "I think he misremembers" (CoO&GR, 2008b, p. 87). Clemens remained forceful in his answers.

After the second time Clemens stated that Pettitte "misremembered," Cummings emphasized the credibility of Pettitte's version (CoO&GR, 2008b, p. 88). Undeterred, Clemens (CoO&GR, 2008b) deflected Cummings' assertion by agreeing that Pettitte is "a fine gentleman" and a very close friend, but "I think he misremembers" (p. 89). Cummings returned to the point later in the hearing to restate his position:

As I said before, I have listened to you very carefully and I—I take you at your word. And your word is that Andy Pettitte is an honest man and his credibility pretty much impeccable. Your lawyer says the same thing. But suddenly—and the committee gave him time after time after time to clear up his testimony and he consistently said the same thing under oath. Not only that, his wife, he goes and tells his wife everything and she says the same thing. But suddenly he misunderstood you. All I'm saying is it's hard to believe, it's hard to believe you, sir. I hate to say that as—you're one of my heroes. But it's hard to believe. (CoO&GR, 2008b, p. 157)

Republican Tom Davis followed Cummings' opening questions by focusing on the inconsistencies in the information McNamee had given to federal authorities. Davis (CoO&GR, 2008b) also questioned McNamee about a telephone conversation that Clemens had taped. In it, Clemens stated: "I just need you to come out and tell the truth," Davis noted. "And you didn't respond." Why, Davis continued, did McNamee not simply say, "I did tell the truth"? (p. 92).

McNamee (CoO&GR, 2008b) responded vaguely, saying he knew he was being taped and was not sure if someone was listening (p. 92). McNamee was apparently still protecting Clemens (see Thompson et al., 2009), but he did say, "[I]f you listen to it and you know my jargon, I did say that. It is what it is" (p. 92). Although Davis' questions had seemed to undermine McNamee's credibility, Democrat Mark Souder (CoO&GR, 2008b, p. 151) returned to that point later, noting that "it is what it is" is an expression New Yorkers use for telling the truth and asked the chairman to have that clarification on record because the phrase was of pivotal importance.

Davis also focused on McNamee's assertion that Clemens had attended a barbecue at Canseco's in June 1998. McNamee reaffirmed that was true, at which point Davis referred to affidavits by Canseco and his wife contradicting McNamee. Davis pushed the point further by allowing Clemens to explain that a golf pro shop receipt corroborated his claim that he was golfing and not at Canseco's party. Finally, Davis asked Clemens about the color of B-12, a steroid injection, and HGH to confirm that Clemens would know if McNamee had injected him with B-12 as Clemens maintained.

Democrat John Tierney began by questioning McNamee but then directed several pointed questions at Clemens over his contention that he and McNamee had never spoken to each other about HGH. Tierney used Clemens' earlier sworn deposition to the committee to illustrate some apparent inconsistencies between Clemens' claim and the facts related to McNamee injecting Clemens' wife Debbie with HGH. "Well, help us out, Mr. Clemens," Tierney (CoO&GR, 2008b) emphasized. "How do you reconcile three times saying you didn't [have a conversation with McNamee about HGH] and then later when somebody specifically finally asks you about your wife you have a recollection of two very distinct and memorable conversations?" (p. 98).

Burton began by insisting that McNamee was a chronic liar who could not be trusted. With his time running short, Burton asserted his main theme: "You're here as a sworn witness. You're here to tell the truth. You're here under oath." Conflating McNamee's past deeds with the issues before the committee, Burton continued: "And yet we have lie after lie after lie after lie of where you—you've told this committee and the people of the country that Roger Clemens did things, and I don't know what to believe." "I know one thing I don't believe," he noted with great flourish, "and that's you" (CoO&GR, 2008b, p. 103).

Democrat Stephen Lynch directed the committee's attention to a question of physical evidence—a July 28, 1998, magnetic resonance image (MRI) of a palpable mass in Clemens' right buttock. Lynch cited the conclusion of an independent analysis conducted by Dr. Mark Murphy from the Armed Forces Institute of Pathology, who believed that the MRI image was most likely due to a steroid injection (CoO&GR, 2008b, p. 105). One of Clemens' lawyers tried to intervene but was ruled out of order. Lynch chose his words carefully: "Given the—given the physical testimony—the physical evidence that we've had there that seems to be consistent with much of what Mr. McNamee is saying." He asked Clemens how the physical evidence could be wrong.

Davis interjected, asking for unanimous consent to enter into the committee record a report by Dr. Burt O'Malley, a molecular and cell biologist, who had reached very different conclusions, even though that report, provided by Clemens attorneys, did not actually discuss the abscess or the MRI (see CoO&GR, 2008b, pp. 109–11). Nevertheless, the manner in which Davis made the interjection appeared to counter Lynch's argument.

Although he had spoken once already, Davis was recognized by the chair to speak again. Davis began to defend Clemens from Lynch's questions, indicating that because Clemens was not a doctor that he should not be expected to respond to Murphy's report. Davis indicated that the physician who had ordered the MRI would submit a deposition that afternoon indicating that his conclusions would differ from those Murphy made. Davis claimed that there was no evidence or even a suspicion that drugs had caused the palpable mass in question (CoO&GR, 2008b, pp. 110–1). Davis confirmed the damage that Lynch's questions had caused by dismissing them as a type of lynching.

In view of Clemens' apparent struggle with the questions at the hearing, several Republican members dismissed the proceedings: Lynn Westmoreland labeled them "a show trial" and Christopher Shays compared them to "a Roman circus, seeing the gladiators fight it out" (CoO&GR, 2008b, pp. 147, 157). A minority report prepared by the Republicans referred to the session as "a nationally televised show trial" (Davis, 2008, p. 3).

In his summary statement, Davis (CoO&GR, 2008b) argued that the Mitchell report "remains largely intact" as he minimized the day's proceedings as simply a "bone of contention" (pp. 160–1). By emphasizing that the real goal of the committee hearings was to rid baseball of steroids,

Davis tried to deflect attention away from how much Clemens had appeared to struggle with establishing his credibility and arguments.

Waxman's summary was more overtly partisan and definitive. Waxman (CoO&GR, 2008b) reaffirmed Davis' point that each committee member and everyone watching would reach his or her own conclusions, but he was certain of what he had learned:

> Chuck Knoblauch and Andy Pettitte confirm what Brian McNamee told Senator Mitchell. We learned of the conversations that Andy Pettitte believed he had with Roger Clemens about HGH. And even though Mr. Clemens says his relationship with Mr. Pettitte was so close that they would know and share information with each other, evidently Mr. Pettitte didn't believe what Mr. Clemens said in that 2005 conversation. (p. 161)

Waxman apologized to McNamee for the way some committee members had treated him before concluding that steroids had to be taken out of professional sports because they were making their way from the professionals into the high schools.

How Entertainment Has Captured Reality

From 2003 onward, the issue of steroid use in high-performance and professional sports has gained a higher and higher public profile, but at the same time, the lens under which it has been investigated has tightened in on personalities and athlete-celebrities. Steroid use became a high-profile issue with the exposure of BALCO, Conte, Montgomery, White, and Jones. However, as important as those athletes were as international world-class athletes, their profile among most North Americans was considerably lower than that of NFL and MLB players. As a result, when the BALCO investigation introduced the names of professional athletes—especially Bonds—the media and the general public began to pay closer attention.

President Bush's State of the Union address brought the claims-making process to the highest office in the United States, and his remarks—directed explicitly at baseball and football players and owners—opened the way for three nationally televised hearings on steroid use in professional sports and a dramatic report that named names and garnered considerable media coverage.

In each case, the medium became the dominant message; the entertainment form suppressed the real investigative potential of each of those media events. For example, unlike the Dubin inquiry—which tried to gather information from a wide variety of sources and organize it on the basis of some fundamental principles—the events from 2003 onward have been reduced to celebrity personalities. There has been a disturbing irony in the recent coverage of steroid use in professional and high-performance sports; the more that the issue has been covered, the shallower the information has become. While earlier discussions were limited in many ways, they at least struggled with some of the context within which athletes were using steroids; there was some attention to the principles on which the steroid ban was based, leaving open the question about whether those principles still applied. The events since 2003 have reduced the question of steroid use in sports to a series of "he says" contests.

As a result, even though there is a large and growing body of serious scholarly research into steroids' physiological and psychological impact and the reasons why athletes use them, few outside the community of experts read it. Even the brilliantly titled *Testosterone Dreams* (Hoberman, 2005) and its near genius cover design—despite its excellent scholarly content—cannot compete with such heavily advertised mass market trade books as *Bases Loaded* (Radomski, 2009), *American Icon* (Thompson et al., 2009); *Vindicated* (Canseco, 2009); *A-Rod: The Many Lives of Alex Rodriguez* (Roberts, 2009); or *Juicing the Game* (Bryant, 2006).

What the average North American "knows" about steroids and their use has been overwhelmingly shaped by "life the movie" and little, if at all, by the complex reality that needs to be understood. On the basis of the contradictory, incomplete, and agenda-driven knowledge that does exist, there is no doubt that the average North American voter needs to revive *Homo sapiens* and force *Homo scaenicus* to the sidelines so the real issues of steroid use in sports can be fully examined and appropriate policies developed and implemented. Naming names and televised show trials have diverted attention from the real concerns of professional and high-performance sports in the modern era.

Conclusion: Sports, Modernity, and Steroids

Three threads have run through this study: Raymond Williams' notion of dominant, residual, and emergent; Michel Foucault's and Anthony Giddens' insights into the nature of modernity; and the process of social constructionism. Together, these threads have brought to the fore important although often invisible or neglected aspects of the use of steroids in sports.

The most significant points of emphasis that emerged from the discussion thus far were the nature of Baron Pierre de Coubertin's Olympic project—an inspired and inspirational vision of the role that sports could play in resisting the forces of modernity and create—through appropriately constructed and philosophically grounded athletic experiences and the resulting larger spectacle as a whole—a new elite leadership for Europe. Coubertin's vision was drawn heavily from his own romanticized conception of medieval Europe and Victorian England. Through the intensity of the experiences that young men would encounter as they tested their physical abilities and mental will within athletic contests based on the fundamental principles of fair play, the Olympic Games would bond chivalrous brothers-in-arms into a new European elite. The Olympic spectacle would exude beauty and reverence, creating a religious experience. From within this context, not only would the use of steroids be inappropriate, but any practices that placed the pursuit of victory above the Olympic Games' educational mission would contradict Coubertin's philosophy, his aspirations for the Olympics, and the goal of overturning the forces of modernity.

From the very outset, Coubertin's project faced serious obstacles and in each instance had to yield to the growing powers of modernity within Europe to keep the Olympic Games alive. The problems were compounded as nation-states began to use their athletes' successes as symbolic expressions of national strength and vitality. The Berlin Games were an early example of how a nation-state's interests and the forces of modernity—the systematic training of athletes to ensure victory—would divert Coubertin's project to a far different course than he had intended. The rise of the Cold War exacerbated the situation further.

Throughout the post-WWII period, the massive expansion of the market economies of the West, the growing importance of television as an entertainment medium and an overwhelmingly powerful vehicle for stimulating consumer demand through advertising, and the Olympic Games' own success as an entertainment spectacle created the ideal conditions for the professionalization of high-performance sports and the modernization of athlete training and development. By the 1970s, nations as diverse as Australia, Canada, the FRG, and GDR had joined the United States and USSR in the struggle to dominate international sports through heavy state investment in ever-expanding systems of athlete preparation, drawing heavily upon the latest developments in the applied sports sciences. Modernity was already the dominant social force when Coubertin launched his Olympic project; by the 1960s, the world of high-performance sports was thoroughly imbued with the philosophy and practices of the modern world. There was no realm of sports that was immune to the competitive, scientifically based, progress-oriented ethos of modernity—not children's or youth sports and most certainly not the Olympic Games. As a televised spectacle, supported by the interests of nation-states on both sides of the Cold War divide, the Olympics were thoroughly infused with the forces of modernism even though IOC rhetoric, policies, and statements of principle stood as residual forces of (modest) resistance from the nineteenth century.

Although steroids and other performance-enhancing substances had entered the Olympic Games as early as 1952 and always run counter to Coubertin's philosophy, the IOC did not take any steps to curb their use until the mid-1960s. By the time the IOC established its first banned list in 1968, the Olympic Games had become thoroughly modernized, more and more athletes were training full time, and every aspect of the Olympic Games was becoming increasingly professionalized. Nevertheless, the IOC continued to invoke the rhetoric of Coubertin's philosophy and claimed that amateurism remained a fundamental principle, differentiating the Olympics from the world of professional sports. On the basis of the claim that it was still upholding Coubertin's philosophy and principles, the IOC justified the exclusion of selected performance-enhancing substances by maintaining that their use represented the professionalization of the Olympic Games— a distorted overcommitment to the quest for victory—and gave some athletes an unfair advantage over others. The zeal for Olympic gold associated with the use of performance-enhancing substances was inconsistent with the ideals of Olympism.

By 1974—two years before it began testing for steroids at the Olympics—the IOC removed the formal requirements of amateurism from the *Olympic Charter* and introduced a new eligibility code that reflected the nature of the athletes who were actually competing at the Olympic Games. With that decision, the IOC abandoned the central principle of Coubertin's project and brought the Olympics into line with the forces of modernity that thoroughly dominated social life in the latter decades of the twentieth century. The central principle on which the ban on selected performance-enhancing substances had been justified was gone; the IOC had to find a new rationale.

The new principle on which the banned list was legitimated centered on the claim that the Olympic Games embodied the most essential element of sports—the principle of "fair play." Fair play became the Olympics' new brand image, and even though this principle was far different than Coubertin's founding vision—particularly insofar as "fair play" was constituted under the conditions of modernity—and did not fundamentally disqualify the use of performance-enhancing substances and practices, it contained enough resonance with the Olympic Games' early history that the IOC could continue to claim moral legitimacy for its ban on selected performance-enhancing substances.

Throughout the 1960s, as the IOC wrestled with the presence of steroids and other performance-enhancing substances in the Olympic Games, it relied on the residual significance and principled importance of Coubertin's original conception of the Olympic Games to justify the exclusion of steroids and other substances (even though the IOC allowed the Olympic Games to become thoroughly dominated by a victory-oriented philosophy and actually needed athletes to perform at the outer limits of human potential so the Olympics would remain a highly sought after, lucrative, televised, international spectacle). At the same time, the emergent forces of nationalism, commercialism, and the use of applied sports science had become the dominant forces guiding the Olympic Games' trajectory.

The new forces of resistance to the ongoing modernization of the Olympic Games would rest with a number of claims-makers who would construct steroid use as deviant and socially problematic in two different ways. One approach—the strategy followed by Chief Justice Charles Dubin—was to restate the fundamental principles of Coubertin's project and maintain that these were the principles on which the Olympic Games should be based. And while there is no doubt that Coubertin's vision and aspirations are moving and inspirational and have been used by politicians to impress voters about how much they cherish certain values and beliefs, the reality is that from the inaugural Olympic Games of 1896, the Olympics have been completely unsuccessful in either overturning the forces of modernity or even escaping the impact of modernity's forces. The sociohistorical context within which the Olympic Games have developed and flourished is thoroughly modernist, and they have been fundamentally shaped by the social forces of modernity—no matter how much a federal commission of inquiry might believe or wish it could be otherwise.

The second strategy was to link steroid use in sports with the broader social war on drugs. This strategy was the most successful; federal legislators sought to demonize steroids by linking them to crack, cocaine, and heroin, despite the claim's fallacy. The success of this undertaking, like all claims-making processes, involved the construction of a very specific conception of steroid use and an ensuing focus on a particular, seriously deleterious aspect of that conception. The simple allegation that steroids killed or imperiled the lives of American youth became that claim. This outcome was, allegedly, the result of high-profile athletes, through their use of steroids, serving as role models leading youth astray. Publicity for that claim came from media and congressional prosecution of select high-profile athletes—in particular, Mark McGwire, Barry Bonds, and Roger Clemens.

Finally, while part of the success of the claims-making process is due to its intense focus on a few celebrity athletes, the larger reason is the manner in which the claims have been constructed as entertainment programming within an entertainment- and celebrity-obsessed culture. If the claims-making process in general is almost always divorced from a firm factual foundation, the claims-making process around steroids has moved from one realm of entertainment—the Olympic Games—to another one—televised congressional hearings involving celebrity athletes—where appearances are paramount and the complexity of argument and counterargument are completely absent. While the real concerns over steroids should center on the impact they may have on athletes' health within the current regime of prohibition, the claims-making process has reduced everything to tabloid-like gossip: "Did McNamee inject Clemens with steroids, as Pettitte reveals Clemens told him?" "Did Bonds commit perjury?" "Who is next?"

The Critique of Antidoping Policies

The current, socially constructed image of the specter of steroids is highly problematic and of considerable concern. Not only have claims-makers succeeded in simplifying the issue of steroid use, they have created a seriously distorted perception of why steroids are banned and completely ignored a number of significant, unintended consequences resulting from the ban and the claims-making process itself. Steroid use by athletes is a complex issue; the current social construction is completely incapable of addressing steroid use constructively.

Fortunately, there is a fairly large and growing contingent of international scholars—from disciplines as different as applied sports science, cultural studies, kinesiology, management studies, medicine, philosophy, and sociology, to name a few areas of specialization—who have begun to contribute to the public and scientific debates over steroid use in sports. Thus, for example, Bengt Kayser and Aaron Smith (2008)—with the support of more than 30 other scholars—published an article in the *British Medical Journal* that challenged conventional wisdom and the socially constructed image of steroid use while indicating the negative impacts and unintended consequences of the current ban. The article developed themes that Kayser, Alexandre Mauron, and Andy Miah (2005) had presented in a special issue of *Lancet* dedicated to sports in the International Year of Sport and Physical Education and a longer version of their position, which appeared in *BMC Medical Ethics* (Kayser, Mauron, & Miah, 2007).

In *Lancet*, Kayser, Mauron, and Miah (2005) were direct and to the point: "The rules of sport define a level playing field on which athletes compete. Anti-doping policies exist, in theory, to encourage fair play. However, we believe they are unfounded, dangerous, and excessively costly" (p. S21). In the *BMC Medical Ethics* article, Kayser, Mauron, and Miah (2007) elaborated on their position but remained equally as pointed in their assessment of antidoping policies. Noting that the creation of WADA intensified the pursuit of athletes using banned performance-enhancing substances as substantially more resources were invested in antidoping programs, they argued that those "severe anti-doping control measures" were based on "questionable ethical grounds." "The ethical foundation of the war on doping," they continued,

> consists of largely unsubstantiated assumptions about fairness in sports and the concept of a "level playing field." Moreover, it relies on dubious claims about the protection of an athlete's health and the value of the essentialist

view that sports achievements reflect natural capacities. In addition, costly anti-doping efforts in elite competitive sports concern only a small fraction of the population. From a public health perspective this is problematic since the high prevalence of uncontrolled, medically unsupervised doping practiced in amateur sports and doping-like behaviour in the general population (substance use for performance enhancement outside sport) exposes greater numbers of people to potential harm. In addition, anti-doping has pushed doping and doping-like behaviour underground, thus fostering dangerous practices such as sharing needles for injection. Finally, we argue that the involvement of the medical profession in doping and anti-doping challenges the principles of non-maleficience and of privacy protection. As such, current anti-doping measures potentially introduce problems of greater impact than are solved, and place physicians working with athletes or in anti-doping settings in an ethically difficult position. In response, we argue on behalf of enhancement practices in sports within a framework of medical supervision. (Kayser, Mauron, and Miah, 2007)

There have been four principal reasons used to justify the ban on steroids and other performance-enhancing substances in sports: The ban ensures a fair and level playing field, protects the integrity of sports, safeguards the health of athletes, and ensures that athletes set a wholesome example for others. Whether one turns to Kayser and his colleagues, Beamish and Ritchie (2006), Møller (2010), Waddington (2010), Waddington and Smith (2009), any of the scholars associated with the International Network for Humanistic Doping Research, or others who have systematically studied steroid use in sports, there is a well-developed body of scholarship that demonstrates why each claim is flawed.

Steroid use does not create an uneven playing field; there are innumerable factors that provide some athletes with advantages over others. A level playing field simply does not exist due to the basic facts of heredity. More importantly, such social realities as global inequalities in funding, the differing social and personal investment athletes and nation-states make in sports, and fundamental problems of inequality of condition and inequality of opportunity ensure that the playing field is not level and never can be (Beamish, 2008). At the same time, sports in the modern era are continually employing scientific technologies to improve performance, but the decision to ban some substances and technologies and not others does not rest on a consistent set of principles; the decisions are motivated by the particular perceptions and values of specific decision-makers who are not directly accountable to the athletes whom their regulations govern.

As a result, a number of substances and performance-enhancing technologies accepted by WADA, the IOC, and professional sports leagues also negate a level playing field.

The claim that steroids undermine the integrity of sports is based on the assertion that their use compromises the ethical foundation and authenticity of sports. However, as Kayser and Smith (2008) have noted: "The idea that all sport is bound by common values and customs ignores the cultural histories and evolution of different sports and the impact of science, technology, and commercialisation on their structure and operation" (p. 86).

Similarly, as Beamish and Ritchie (2006) have documented in detail, sports do not exist as transhistorical phenomena with specific essentialist cores. Sports are socially created and determined sets of social practices located in particular sociohistorical contexts. Within the context of contemporary modernity, high-performance sports are specific, socially constructed entertainment commodities that are characterized by the drive to produce athletic performances at the outer limits of human potential through the use of scientifically informed regimes of athlete preparation with the assistance of teams of applied sports scientists and other support personnel. Within this environment, banning the use of various performance-enhancing technologies actually undermines the integrity of the ethos of modernist sports.

The issue of athletes' health is a bit more complex than most recognize. When the IOC created, imposed, and monitored the banned list, protecting the health of athletes was one of its basic fundamental concerns. Thus, for example, in the Olympic Movement: Anti-Doping Code, which was put into effect in January 2000 and remained as IOC policy until it was replaced by WADA's Anti-Doping Code, the IOC (2000) referred directly and indirectly to athletes' health in four of the six premises justifying the code. The IOC noted its commitment to "prevent endangering the health of athletes," the "Movement's duty to protect the health of athletes," the IOC's desire to "safeguard the health of athletes," and its obligation to "act in the best interests of athletes."

From the first version of the Anti-Doping Code to its most recent version, WADA (2003, 2009a) has been more circumspect. The WADA code formally eliminated protection of athletes' health as the basic grounds for the banned list. Under WADA, the fundamental principle behind the code is to protect athletes' "fundamental right to participate in doping-free sport." The code will seek to "*promote* health, fairness, and equality" for athletes, but WADA does not claim that it is safeguarding athletes' health through its banned list (WADA, 2009a, p. 11, emphasis added). This is not simply a matter of semantics. Recognizing that steroid use is widespread in high-performance sports—hence, the exorbitant measures and costs dedicated to detecting banned substance use—WADA's policies do not protect athletes' health. More importantly, they may be placing athletes' health at greater risk than would be the case without the ban.

In view of the ban and the legal restrictions on steroid use, athletes do not have direct access to the best informed, medically supervised use of unadulterated steroids taken under appropriately sterile conditions. Relying on an elaborate, trial-and-error-based ethnopharmacology, athletes use steroids of unknown quality purchased on the black market through self-administration or injection in unsterile conditions. In addition, the substances or steroids that clear athletes' systems quickly and are difficult to detect are among those which are the hardest on athletes' physiology and long-term health (Beamish & Ritchie, 2006; Voy, 1991). The presence of the ban pressures athletes who choose to use steroids to select them based on detection criteria rather than their health impacts. WADA is very careful to not claim that the steroid ban protects athletes' health because it simply does not.

Finally, the notion that substances are banned because athletes are important role models is naïve in two fundamental senses. First, it maintains that high-performance and professional athletes must be "model citizens," judging them with criteria "that are not imposed on any other category of admired citizen" (Kyser & Smith, 2008, p. 86). Second, it suggests that athlete behavior is a key variable in youths' steroid use. The decision to take steroids is a complex one and none of the current research has proposed or supported a monocausal model nor has it shown that athlete role models are the predominant cause of steroid use among youth (DuRant, Escobedo, & Heath, 1995; Kanayama et al., 2006; Kindlundh et al., 1999; Miller et al., 2002; Parkinson & Evans, 2006).

Socially Constructed Absences: Neglected Issues in Performance-Enhancing Substances

While the current social construction of steroids as demonized substances has tended to suppress debate over the philosophical, medical, and sociological rationales for the banned list, it has also structured the agenda of concerns in a manner that completely overlooks some fundamental questions about steroids and sports. Five examples will not only make the point but also indicate the importance of each of these issues for the world of high-performance sports today.

The first issue one might focus on—one that truly merits extensive public discussion—concerns risk and acceptable levels of risk. There is no doubt that high-performance sports involve risk (Parkkari, Kujala, & Kannus, 2001; Pipe, 2001). The risks involved in high-performance sports—muscle and ligament tears, broken bones, multiple concussions, overuse injuries—are often seen as "part of the game" and thus justified. The risks associated with performance-enhancing substances are usually excluded from this category because, it is argued, they are not integral to competing. But this claim buries two issues.

First, does the use of banned performance-enhancing substances, including steroids, risk athletes' health? If so, what is the level of risk, and how would that level of risk be altered under medical supervision and on the basis of thorough, publically scrutinized scientific study of steroids and other substances?

Second, is it true that athletes striving to be the best in the world, performing at the outer limits of human athletic performance and engaging in demanding, repeated practice regimes on an ongoing basis over years of athlete development, do not need certain pharmacological substances? The demands of athlete preparation require adequate recovery to prevent injury, but this creates a dilemma that requires extensive analysis. There is a fine line between a substance serving as an ergogenic aid (directly enhancing performance) and its use as a therapeutic treatment (speeding recovery and reducing the risk of further injury). Athletes committing their lives and careers to sports have a right to the best therapeutic treatment possible, and the current ban on certain substances denies them that access, shortening their careers and depriving them of earning potential. There is an additional question: If some physical and pharmaceutical treatments reduce injury and are accepted while others are banned, what is the basis for the distinction? None of these issues are black and white.

This question of acceptable risk leads directly into a second major issue that the current social construction of steroids leaves unexamined. The current ban itself creates a number of significant health risks for athletes who choose to use those substances. Many of those risks have already been mentioned. Removing the ban on proscribed substances may significantly reduce the risk to athletes using them and advance the medical community's ability to protect their health. Kayser, Mauron, and Miah (2007) have argued that "allowing medically supervised doping within the framework of classical medical ethical standards, particularly with regard to the principle of non-maleficience [not doing harm to others], would potentially have a number of positive consequences." They emphasized three points.

First, medically supervised use would allow physicians, physiologists, sports scientists, and athletes to determine the real risks associated with particular substances. At present, the real epidemiology of steroid use, in the manner employed by high-performance athletes, is not known. Rather than relying on anecdotal evidence, researchers could monitor the controlled use of substances of known qualities over the short and long term.

Second, as noted already, high-performance sports result in injury. It is already the case that several substances that physicians use for therapeutic reasons are proscribed when an athlete is healthy or involved in competition. Athletes can apply for and receive a therapeutic use exemption (TUE). But the very existence of TUEs raises three questions that need thorough consideration. First, on what real basis can the decision be made that at one level of injury that an athlete may receive a TUE but at a later point in time no longer merit that exemption? What assurances are there that TUEs are granted equitably and on the basis of the same standards? Third, what criteria determine that one and the same substance is in one set of circumstances permissible to use but under slightly different circumstances is no longer permissible? Not only do all these distinctions create significant scientific and ethical problems, but they also may impede some athletes from receiving the best medical care possible as they train and compete.

Third, as Kayser, Mauron, and Miah (2007) have emphatically stated, "the concern about doping is largely disingenuous, if it is supposed to reflect a genuine moral concern for health."

> There is no lack of moral entrepreneurs, poised to preach the war on doping: sports authorities, politicians, opinion leaders, ethicists, and the media. They claim the moral high ground by waging what has become, in effect, what social scientists call a "symbolic crusade." Yet, while high-level sports is touted as embodying the positive values of health, meritorious effort, harmonious development of body and mind, this downplays the very real health risks of elite sports as well as accepted levels of foul play with considerable health damage in certain sports such as soccer or ice-hockey. Today's medical reality of high-level athletics little resembles the quaint image of an ideal harmony between beauty, strength and health dreamed up by the early Olympic movement. Elite sports have become thoroughly alien to the sort of physical exercise that is a legitimate general public health concern. In

addition, high-level athletes are singled out for attention and their health-related behaviours subjected to an invasive scrutiny that would be impractical—and unethical—if it were applied to the general public.

The war on drugs in sports funnels scarce resources into a program of intense and intrusive surveillance that makes little public health sense due to the tiny fraction of the population involved. If there is a genuine public health concern related to steroids—and data on youth use suggests that may be the case—then strategies should be developed that will address the broader public issue rather than the artificially created one within high-performance sports.

The current repressive approach to steroids has created the conditions where a black market flourishes. As a result, youths and athletes use steroids of dubious quality, frequently sharing needles—thereby increasing the possible spread of HIV, hepatitis, and other diseases (Aitken, Delalande, & Stanton, 2002; Midgley et al., 2000). Because steroid use extends well beyond high-performance sports, a much broader approach needs to be developed. The vast resources currently invested in tracking and testing the tiny population of elite athletes should be directed more broadly and wisely. Repression and testing have not been effective in any aspect of the broader war on drugs; the resources spent on high-performance sports should be invested in a well-developed education program, including an assessment of the cultural shift associated with an increasing acceptance of body modification in its many forms.

A third area of debate that the current social construction of steroid use in sports ignores engages with the simple question of what would happen if the steroid ban were lifted? Would there be more deaths, chronic illnesses, shorter life spans, more athletes taking health risks? Kayser, Mauron, and Miah (2007) have argued that if steroid use were allowed within an ethical framework based on the principle of not doing harm to others, there would likely be increased use of ergogenic drugs, but that would not necessarily lead to increases in morbidity and mortality. Under the appropriate conditions of medical supervision, athletes using steroids and other performance-enhancing substances would be better informed about the substances they were taking and the risks involved. Removing the ban on steroids would make this aspect of high-performance sports less risky.

The prospects of removing the ban are slim; indeed, it is debatable that one could even initiate that discussion within the current political climate. Sports policy analyst Barry Houlihan (1999) has emphasized that the major decisions regarding drug policy—"what to test for, who to test and what penalties to impose for doping infractions are all tightly controlled by the federations and the IOC, or occasionally governments" (p. 332). The failure to form what Houlihan terms "an epistemic community" of all the various parties that have a stake in the use or proscription of performance-enhancing substances means that the agenda is controlled by a few powerful and influential bodies—WADA in particular. As a result, there has not been a sustained, open discussion about the ethical foundations and principles behind the proscription of steroids and other substances since the 1960s—and that discussion was circumscribed by certain vested interests.

The final question that the current social construction of steroid use in sports overlooks is the critical issue of physicians' roles in high-performance sports. The current structure of high-performance sports places physicians in professionally and ethically compromising situations. Kayser, Mauron, and Miah (2007) have pointed out that in 1983, Thomas Murray (1983), president of The Hastings Center—a leading institute for ethics—and current chair of WADA-AMA's Ethical Issues Review Panel, indicated that within the context of high-performance sports, physicians face conflicting pressures. The decision of a sponsor, coach, owner, or government official may trump that of a physician's professional judgment about an athlete's best interests. Kayser, Mauron, and Miah (2007) agree with Murray's assessment and have argued that, consistent with the prevailing ethical standards of the medical profession, "the role of the physician involved in the athlete's health supervision should be one of preserving the athlete's autonomy." This would involve a "balance between ensuring that treatment leads to the highest degree of present and future health, while acknowledging the athlete's interest to maintain a chosen style of life."

Kayser, Mauron, and Miah (2007) have recognized that there will be conflicts between the optimization of performance and the possible risk to an athlete's health—looking for performance advantages when downhillers already career down slopes at 100 kilometers an hour is a good example—but the dilemma already exists when "therapeutic measures are applied to keep an athlete in the game despite an existing injury." "Ethical reasoning," they wrote,

> should be based on proportionality, assessing the benefits and risks as objectively as possible. Admittedly, this is not an easy task, since it requires a process of negotiation to face the difficult question about what kinds of health

risks are acceptable for an athlete to take. While further elaboration on this is beyond the scope of this paper, we would suggest that the solution lies partly in the structures of sport that permit such risk taking. Nevertheless, we believe that by carefully helping an athlete enhance her performance (by utilizing currently banned methods), in keeping with the principle of autonomy, using any safe technology available, the physician should again become the direct partner of the athlete in pursuit of ever increasing performance. As a result, a physician in the role of caring performance enhancer should be accountable for ill effects from the use of any medical technology. This would be analogous to the usual role of physicians. They are free in their choice of intervention, pharmacologic or other, as long as these are in agreement with current medical knowledge and without disproportionate iatrogenic ill effects. Rather than speculate on anti-doping test procedures, resources should be invested into protecting the integrity of physicians who make such judgments.

The growth and development of high-performance sports systems has resulted in teams of support personnel surrounding athletes. Each of those support groups has professional and ethical guidelines that it must follow, but the decision to ban selected substances that have more than one purpose creates impossible conundrums for everyone within the integrated sports system. These fundamental issues need to be examined fully, critically, and openly by everyone involved in the modern world of high-performance sports. Unfortunately, the existing social construction of steroids prevents that examination from taking place.

Modernity, Power-Knowledge, and the High-Performance Athlete

There is one final issue that merits attention—one that may be so obvious that it is continually overlooked or so profound that few are willing to face it directly: the simple matter that as an athlete rises through the age-class feeder system of sports—from the local to the regional, then state (or provincial), national, and, finally, the international or professional level of competition—he or she becomes—indeed, *must become*—fully committed to the social relations of elite-level sports under the conditions of modernity. The works of Foucault and Giddens are particularly instructive on this issue.

In a number of different texts and interviews, Foucault (2003) emphasized that the main objective of his work as a whole was to examine specific histories (or genealogies) of different ways in which humans have structured knowledge and produced conceptions of themselves as "subjects." This project meant Foucault (2003) was continually engaged in issues of power but "not Power with a capital P," which employs the notion of power "dominating and imposing its rationality upon the totality of the social body" (p. 95). For Foucault, power can only be grasped as "a field" comprised of multiple relations, generated/imposed through a variety of "technologies" or "modalities."

Critical to his work on power, the constitution of subjects, and technologies of power is the relation of power and knowledge—a relation he identifies as power/knowledge. Power/knowledge relations, Foucault (1978) maintained, must involve "the subject who knows, the objects to be known and the modalities of knowledge" (pp. 27–8). This approach to power requires an understanding of how power is present in immediate, everyday life situations and the manner in which it "categorizes the individual, marks him by his own individuality, attaches him to his own identity, imposes a law of truth on him that he must recognize and others have to recognize in him" (Foucault, 2003, p. 130).

To underscore the point, Foucault (1991) noted that even in *Discipline and Punish*, "the target of analysis wasn't 'institutions', 'theories', or 'ideology', but *practices*" (p. 75). To understand "disciplinary society" and the formation of subjects within modernity, it is "a question of analyzing a 'regime of practices'—practices being understood here as places where what is said and what is done, rules imposed and reasons given, the planned and the taken for granted meet and interconnect" (p. 75). Practices are the manner in which people live. The most significant determinant of action is not power exerted from above or from outside the individual; it is the internalized power/knowledge that constitutes what people believe and actually enact in practice, thereby reproducing it.

The primary practice under consideration here is steroid use by athletes at the elite level of sports within modernity. Modernity, Foucault (1978) argued, is the era of the individual—"a reality fabricated by this specific technology of power that I have called 'discipline' " (p. 194). To understand and explain discipline, Foucault turned to Jeremy Bentham's Panopticon to illustrate and explore the processes of surveillance, self-surveillance, self-discipline, and different technologies of power/knowledge within modernity. Discipline, as it is established through panopticism, makes it possible "to bring the effects of power to the most minute and distant elements [of life]. It assures an infinitesimal distribution of power relations" (Foucault, 1978, p. 216).

The panopticon did not just solve a technical problem, Foucault argued; through its principles, "a whole type of society emerges." Modernity is a social formation based on panoptic discipline where individuals engage in self-surveillance, self-discipline, self-constraint, and self-measurement. "Our society is one not of spectacle, but of surveillance," Foucault (1978) emphasized;

> under the surface of images, one invests bodies in depth; behind the great abstraction of exchange, there continues the meticulous, concrete training of useful forces; the circuits of communication are the supports of an accumulation and a centralization of knowledge; the play of signs defines the anchorages of power; it is not that the beautiful totality of the individual is amputated, repressed, altered by our social order, it is rather that the individual is carefully fabricated in it, according to a whole technique of forces and bodies. We are much less Greeks than we believe. We are neither in the amphitheatre, nor on the stage, but in the panoptic machine, invested by its effects of power, which we bring to ourselves since we are part of its mechanism. (p. 217)

The nature of power/knowledge in modernity fashions the practices that create the individual athlete-subject and structure his or her actions. The predominant scientific knowledge framework centers on painstaking, exacting analyses of clearly identified variables to produce better means (techniques and practices) to a particular end (victory)—all part of the continual pursuit of progress. The power/knowledge technologies of surveillance range from the global (the standards of world records, the current performances of other elite athletes, the televised spectacle, media assessments and commentaries, etc.), to the components of a national athlete development and assessment system (an athlete's world ranking, national expectations, performance criteria for funding, etc.), to an athlete's coaches and closest confidants. The technologies of self-surveillance involve fragile conceptions of identity, the "objectivity" of performance results, the continuous demands of self-discipline, a totalized commitment to training practices aimed at performance increments measured in hundredths of a second, millimeters of distance, grams of weight, or near instantaneous reactions or decision-making processes. Ironically, those practices are continually intensified for those who are most successful; failure to comply with/succumb to the technologies of discipline leads to an athlete's elimination from elite-level modern sports—the "prison of measured time," to use Jean-Marie Brohm's (1978) apt designation.

Thus, for Foucault, the key terms and conceptualizations are the genealogies and structure of knowledge; fields, technologies, and modalities of power; power/knowledge; panopticism; disciplinary society; and regimes of practices, surveillance, self-surveillance, self-discipline, self-constraint, and self-measurement. They reflect the disciplinary society of modernity with which elite-level athletes must inescapably engage.

Giddens' work on modernity and self-identity focuses much more on the micro level of the disciplinary world of modernity. It stands as an important complement to Foucault.

Giddens (1991) has emphasized that within the context of modernity and the wide, complex variety of experiences it presents to an individual, the constitution of self-identity is a "reflexive project" that consists "in the sustaining of coherent, yet continuously revised, biographical narratives" within "the context of multiple choice as filtered through abstract systems" (p. 5). As a "reflexive project," individuals are continually assessing themselves with reference to the larger social formation within which they are acting and the knowledge systems that are available, drawing upon specific resources and understandings of each social situation and the social context as a whole. Within sports—aside from the overarching modernist ethos and its emphasis on dynamic change and progress—the role of scientific knowledge and the competitive nature of sports are the dominant "abstract systems" through and against which athletes filter and constitute their self-identities.

Giddens breaks down the formation of self-identity within the context of modernity into a number of different dimensions or aspects—each of which applies to high-performance athletes constituting themselves as world-class competitors. Within the context of modernity, the "self is seen as a reflexive project, for which the individual is responsible" (Giddens, 1991, p. 75). "We are not what we are, but what we make ourselves," he emphasized. As a result, self-identity is conceptualized as an individual responsibility (project), constituted within a trajectory of progress that strives to represent and achieve a coherent developmental process. "The reflexivity of the self is continuous," Giddens (1991) noted, "as well as all-pervasive."

> At each moment, or at least at regular intervals, the individual is asked to conduct a self-interrogation in terms of what is happening. Beginning as a series of consciously asked questions, the individual becomes accustomed to asking, "how can I use this moment to change?" Reflexivity in this sense

belongs to the reflexive historicity of modernity, as distinct from the more generic reflexive monitoring of action.

Self-identity as a "coherent phenomenon" takes the form of a narrative in which the self and the individual's identity and thus aspirations are made explicit. For world-class athletes, there is no question about how that narrative should unfold and how each chapter in the story should end nor the level of commitment, pain, and sacrifice it will entail.

The formation of a self-identity, Giddens (1991) indicated, "implies the control of time—essentially, the establishing of zones of personal time which have only remote connections with temporal orders" (p. 77). Because self-identity within modernity is continually focused on the future as possibility, individuals want to ensure as much as possible that nothing is left to chance or contingency. As a result, all aspects of time—daily schedules, practice regimes, work/recovery ratios, speed of execution, etc.—are tightly controlled so every preparation possible is made along the route to each specific goal. It is little wonder that to ease the psychological burden of near obsessive attention to detail that so many athletes rely on superstition to alleviate some of the reflexivity and personal responsibility for success.

Finally, Giddens' (1991) conception of self-identity formation recognizes that the "reflexivity of the self *extends to the body*, where the body is part of an action system rather than merely a passive object" (p. 77). " 'The body' sounds a simple notion," Giddens wrote, "particularly as compared to concepts like 'self' or 'self-identity.' " But, he continued, "the body is not just a physical entity which we 'possess', it is an action-system, a mode of praxis, and its practical immersion in the interactions of day-to-day life is an essential part of the sustaining of a coherent sense of self-identity" (p. 99).

Giddens recognized that the body is central to all processes of self-identity formation within high modernity, but this is of particular significance for athletes—especially world-class athletes—because it is this embodied dimension of self-identity that leads Giddens to focus on "regimes of the self." The embodied character of self-identity formation, its particular types of reflexivity, and the control of time are all focused on shaping the body and expanding its powers and capacities. One is now at the core of how athletes become deeply imbedded in regimes that involve an embodied self but hinge on the continual improvement of physical performance potential, skills, and execution. The body—the body striving to perform at the outer limits of human athleticism—becomes the athlete's main instrument of self-identity, self-expression, and self-definition. In concise terms, ongoing embodied performances progressing along a specific trajectory become the high-performance athlete.

In view of the processes Giddens has examined and detailed, the wonder is not that a number of athletes turn to banned performance-enhancing substances to sustain their self-identities in modern world-class sports; it is surprising that not every athlete is using them.

In view of all the arguments presented in this book, steroids are not the demons that loom ominously over the world of elite sports; it is the way athletes must embody self-identities under the disciplinary technologies of high-performance sports in the modern era that should be disturbing. Unfortunately, the current social construction of steroid use does nothing to help athletes, policymakers, legislators, or the public at large recognize the depth and scope of the real issues confronting high-performance athletes or how those problems could be adequately addressed.

Bibliography

A business built on bulk. (1985, May 13). *Sports Illustrated*, 56–61.

Agence mondiale antidopage. (1999). Constitutive instrument of foundation of the Agence mondiale antidopage, World Anti-Doping Agency. Available from http://www.wada-ama.org/rtecontent/document/constitutive_instrument _foundation.pdf.

Aitken, C., Delalande, C., & Stanton, K. (2002). Pumping iron, risking infection? Exposure to hepatitis C, hepatitis B and HIV among anabolic-androgenic steroid injectors in Victoria, Australia. *Drug and Alcohol Dependence*, 65(3), 303–8.

Alfano, P., & Janofsky, J. (1988, November 19). A guru who spreads the gospel of steroids. *New York Times*. Available from http://www.nytimes.com/1988/11/ 19/sports/a-guru-who-spreads-the-gospel-of-steroids.html?pagewanted=all.

Allinger, C., & Allinger, T. (2004, September 10). Own the podium–2010: Final report with recommendations of the independent task force for winter NSOs and funding partners. Available from http://www.sportmatters.ca/ Groups/SMG%20Resources/Sport%20and%20PA%20Policy/otp_report _-_final_-_e.pdf.

Alzado, L. (1991, July 8). I'm sick and I'm scared. *Sports Illustrated*, 20–7.

American Medical Association. (1991). Statement of the American Medical Association to the Committee of the Judiciary, United States Senate, re: scheduling of anabolic steroids. In W. Taylor, *Macho medicine: A history of the anabolic steroid epidemic* (pp. 120–2).

American Psychiatric Association. (1987). *Diagnostic and statistical manual of mental disorders* (3rd ed., rev. [*DSM-III-R*]). Washington, DC: Author.

American Psychiatric Association. (1994). *Diagnostic and statistical manual of mental disorders* (4th ed. [*DSM-IV*]). Washington, DC: Author.

Assael, S. (2007). *Steroid nation: Juiced home run totals, anti-aging miracles, and a Hercules in every high school—the secret history of America's true drug addiction*. New York: ESPN Books.

Associated Press. (2004, January 21). Text of President Bush's State of the Union address. Available from http://www.post-gazette.com/pg/04021/263842 .stm#drugs.

Associated Press. (2007, December 13). List of names in Mitchell report. *Sporting News* (December 13). Available from http://www.sportingnews.com/mlb/article/2007-12-13/list-names-mitchell-report.

Baird, J. (1990). *To die for Germany: Heroes in the Nazi pantheon.* Bloomington, IN: Indiana University Press.

Bale, J. (2004). *Roger Bannister and the four-minute mile.* London and New York: Routledge.

Barney, R., Wenn, S., & Martyn, S. (2002). *Selling the five rings: The International Olympic committee and the rise of Olympic commercialism.* Salt Lake City: The University of Utah Press.

Barron, S. (Ed.). (1991). *"Degenerate Art": The fate of the avant-garde in Nazi Germany.* Los Angeles: Harry N. Abrams.

Barry Bonds talks about ZMA in Muscle & Fitness! (2010). SNAC: Scientific Nutrition for Advanced Conditioning. Available from http://www.snac.com.

Bartov, O. (1991). *Hitler's army.* New York: Oxford University Press.

Bascomb, N. (2004). *The perfect mile: Three athletes, one goal, and less than four minutes to achieve it.* Boston: Houghton Mifflin.

Beamish, R. (2008). Sport and social stratification. In J. Crossman (Ed.), *Canadian Sport Sociology* (2nd ed., pp. 61–78). Toronto: Thomson Nelson.

Beamish, R., & Ritchie, I. (2005). "Training" and performance-enhancing substances. *Sport in History, 25*(3), 434–51.

Beamish, R., & Ritchie, I. (2006). *Fastest, highest, strongest: A critique of high-performance sport.* London: Routledge.

Beckett, A., & Cowan, D. (1978). Misuse of drugs in sport. *British Journal of Sports Medicine, 12*(4), 185–94.

Beevor, A. (1999). *Stalingrad: The fateful siege, 1942–1943.* Toronto: Penguin Books.

Bell, C. (Director). (2008a). *Bigger, stronger, faster* [Film]. Magnolia Pictures.

Bell, C. (2008b). Rep. Henry Waxman clueless in bigger stronger faster. Available from http://www.youtube.com/watch?v=xxLNKnLaDG8.

Bentley, E. (Ed.). (1971). *Thirty years of treason: Excerpts from hearings before the House Committee on Un-American Activities, 1938–1968.* New York: The Viking Press.

Berendonk, B. (1991). *Doping Dokumente: Von der Forschung zum Betrug* [Doping documents: From research to deceit]. Berlin: Springer-Verlag.

Berger, P., & Luckmann, T. (1966). *The Social construction of reality: A treatise in the sociology of knowledge.* Garden City, NY: Doubleday Anchor.

Berman, M. (1988). *All that is solid melts into air.* Toronto: Penguin Books.

Bette, K. H. (1984). *Strukturelle Aspekte des Hochleistungssports in der Bundesrepublik* [Structural aspects of high-performance sport in the Federal Republic]. St. Augustin: Verlag Hans Richarz.

Bloch, M. (1961). *Feudal society.* London: Routledge & Paul.

Bodlander, J. (2008, January 15). Baseball officials grilled over steroids. Available from http://www.youtube.com/watch?v=BJpE_aA80-w&NR=1.

Boniface VIII, Pope. (1302, November 18). *Unam Sanctam* [One Holy Catholic and Apostolic Church]. Available from http://www.americancatholic truthsociety.com/docs/unamsanctum.htm.

Breo, D. (1985, Oct. 11). Hitler's final days recalled by physician. *American Medical News, 1,* 34–43.

Brohm, J.-M. (1978). *Sport, a prison of measured time.* Translated by I. Fraser. London: Ink Links Ltd.

Brower, K. (1989). Rehabilitation for anabolic-androgenic steroid dependence. *Clinical Sports Medicine 1,* 171–81.

Brower, K. (2002). Potential for physical and psychological dependence. In C. Yesalis (Ed.), *Anabolic steroids in sport and exercise* (pp. 279–303). Champaign, IL: Human Kinetics.

Brower, K., Blow, F., Beresford, T., & Fuelling, C. (1989). Anabolic-androgenic steroid dependence. *Journal of Clinical Psychiatry, 50*(1), 31–3.

Brown, D. (2001). Modern sport, modernism and the cultural manifesto: De Coubertin's *Revue Olympique. The International Journal of the History of Sport, 18*(2), 78–109.

Brundage, A. (1969). On Amateurism. A paper presented at the 68th Session of the International Olympic Committee, Warsaw, Poland.

Bryant, H. (2006). *Juicing the game: Drugs, power, and the fight for the soul of major league baseball.* New York: Plume.

Buckley, W., Yesalis, C., Friedl, K., Anderson, W., Streit, A., & Wright, J. (1988). Estimated prevalence of anabolic steroid use among high school seniors. *Journal of the American Medical Association, 260*(23), 3411 5.

Burke, E. (1793). *Reflections on the revolution in France in a letter intended to have been sent to a gentleman in Paris* (a new edition). London: J. Parsons.

Campagnolo, I. (1979). *Partners in pursuit of excellence.* Ottawa: Minister of State, Fitness and Amateur Sport.

Canada. (1989). *Hearings: Commission of inquiry into the use of drugs and banned practices intended to increase athletic performance* (86 vols.). Ottawa: Government of Canada.

Canadian Olympic Association. (1984). *Policy on doping and drug usage.* Montreal: Canadian Olympic Association.

Canadian Olympic Association. (1987, July). Policy on the use of banned substances and procedures in sport. *Olympinfo, 35,* 1–2.

Canseco, J. (2005a). *Juiced.* New York: HarperCollins.

Canseco, J. (2008). *Vindicated.* New York: Simon Spotlight.

Chaikin, T., & Telander, R. (1988, October 24). The nightmare of steroids. *Sports Illustrated,* 82–102.

Christie, J., & Fisher, M. (1984, July 30). Steroid use in weightlifting another setback for sport. *The Globe and Mail*, pp. S1, S5.

Clark, T. (1997). *Art and propaganda in the twentieth century*. New York: Calmann and King.

Clemens, R. (2007, December 22). Denial of steroid use as claimed in Mitchell report. Available from http://www.youtube.com/wrclemens.

Clemens, R. (2008). Deposition against Brian McNamee. Available from http://assets.espn.go.com/media/pdf/080107/mlb_clemens.pdf.

Cohen, J., Collins, R., Darkes, J., & Gwartney, D. (2007). A league of their own: Demographics, motivations and patterns of use of 1,955 male adult non-medical anabolic steroid users in the United States. *Journal of the International Society of Sports Nutrition, 4*, 12–26.

Cole, C. (2004, August). Drafting Kelli White. *Journal of Sport and Social Issues, 28*, 219–22.

Committee on Government Reform. (2005, March 17). Restoring faith in America's pastime: Evaluating Major League Baseball's efforts to eradicate steroid use. Available from http://ftp.resource.org/gpo.gov/hearings/109h/23038.pdf.

Committee on Oversight and Government Reform. (2008a, January 15). The Mitchell report: The illegal use of steroids in Major League Baseball. Available from http://frwebgate.access.gpo.gov/cgi-bin/getdoc.cgi?dbname=110_house_hearings&docid=f:55749.pdf.

Committee on Oversight and Government Reform. (2008b, February 13). The Mitchell report: The illegal use of steroids in Major League Baseball, day 2. Available from http://frwebgate.access.gpo.gov/cgi-bin/getdoc.cgi?dbname=110_house_hearings&docid=f:43333.pdf.

Copenhagen Declaration on Anti-Doping in Sport. (2003). Available from http://www.wada-ama.org/Documents/World_Anti-Doping_Program/Governments/WADA_Copenhagen_Declaration_EN.pdf.

Davis, T. (2008, March 25). Weighing the committee record: A balanced review of the evidence regarding performance enhancing substances in baseball: Staff report, U.S. House of Representatives, 110th Congress, Committee on Oversight and Government Reform. Available from http://hosted.ap.org/specials/interactives/_sports/baseball08/clemens_congress/MinorityReport.pdf.

Deford, F. (1988, October 10). Olympian changes: Politics and money are dead issues, drugs and new sports aren't. *Sports Illustrated*, 126–7.

Descartes, R. (1993 [1637]). *Discourse on method and meditations on first philosophy* (3rd ed.). Indianapolis, IN: Hackett Publishing.

Dimeo, P. (2007). *A history of drug use in sport, 1876–1976: Beyond good and evil.* London: Routledge.

Donati, A. (2004). The silent drama of the diffusion of doping among amateurs and professionals. In J. Hoberman & V. Møller, *Doping and Public Policy* (pp. 45–90). Odense: University Press of Southern Denmark.

Dubin, C. (1990). *Commission of inquiry into the use of drugs and banned practices intended to increase athletic performance.* Ottawa: Canadian Government Publishing Centre.

Duchaine, D. (1982). *Underground steroid handbook for men and women.* Venice Beach: OEM Media.

Dunning, E., & Sheard, K. (2005). *Barbarians, gentlemen and players* (2nd ed.). London: Routledge.

DuRant, R., Escobedo, L., & Heath, G. (1995). Anabolic-steroid use, strength training and multiple drug use among adolescents in the United States. *Pediatrics, 96*, 23–8.

Durkheim, E. (1933 [1893]). *The division of labor in society.* Translated by G. Simpson. Glencoe, IL: The Free Press.

Evans, R. (2002). Just-say-no campaign. In L. Breslow (Ed.), *Encyclopedia of Public Health* (vol. 2), (p. 666). New York: Macmillan Reference.

Evans, R. (2004). *The coming of the Third Reich.* New York: The Penguin Press.

Faigenbaum, A., Zaichkowsky, L., Gardner, D., & Micheli, L. (1998). Anabolic steroid use by male and female middle school students. *Paediatrics, 101*(5), 1–6.

Fainaru-Wada, M., & Williams, L. (2006). *Game of shadows: Barry Bonds, BALCO, and the steroid scandal that rocked professional sports.* New York: Gotham Books.

Fair, J. (1993). Isometrics or steroids? Exploring new frontiers of strength in the early 1960s. *Journal of Sport History, 20*(1), 1–24.

Foucault, M. 1978. *Discipline and Punish.* Translated by A. Sheridan. New York: Vintage Books.

Foucault, M. (1991). Questions of method. In G. Burchell, C. Gordon & P. Miller (Eds.), *The Foucault effect: Studies in governmentality* (pp. 73–86). Chicago: University of Chicago Press.

Foucault, M. (2003). *The essential Foucault.* Edited by P. Rabinow & N. Rose. New York: The New Press.

Foucault, M. (2007). *Security, territory, population: Lectures at the Collège de France, 1977–78.* Translated by G. Burchell. New York: Palgrave Macmillan.

Francis, C. (1990). *Speed trap: Inside the biggest scandal in Olympic history.* Toronto: Lester & Orpen Dennys.

Franke, W., & Berendonk, B. (1997). Hormonal doping and androgenization of athletes: A secret program of the German Democratic Republic government. *Clinical Chemistry, 43*(7), 1262–79.

Fraser, G. (1983, August 23). Steroid use strips Canadians of five Pan-Am Games medals. *The Whig Standard*, pp. 1–2.

Gabler, N. (2000). *Life: The movie–how entertainment conquered reality.* New York: Vintage Books.

Gafner, R. (1995). *The International Olympic Committee one hundred years: The idea–the presidents the achievements* (vols. 2–3). Lausanne: The International Olympic Committee.

Galanter, M., & Kleber, H. (2008). *The American psychiatric Publishing textbook of substance abuse treatment*, 4th ed. American Psychiatric Publications, Washington, D.C.

Gesellschaft zur Förderung des olympischen Gedankens in der DDR [Society for the promotion of the Olympics' ideals in the GDR] (Ed.). (1973). *Spiele der XX. Olympiade, München 1972* [Games of the XX Olympiad: Munich, 1972]. Berlin: Sportverlag.

Getting physical and chemical. (1985, May 13). *Sports Illustrated*, 50–5.

Giddens, A. (1971). *Capitalism and modern social theory: An analysis of the writings of Marx, Durkheim and Max Weber*. Cambridge, England: Cambridge University Press.

Giddens, A. (1984). *The constitution of society*. Los Angeles: University of California Press.

Giddens, A. (1985). *The nation-state and violence*. Los Angeles: University of California Press.

Giddens, A. (1987). *Social theory and modern sociology*. Stanford, CA: Stanford University Press.

Giddens, A. (1990). *The consequences of modernity*. Stanford, CA: Stanford University Press.

Giddens, A. (1991). *Modernity and self-identity*. Stanford, CA: Stanford University Press.

Gies, F. (1984). *The knight in history*. New York: Harper & Row.

Gilbert, D. (1980). *The miracle machine*. New York: Coward, McCann & Geoghegan.

Girouard, M. (1981). *The return to Camelot*. New Haven, CT: Yale University Press.

Goldman, B. (1984). *Death in the locker room: Steroids and sports*. South Bend, IN: Icarus Press.

Government of Canada. (1989). *Hearings: Commission of inquiry into the use of drugs and banned practices intended to increase athletic performance* (vols. 1–86). Ottawa, Canadian Government Publishing Centre.

Graham, C. (1986). *Leni Riefenstahl and Olympia*. Metuchen, NJ: The Scarecrow Press.

Gruneau, R., & H. Cantelon. (1998). Capitalism, commercialism and the Olympics. In J. Seagrave & D. Chu (Eds.), *The Olympic games in transition* (pp. 345–64). Champaign, IL: Human Kinetics.

Guttmann, A. (1984). *The Games must go on: Avery Brundage and the Olympic movement*. New York: Columbia University Press.

Guttmann, A. (2002). *The Olympics, a history of the modern games* (2nd ed.). Urbana, IL: University of Illinois Press.

H.R.3421.IH. To provide for the control of anabolic steroids under the Controlled Substances Act and for other purposes. (Introduced in House - IH). (1989). Available from http://thomas.loc.gov/cgi-bin/query/z?c101:H.R.3421:.

H.R.5269.EAS (Engrossed Amendment Senate). (1990). An act to control crime. Available from http://thomas.loc.gov/cgi-bin/query/z?c101:H.R.5269:.

H.R.5269.RH (Reported in House). (1990). Comprehensive crime control act. Available from http://thomas.loc.gov/cgi-bin/query/z?c101:H.R.5269:.

Harvey, D. (2003). *Paris: Capital of modernity.* New York: Routledge.

Hemming, A. (1946, April). The truth about testosterone. *Science Digest,* 75–6.

Hitler, A. (1939). *Mein Kampf* [My struggle]. Translated under the auspices of A. Johnson. New York: Reynal and Hitchcock.

Hoberman, J. (2005). *Testosterone dreams: Rejuvenation, aphrodisia, doping.* Berkeley: University of California Press.

Hobsbawm, E. (1995). *The age of extremes: The short twentieth century.* London: Abacus.

Hoffman, J., Faigenbaum, A., Ratamess, N., Ross, R., Kang, J., & Tenenbaum, G. (2008). Nutritional supplementation and anabolic steroid use in adolescents. *Medicine and Science in Sports and Exercise, 40*(1), 15–24.

Hormones in geriatrics. (1954, April 17). *Journal of the American Medical Association, 154,* 1336.

Hormones for he-men. (1945, May 28). *Newsweek,* 90.

Houlihan, B. (1999). Anti-doping policy in sport: The politics of international policy co-ordination. *Public Administration, 77*(2), 311–34.

Houlihan, B. (2004). Harmonising anti-doping policy: The role of the World Anti-Doping Agency. In J. Hoberman & V. Møller (Eds.), *Doping and public policy* (pp. 19–30). Odense: University Press of Southern Denmark.

House of Representatives. (1989). *The anabolic steroid restriction act of 1989: Hearings before the Subcommittee on Crime of the Committee of the Judiciary of the House of Representatives,* 101st Congress, 1st Session.

House of Representatives. (1990). *The anabolic steroid restriction act of 1990: Hearings before the Subcommittee on Crime of the Committee of the Judiciary of the House of Representatives,* 101st Congress, 2nd Session.

International Olympic Committee. (1984). *Medical guide.* Lausanne: IOC Press.

International Olympic Committee. (2000). *Olympic movement: Anti-doping code.* Available from http://www.medycynasportowa.pl/download/doping_code _e.pdf.

International Olympic Committee. (2010). *Olympic charter.* Available from http://www.olympic.org/Documents/Olympic%20Charter/Charter_en_2010.pdf.

James, C. L. R. (1937). *World revolution, 1917–1936: The rise and fall of the Communist International.* London: M. Secker and Warburg.

Johnson, W. O. (1985, May 13). Steroids: A problem of huge dimensions. *Sports Illustrated,* 38–49.

Johnson, W. O. (1988a, September 19). Hit for a loss. *Sports Illustrated,* 50–7.

Johnson, W. O. (1988b, September 26). The spirit flames a new. *Sports Illustrated,* 42–57.

Johnson, W. O. and Moore, K. (1988, October 3). The loser. *Sports Illustrated*, 20–7.

Kanayama G., Barry, S., Hudson, J., & Pope, H. (2006). Body image, self-esteem, and attitudes towards male roles in anabolic-androgenic steroid users. *American Journal of Psychiatry*, 163(4), 697–703.

Kanayama G., Boynes, M., Hudson, J., Field, A., & Pope, H. (2007). Anabolic steroid abuse among teenage girls: An illusory problem? *Drug and Alcohol Dependence*, 88(2–3), 156–62.

Kando, T. (1975). *Leisure and popular culture in transition*. St. Louis, MO: Mosby.

Katz, D., & Pope, H. (1990). Anabolic-androgenic steroid-induced mental status changes. In G. Lin & L. Erinoff (Eds.), *Anabolic steroid abuse*. (pp. 215–23). Washington, DC: U.S. Government Printing Office.

Kayser, B., Mauron, A., & Miah, A. (2005, December). Legalisation of performance-enhancing drugs. *Lancet*, 366, S21.

Kayser, B., Mauron, A., & Miah, A. (2007). Current anti-doping policy: A critical appraisal. *BMC Medical Ethics* 8(2). Available from http://www.biomed central.com/1472-6939/8/2.

Kayser, B., & A. Smith. (2008, July 12). Globalisation of anti-doping: The reverse side of the medal. *British Medical Journal*, 337, 85–7.

Kershaw, I. (1987). *The Hitler myth: Image and reality in the Third Reich*. New York: Oxford University Press.

Kershaw, I. (1991). *Hitler*. New York: Longman.

Keys, B. (2003). Soviet sport and transnational mass culture in the 1930s. *Journal of Contemporary History*, 38(3), 413–34.

Kidd, B. (1988). The elite athlete. In J. Harvey & H. Cantelon (Eds.), *Not just a game: Essays in Canadian sport sociology* (pp. 287–307). Ottawa: University of Ottawa Press.

Killanin, Lord. (1976). Eligibility and amateurism. In L. Killanin & J. Rodda (Eds.), *The Olympic Games: 80 years of people, events and records* (pp. 143–53). Don Mills: Collier-Macmillan.

Kindlundh, A., Isacson, D., Berglund, L., & Nyberg, F. (1999). Factors associated with adolescent use of doping agents: Anabolic-androgenic steroids. *Addiction*, 94(4), 543–53.

Kingsley, C. (1887). *Health and education* (new edition). London: Macmillan.

The kitchen debate. (1959). Available from http://www.teachingamerican history.org/library/index.asp?document=176

Klemperer, V. (1999). *I will bear witness, 1933–1941: A diary of the Nazi years*. Translated by M. Chalmers. New York: The Modern Library.

Knorr-Cetina, K. (1981). *The manufacture of knowledge: An essay on the constructivist and contextual nature of science*. New York: Pergamon Press.

Knorr-Cetina, K. (1999). *Epistemic cultures: How the sciences make knowledge*. Cambridge, MA: Harvard University Press.

Kotler, P. (1994). *Marketing management: Analysis, planning, implementation and control.* Englewood Cliffs, NJ: Prentice Hall.

Kreimeier, K. (1996). *The UFA story: A history of Germany's greatest film company, 1918–1945.* Translated by R. Kimber and R. Kimber. Berkeley: University of California Press.

Krüger, A. (2003). Germany: The propaganda machine. In A. Krüger & W. Murray (Eds.), *The Nazi Olympics: Sport, politics, and appeasement in the 1930s.* Champaign, IL: University of Illinois Press.

Kruif, P. (1945a). *The male hormone.* Garden City, NY: Garden City Publishing Company.

Kruif, P. (1945b, July). Can man's prime be prolonged? *Reader's Digest, 45,* 21–4.

Labre, M. (2002). Adolescent boys and the muscular male body ideal. *Journal of Adolescent Health, 30*(4), 233–42.

Langston, E. (1991). Statement of the American Medical Association to the Committee of the Judiciary presented by Edward Langston, MD, re: scheduling of anabolic steroids. In W. Taylor, *Macho medicine: A history of the anabolic steroid epidemic* (pp. 120–2).

Latour, B. (1987). *Science in action.* Cambridge MA: Harvard University Press.

Latour, B. (1993). *We have never been modern.* Translated by C. Porter. New York: Harvester Wheatsheaf.

Lausanne declaration on doping in sport. (1999, February 4). *Olympic Review* (February–March), 17–8.

Lehnertz, K. (1979). *Berufliche Entwicklung der Amateurspitzensportler in der Bundesrepublik Deutschland* [Occupational development of elite amateur athletes in the Federal Republic of Germany]. Schorndorf: Karl Hofmann.

Library of Congress. (1986). Bill summary & status, 99th Congress (1985–1986), H.R.5484 All Information. Available from http://thomas.loc.gov/cgi-bin/bdquery/z?d099:HR05484:@@@L&summ2=m&%7CTOM:/bss/d099query.html%7C#summary.

Library of Congress. (1988a). Bill summary & status, 100th Congress (1987–1988), H.R.5210 All Information. Available from http://thomas.loc.gov/cgi-bin/bdquery/z?d100:HR05210:@@@L&summ2=m&%7CTOM:/bss/d100query.html%7C.

Library of Congress. (1988b). Bill summary & status, 100th Congress (1987–1988), H.R.5210 CRS Summary. Available from http://thomas.loc.gov/cgi-bin/bdquery/z?d100:HR05210:@@@D&summ2=0&lTOM:/bss/d100query.html.

Library of Congress. (1989a). Bill summary & status, 101st Congress (1989–1990), H.R.3421. Available from http://www.thomas.gov/cgi-bin/bdquery/z?d101:H.R.3421:.

Library of Congress. (1989b). Bill summary & status, 101st Congress (1989–1990), S.1829. Available from http://thomas.loc.gov/cgi-bin/bdquery/z?d101:s1829:.

Library of Congress. (1989c). Bill summary & status, 101st Congress (1989–1990), H.R.995. Available from http://thomas.loc.gov/home/bills_res.html.

Library of Congress. (1989d). Bill summary & status, search results. Available from http://thomas.loc.gov/cgi-bin/bdquery/?&Db=d101&querybd=@FIELD (FLD003+@4((@1(Rep+Stark++Fortney+Pete))+01101)).

Library of Congress. (1990). Bill summary & status, 101st Congress (1989–1990), S.3266. Available from http://thomas.loc.gov/cgi-bin/bdquery/z?d101:S.3266:.

Library of Congress. (1990b). Bill text, 101st Congress (1989–1990), S.3266.ENR. Available from http://thomas.loc.gov/cgi-bin/query/z?c101:S.3266.ENR:.

Littman, J. (2004, May). Gunning for the big guy. *Playboy*, 66–70, 78, 142–5.

Littman, J. (2009a, January 14). Bonds blockbuster: 'The clear' was legal. *Yahoo! Sports*. Available from http://sports.yahoo.com/mlb/news;_ylt=Am3dP.nX 4rxHLoKhbkHn2bo5nYcB?slug=li-clear011409&prov=yhoo&type=lgns.

Littman, J. (2009b, February 4). Novitzky was target of secret probe. *Yahoo! Sports*. Available from http://sports.yahoo.com/mlb/news;_ylt=AoRDnSkgKpa0HfY NXaojUtgRvLYF?slug=li-novitzky020309&prov=yhoo&type=lgns.

Litzky, F. (1999, April 14). TRACK AND FIELD; Slaney suing the I.A.A.F. in dispute over a drug test. *New York Times*. Available from http://www.nytimes com/1999/04/14/sports/track-and-field-slaney-suing-the-iaaf-in-dispute-over-a -drug-test.html?scp=2&sq=Frank+Litsky&st=nyt.

Lovejoy, A. (1936). *The great chain of being*. Cambridge, MA: Harvard University Press.

Macintosh, D., Bedecki, T., & Franks, C. (1987). *Sport and politics in Canada*. Kingston, Ontario: McGill-Queen's University Press.

Mandell, R. (1987). *The Nazi Olympics*. Urbana and Chicago: University of Illinois Press.

Mangan, J. (1981). *Athleticism in the Victorian and Edwardian public school*. New York: Cambridge University Press.

Marx, K & Engels, F. (1934 [1848]). *The manifesto of the communist party*. London: Martin Lawrence.

Mason, P. (1982). *The English gentleman*. London: Andre Deutsch.

McAuley, L. (1986, July 17). Drug use ends 6 athletes' amateur careers. *The Citizen*, pp. A1, A16.

Midgley, S., Heather, N., Best, D., Henderson, D., McCarthy, S., & Davies, J. (2000). Risk behaviours for HIV and hepatitis infection among anabolic-androgenic steroid users. *AIDS Care*, *12*, 163–70.

Miller, K., Barnes, G., Sabo, D., Melnick, M., & Farrell, M. (2002). Anabolic-androgenic steroid use and other adolescent problem behaviors: Rethinking the male athlete assumption. *Sociological Perspectives*, *45*(4), 467–89.

Mitchell, G. (2007, December 13). *Report to the Commissioner of Baseball of an independent investigation into the illegal use of steroids and other performance enhancing substances by players in Major League Baseball*. Available from http://files.mlb.com/mitchrpt.pdf.

Møller, V. (2005). Knud Enemark Jensen's death during the 1960 Rome Olympics: A search for truth? *Sport in History, 25*(3), 452–71.

Møller, V. (2010). *The ethics of doping and anti-doping.* London: Routledge

Monaghan, L. (2001). *Bodybuilding, drugs and risk.* London: Routledge.

Morford, R., & McIntosh, M. (1993). Sport and the Victorian gentleman. In A. Ingham & J. Loy (Eds.), *Sport in social development* (pp. 51–76). Champaign IL: Human Kinetics.

Munro, J. (1970). *A proposed sports policy for Canadians.* Ottawa: Department of National Health and Welfare.

Murray, T. (1983). The coercive power of drugs in sports. *Hastings Center Report, 13*(4), 24–30.

Murray, W. (1992). France, Coubertin and the Nazi Olympics. *Olympika, 1,* 46–69.

National Public Radio. (2007, April, 2). Timeline: America's war on drugs. Available from http://www.npr.org/templates/story/story.php?storyId =9252490.

National Sports Policy Task Force. (1988). *Toward 2000: Building Canada's sport systems.* Ottawa: Government of Canada, Fitness and Amateur Sport.

Navasky, V. (1980). *Naming names.* New York: The Viking Press.

Nisbet, R. (1978). Conservatism. In T. Bottomore and R. Nisbet (Eds.), *A history of sociological analysis* (pp. 80–117). London: Heinemann Books.

Nixon, R., & Khrushchev, N. (1950, July 24). The kitchen debate. Available from http://www.youtube.com/watch?v=VPWG1i6YqVo.

Novitzky, J. (2003, September 3). Affidavit of special agent Jeff Novitzky in support of request for search warrants. Available from http://www.sfgate.com/ chronicle/acrobat/2004/02/13/affidvt.pdf.

Okeeffe, M. (2005, February 6). Canseco confessions: Tell-all outs steroid users. Available from http://www.nydailynews.com/archives/news/2005/02/06/ 2005-02-06_canseco_confessions_tell-all.html.

Okeeffe, M., & Quinn, T. J. (2005, February 7). Book juices fame voters may keep stars out. Available from http://www.nydailynews.com/archives/sports/2005/ 02/07/2005-02-07_book_juices_fame_voters_may_.html.

Own the Podium. (2010). *Pillars of excellence.* Available from http://www .ownthepodium2010.com/About/objectives.aspx.

Parkinson, A., & Evans, N. A. (2006). Anabolic androgenic steroids: A survey of 500 users. *Medicine and Science in Sports and Exercise, 38*(4), 644–51.

Parkkari J., Kujala U. M., & Kannus, P. (2001). Is it possible to prevent sports injuries? Review of controlled clinical trials and recommendations for future work. *Sports Medicine, 31*(14), 985–95.

Pedersen, W., Wichstrøm, L., & Blekesaune, M. (2001). Violent behaviours, violent victimization, and doping agents: a normal population study of adolescents. *Journal of Interpersonal Violence, 16,* 808–32.

Pfetsch, F., Beutel, P., Stork, H.-M., & Treutlein, G. (1975). *Leistungssport und Gesellschaftssystem* [High-performance sport and the social system]. Schorndorf: Karl Hofmann Verlag.

Pipe, A. (2001). The adverse effects of elite competition on health and well-being. *Canadian Journal of Applied Physiology, 26*(Suppl.), S192–S201.

Polanyi, K. (1944). *The great transformation.* Toronto: Farrar & Rinehart.

Pope, H., & Brower, K. (2008). Treatment of anabolic-androgenic steroid-related disorders. In M. Galanter & H. Kleber (Eds.), *The American psychiatric publishing textbook of substance abuse treatment* (4th ed., pp. 237–45). Washington, DC: American Psychiatric Press.

Pope, H., & Katz, G. (1988). Affective and psychotic symptoms associated with anabolic steroid use. *American Journal of Psychiatry, 145*(4), 487–90.

Radomski, K. (2009). *Bases loaded.* New York: Hudson Street Press.

Real, M. (1996). The postmodern Olympics: Technology and the commodification of the Olympic movement. *Quest, 48*(1), 9–24.

Regan, G. (1981). *A challenge to the nation: Fitness and amateur sport in the '80s.* Ottawa: Ministry of State, Fitness and Amateur Sport.

Rentschler, E. (1996). *The ministry of illusion: Nazi cinema and its afterlife.* Cambridge, MA: Harvard University Press.

Riefenstahl, L. (Director). (2001). *Triumph des Willens* [Triumph of the will] [DVD]. Bloomington, IL: Synapse Films.

Riefenstahl, L. (Director). (2006). *Olympia* [DVD]. Venice, CA: Pathfinder Home Entertainment.

Ritchie, I. (2003). Sex tested, gender verified: Controlling female sexuality in the age of containment. *Sport History Review, 34*(1), 80–98.

Roberts, S. (2009). *A-Rod: The many lives of Alex Rodriguez.* New York: Harper Collins.

Röder, H. (n.d.). *Nachwuchsleistungssport* [High-performance sport aspirants]. Available from http://www.sport-ddr-roeder.de/nachwuchsleistungssport.html.

Rürup, R. (Ed.). (1991). *Der Krieg gegen die Sowjetunion, 1941–1945* [The war against the Soviet Union, 1941–1945]. Berlin: Argon Publishers.

Ryan, A. J. (1976). Athletics. In C. Kochakian (Ed.), *Handbook of experimental pharmacology* (pp. 515–34), New York: Springer-Verlag.

S.1829, the steroid trafficking act of 1989. (1989). Available from http://thomas.loc.gov/cgi-bin/bdquery/z?d101:SN01829:@@@L&summ2=m&S.3266.ENR.

S.3266, crime control act of 1990 (enrolled bill [final—passed both House and Senate]). (1990). Available from http://thomas.loc.gov/cgi-bin/bdquery/z?d101:SN03266:%7CTOM:/bss/d101query.html%7C.

Safai, P. (2007). A critical analysis of the development of sports medicine in Canada, 1955–1980. *International Review for the Sociology of Sport, 42*(3), 321–41.

Safire, W. (2009, July 23). The Cold War's hot kitchen. *New York Times.* Available from http://www.nytimes.com/2009/07/24/opinion/24safire.html?_r=1&ref =williamsafire.

Schmaltz, J. (2003). The king of swing: What fuels baseball super hitter Barry Bonds? *Muscle & Fitness.* Available from http://www.snac.com/mag_king _of_swing.htm.

Schrecker, E. (2002). *The age of McCarthyism: A brief history with documents* (2nd ed.). Boston: Bedford/St. Martin's Press.

Scott, D., Wagner, J., & Barlow, T. W. (1996). Anabolic steroid use among adolescents in Nebraska schools. *American Journal of Health Systems and Pharmacology,* 53, 68–72.

Senate Judiciary Committee. (2002). Report of the Committee of the Judiciary, U.S. Senate, 101st Congress, 2nd Session. In W. Taylor, *Anabolic steroids and the athlete* (2nd ed., pp. 280–300). Jefferson, NC: McFarland.

Senn, A. (1999). *Power, politics and the Olympic Games.* Champaign IL: Human Kinetics.

Selig, A. (2006, March 30). Statement of the Commissioner Allan H. (Bud) Selig. Available from http://www.dlapiper.com/files/upload/selig_statement.pdf.

Shepard, R. (1959, July 26). Debate goes on TV over Soviet protest. *New York Times,* pp. 1–2.

Shirer, W. (1959). *The rise and fall of the Third Reich.* New York: Simon and Schuster.

Shirer, W. (1961). *Berlin diary.* New York: Popular Library.

Silvermann, F. (1984, May). Guaranteed aggression: The secret of testosterone by Nazi troops." *Journal of the American Medical Association,* 129–31.

60 *Minutes.* (2008a, January 8). Roger Clemens. Available from http://www .cbsnews.com/video/watch/?id=3680216n&tag=related;photovideo.

60 *Minutes.* (2008b, January 8). Transcript from Roger Clemens on 60 Minutes. Available from http://www.cbsnews.com/stories/2008/01/03/60minutes/ main3671585.shtml.

Slowikowski, S., & Loy, J. (1993). Ancient athletic motifs and the Modern Olympic Games. In A. Ingham & J. Loy (Eds.), *Sport in social development* (pp. 21–50). Champaign IL: Human Kinetics.

Smith, S. (1991, July 8). A doctor's warning ignored. *Sports Illustrated,* pp. 22–3.

Speer, A. (1969). *Erinnerungen* [Memoirs]. Berlin: Verlag Ullstein.

Sport Canada. (1984a). *Scorecard.* Ottawa: Minister of State, Fitness and Amateur Sport.

Sport Canada. (1984b). *Drug use and doping control in sport: A Sport Canada policy.* Ottawa: Minister of State, Fitness and Amateur Sport.

Sport Canada. (1984c). *Drug use and doping control in sport: Concerns for the amateur athlete.* Ottawa: Minister of State, Fitness and Amateur Sport.

Sport Canada. (1985). *Drug use and doping control in sport: A sport Canada policy update.* Ottawa: Minister of State, Fitness and Amateur Sport.

Sports Illustrated. (1991, July 8). Cover image. Available from http://sports illustrated.cnn.com/vault/cover/featured/9284/index.htm.

SNAC. (2010). SNAC: Scientific Nutrition for Advanced Conditioning. Available from http://www.snac.com/products.htm.

Sokolove, M. (2004, January 18). In pursuit of doped excellence: The lab animal. *New York Times Magazine.* Available from http://www.nytimes.com/2004/01/18/magazine/in-pursuit-of-doped-excellence-the-lab-animal.html.

Stevenson, D. (1997). Olympic arts: Sydney 2000 and the cultural Olympiad. *International Review for the Sociology of Sport, 32*(3), 227–38.

Taylor, F. (1911). *The principles of scientific management.* New York: Harper and Brothers.

Taylor, W. (1982). *Anabolic steroids and the athlete.* Jefferson, NC: McFarland.

Taylor, W. (1985). *Hormonal manipulation: A new era of monstrous athletes.* Jefferson, NC: McFarland.

Taylor, W. (1991). *Macho medicine: A history of the anabolic steroid epidemic.* Jefferson, NC: McFarland.

Taylor, W. (2002). *Anabolic steroids and the athlete* (2nd ed.). Jefferson, NC: McFarland.

Teichler, H.-J. (1982). Coubertin un das Dritte Reich [Coubertin and the Third Reich]. *Sportwissenschaft, 12*(1), 18–55.

Telander, R. (1988, October 24). A peril for athletes. *Sports Illustrated,* 114.

Telander, R. (1989, February 20). The death of an athlete. *Sports Illustrated,* 68–78.

Theberge, N. (2008). The integration of chiropractors into health care teams: A case study from sport medicine. *Sociology of Health and Illness, 30*(1), 19–34.

Thompson, E. (1974). Time, work-discipline, and industrial capitalism. In M. W. Flinn & T. C. Smout (Eds.), *Essays in Social History* (pp. 39–77). Oxford: Oxford University Press.

Thompson, T., Vinton, N., O'Keeffe, M., & Red, C. (2009). *American icon: The fall of Roger Clemens and the rise of steroids in America's pastime.* New York: Alfred A. Knopf.

Todd, J., & Todd, T. (2001). Significant events in the history of drug testing and the Olympic Movement: 1960–1999. In W. Wilson and E. Derse (Eds.), *Doping in elite sport.* (pp. 65–128). Champaign, IL: Human Kinetics.

Todd, T. (1983, August 1). The steroid predicament. *Sports Illustrated,* 62–77.

Todd, T. (1987). Anabolic steroids: The gremlins of sport. *Journal of Sport History, 14*(1), 87–107.

Tönnies, F. (1957 [1887]). *Community and society.* Translated by C. Loomis. New York: Harper Torchbooks.

UK Sport. (2007a, November 12–15). Mission 2012. In UK Sport (Ed.), *World Class Coaching Conference* (pp. 24–7). Available from http://www.uksport .gov.uk/pages/wc-performance-conference.

UK Sport. (2007b, November 12–15). Elite training centres: The vision. In UK Sport (Ed.), *World Class Coaching Conference* (pp. 28–30). Available from http://www.uksport.gov.uk/pages/wc-performance-conference.

UK Sport. (2007c, May 8). UK Sport launches "Mission 2012." Available from http://www.uksport.gov.uk/news/uk_sport_launches_mission_2012_.

UK Sport. (2010). World class performance programme. Available from http:// www.uksport.gov.uk/pages/wc-performance-programme.

UNESCO. (2005a, January 10–14). Oral report of the rapporteur of the 3rd session of the intergovernmental meeting of experts on the draft international convention against doping in sport. Available from http://unesdoc.unesco.org/images/ 0013/001388/138867e.pdf.

UNESCO. (2005b, October 19). International convention against doping in sport 2005. Available from http://portal.unesco.org/en/ev.php-URL_ID=31037 &URL_DO=DO_TOPIC&URL_SECTION=201.html.

UNESCO. (2010). Towards a better sport. Available from http://www.unesco.org/ new/en/social-and-human-sciences/themes/sport/anti-doping/international -convention-against-doping-in-sport/background.

U.S. Army. (1944). *Handbook for military government in Germany prior to defeat or surrender.* CD ROM, U.S. War Department.

U.S. Code. (2006). Available from http://www2.law.cornell.edu/uscode/18/usc_sec _18_00001001——000-.html.

USOC "Podium 2002" Programme. (1999, April-May). *Olympic Review, 26,* p. 35.

U.S. Sentencing Commission. (2006). *2006 steroids report.* Available from http:// www.docstoc.com/docs/9412954/2006-Steroids-Report.

Verroken, M., & Mottram, D. (2005). Doping control in sport. In D. Mottram (Ed.), *Drugs in sport* (4th ed., pp. 309–56). London: Routledge.

Voy, R. (1991). *Drugs, sports, and politics.* Champaign, IL: Leisure Press.

Waddington, I. (1996). The development of sports medicine. *Sociology of Sport Journal,* (13), 176–96.

Waddington, I. (2000). *Sport, health, and drugs.* Leicester: E and FN Spon.

Waddington, I., & Smith, A. (2009). *An introduction to drugs in sport.* London: Routledge.

Wade, N. (1972, June 30). Anabolic steroids: Doctors denounce them, but athletes aren't listening. *Science, 176,* 1399–403.

Weber, M. (1927). *General economic history.* Translated by F. Knight. New York: Greenberg.

Welch, D. (1983). *Propaganda and the German cinema, 1933–1945.* New York: Oxford University Press.

Welch, D. (1993). *The Third Reich: Politics and propaganda.* New York: Routledge.

Williams, R. (1977). *Marxism and literature.* Oxford: Oxford University Press.

Williams, R. (1980). Base and superstructure in Marxist cultural theory. In R. Williams, *Problems in materialism and culture* (pp. 31–49). London: Verso.

Wilstein, S. (1998, August 16). Home-run derby; ROGER THAT; Legendary season grows with every prodigious clout. *Houston Chronicle,* Sports 1.

Wilstein, S. (1998, August 21). "Andro" pill OK in baseball, not in Olympics, *Houston Chronicle,* Sports 1.

World Anti-Doping Agency. (2003). *World Anti-Doping Code* (v. 3). Available from http://www.wada-ama.org/rtecontent/document/code_v3.pdf.

World Anti-Doping Agency. (2009a). *The world anti-doping code.* Available from http://www.ifbb.com/pdf/wadacode.pdf.

World Anti-Doping Agency. (2009b, September 19). *The world anti-doping code: The 2010 prohibited list.* Available from http://www.wada-ama.org/Documents/World_Anti-Doping_Program/WADP-Prohibited-list/WADA_Prohibited_List_2010_EN.pdf.

Wulf, S. (1988, September 5). Scorecard. *Sports Illustrated,* 23–5.

Yesalis, C., & Bahrke, M. (2002). History of doping in sport. *International Sports Studies, 24*(1), 42–76.

Yesalis, C., Bahrke, M., Kopstein, A., & Barsukiewicz, C. (2000). Incidence of anabolic steroid use: A discussion of methodological issues. In C. Yesalis (Ed.), *Anabolic steroids in sport and exercise* (2nd ed., pp. 73–115). Champaign, IL: Human Kinetics.

Yesalis, C., & Cowart, V. (1998). *The steroids game: An expert's inside look at anabolic steroid use in sports.* Champaign, IL: Human Kinetics.

Yesalis, C., Vicary, J., Buckley, W., Streit, A., Katz, D., & Wright, J. (1990). Indications of psychological dependence among anabolic-androgenic steroid abusers. In G. Lin & L. Erinoff (Eds.), *Anabolic steroid abuse* (pp. 196–214). Washington, DC: U.S. Government Printing Office.

Ziegler, J. (1984). Forward. In Bob Goldman, *Death in the locker room: Steroids and sports.* (pp. 1–2). South Bend, IN: Icarus Press.

Index

About the Author

ROB BEAMISH has held a joint appointment in the Department of Sociology and the School of Kinesiology and Health at Queen's University, Kingston, Canada for the past 25 years. During that time, in addition to his teaching and research responsibilities, he has served as the associate dean (studies) and the head of the Department of Sociology. In addition to numerous articles, book chapters, and encyclopedia entries related to social theory, sport sociology, and the use of performance-enhancing substances, Beamish is the author of several books, including: *Question: What Do You Do for a Living? Answer: I'm an Athlete!*; *Fastest, Highest, Strongest: The Critique of High-Performance Sport* (with Ian Ritchie); and *The Promise of Sociology: The Classical Tradition and Contemporary Sociological Thinking*.